HUMAN
BEING

HUMAN BEING

Illuminating the reality beneath the facade

Decoding the fundamental qualities that
drive our decisions, behaviours and results

ASHKAN TASHVIR

First published 2022 by Engenesis Publications

Ashkan Tashvir asserts the moral right to be identified as the author of *HUMAN BEING* and all associated products.

ISBN 978 1 922433 04 6 Paperback (Australian Print)
ISBN 978 1 922433 05 3 Paperback (P.O.D.)
ISBN 978 1 922433 06 0 Hardcover (P.O.D.)
ISBN 978 1 922433 07 7 Kindle
ISBN 978 1 922433 08 4 ePub

publications.engenesis.com

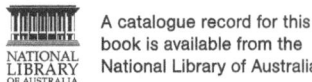 A catalogue record for this book is available from the National Library of Australia

Edited by Phaedra Pym – awaywithwords.net.au
Book design and production by Eric and Thymen Hoek – exlibris.com.au

Disclaimer: This book is intended to give general information only. The material herein does not represent professional advice. The author expressly disclaims all liability to any person arising directly or indirectly from the use of, or for any errors or omissions in, the information in this book. The adoption and application of the information in this book is at the reader's discretion and is his or her sole responsibility.

This book is dedicated to you, the reader,
and to my daughter, Diana.

Contents

Preface

Many important discoveries and ideas in the world are initially triggered by a lightbulb moment of awareness. For me, that moment of clarity occurred in the early hours of the morning at a time when I was dealing with an enormous level of inauthenticity and a lack of integrity from people all around me. I was also acutely present to the misery, dysfunction and unworkability in the world and its devastating impacts everywhere.

Prior to that pivotal awakening, I had been building businesses since my teens and had studied faith, several religions and various disciplines of philosophy and schools of thought. On a personal and professional level, I had also observed and been associated with many people who considered themselves intellectuals or experts, but were leading their lives in a manner that was totally incongruent with their knowledge and what they claimed they were striving to achieve. Many weren't practising what they preached, and some could barely look after themselves and their families, let alone accomplish their professional goals. Rather than authentically looking within, some claimed to be striving to resolve complex, systemic problems of humanity and society. They approached life as if they possessed 'the complete theory of everything'. Although, deep down, they knew their ideologies were failing them, they stubbornly continued to believe they had all the answers to the world's problems despite clearly being stuck and completely miserable in their own lives. While I completely acknowledge that I, too, am imperfect, in that moment, I recognised that I was unwilling to stand by as a passive observer to all these inauthenticities. My profound care and compassion for humanity ignited an irrepressible urge to take action. From that moment on, I knew there was no turning back.

I set out to explore and discover the qualities and attributes that matter most when it comes to performance, effectiveness, influence, wellbeing and fulfilment. What began as a truth-seeking journey sparked by curiosity and care led to a sincere intention to learn the mechanisms behind our decisions and behaviours. This further led me to deeply examine the breadth and depth of fundamental truths about human beings. Over the next ten years, I studied people from all walks of life and corners of the globe to discover why some manage to create a life of effectiveness, prosperity and fulfilment while many others constantly struggle and are never truly fulfilled. My goal was to study human beings objectively and without judgement, including startup founders, entrepreneurs and high achievers. Of the hundreds of startup founders I observed, I discovered multiple similarities behind an alarming failure rate. I also realised that my observations relating to startups applied equally and systemically in society.

Part of my research involved the study and firsthand experience of existing and readily available solutions, tools, practices and products for people who want to transform. On one end of the spectrum, we have the legions of so-called self-help 'experts' and 'gurus' who suggest we can change anything simply by thinking positively or practising any number of tips and tricks offered online or in their latest book. Then at the opposite end of the spectrum are the practitioners who attempt to categorise people into personality types and other categories.

I decided to invest in several sessions with a range of practitioners. I began with clinical psychology, trying various disciplines, including traditional psychoanalysis and behavioural psychology. I went into every session with an open mind but usually left feeling deflated after being categorised as a certain personality type with a defined temperament and being told I needed to develop 'coping mechanisms' to ensure my flaws don't get in the way of what I want to achieve in life. Some practitioners drew my attention to my upbringing and childhood, explaining how they had shaped my character and personality to such an extent that they would be virtually impossible to change at this stage of my life. In other words, these practitioners were insinuating that I am hardwired to be who and how I am and that I should focus on addressing my behaviours or changing my environment in order to distance myself from people and other factors that might be driving my unwanted behavioural patterns.

I am not suggesting that these approaches are devoid of merit. However, they miss the fundamental requirements that facilitate transformation.

That's primarily because, while these and many other disciplines of mainstream modern psychology focus on fixing or refining individual behaviours or, at best, behavioural and cognitive patterns, they ignore the deeper, more subtle, yet far more important qualities which drive our behaviours. It is those deeper qualities and drivers of our decisions, behaviours and actions that I set out to define and map out.

Later, as a business venture builder and investor, it became a high priority for me to find the 'right' people, team members, entrepreneurs and founders to work with and invest in. I knew I was not alone in this quest. Finding the right people to partner with is critical for all venture builders, entrepreneurs and investors, just as it is for other significant endeavours in life, such as building relationships. I became present to the common rhetoric used by many of the world's greatest entrepreneurs and leaders about how important it is to surround yourself with 'talented', 'exceptional', 'amazing', 'great' people, and the list goes on. But what do those words really mean? What are the underlying qualities that define an 'amazing' or 'great' team member, and how can you see those qualities with clarity? These questions led me to ponder: how does one find and choose with discernment people who are the right fit when so many present a facade that hides the truth? And what are the qualities required by a team of people that enables them to perform and build products and services that solve the end users' burning pain despite the enormous level of uncertainties and challenges faced when trying to lift a startup off the ground? The idea that attracting 'top talent' leads to a 'high-performing' team that then serves a customer we have no effective way of understanding just didn't cut it for me. These concepts, while popular, were vague and unclear. It was ambiguities like these that I set out to demystify.

In addition to discovering a lack of clarity around the qualities that make up the 'right' person to partner or work with, I realised that while some people are exceptionally effective in their domain, they understand very little about human beings – the very beings they need to work with to achieve the 'greatness' they are pursuing. I was also astounded to discover how little we human beings know about ourselves. And because of that, we don't know how to be with ourselves or others. As a result, we suffer, individually and collectively. We may marry someone not suited to us, follow the 'wrong' leader, hire the 'wrong' employee or select a business partner whose values are misaligned with ours and the company, etc. In short, a lack of understanding about ourselves and others combined with a lack of clarity around the qualities that underpin our behaviours, decisions and results leads us to make ineffective decisions. This gets in the way of our influence and effectiveness, which hinders our ability to achieve our intentions and therefore prevents us from being fulfilled. Our collective suffering then extends to our community, society and humanity. Indeed, I firmly believe many of the catastrophic problems in the world stem from misperceptions and misconceptions about human beings and the severe consequences of that because, as social creatures, being with others is a necessity; it's as if it's hardwired into our DNA.

I discovered that visionary leaders, on the other hand, have the ability to 'see in the dark' as a result of their vivid awareness. This sets them on the path towards integrity (wholeness) and effectiveness. Furthermore, their effectiveness in their endeavours leads them to fulfil the intentions they set for themselves, which results in a by-product of prosperity and wellbeing in most cases. This paradigm sets them apart from others. They know that while intelligence and material wealth are important, they are not enough to live a truly fulfilling life. Many celebrities and 'successful' people eventually come to a similar conclusion when they realise that there is still something missing in their lives despite their financial and professional success. At some point, it hits them that what and who they have become is their most significant accomplishment in life.

There is an art and science to understanding human beings so that we can interact with each other more effectively. Whether you are building a family, your career, a startup or an organisation, these studies led me to conclude that how you and the people around you are BEING matters. It was the eureka moment of clarity I had been seeking. Coming from an engineering background, my analytical way of thinking fuelled a desire to contextualise my discoveries. This led me to identify the qualities we all possess but relate to or execute differently and the common patterns among the high achievers and those who lead a life of fulfilment, meaning and wellbeing. With the foundations in place, I engineered a tangible framework to support anyone who wants to be the leader of their own life and be in charge of their source of power. And so, the Being Framework™ was born.

For centuries, we have been bombarded with excuses for why people and businesses fail in their endeavours, with the blame typically pointed squarely on external factors. However, my studies revealed that the answer lies, to a significant degree, within ourselves. It all starts with who and how we are BEING. This book provides a high-level walk-through of the Being Framework and, in so doing, explores how to see through one's Being – yours and others – by casting light on the qualities that drive our behaviours, decisions and results.

After launching the Being Framework and its associated tools: the Being Framework Ontological Model, Transformation Methodology and Being Profile®, I embarked on a book writing process to share the Being paradigm with a broader audience. The outcome was a comprehensive body of work published in 2021 that delves deeply into the framework, including the philosophy that underpins it and multiple references. Once that book was launched, I felt compelled to write a second, less technical book for anyone interested to learn more about themselves and others, and who wants to become a more effective human capable of leading a life of fulfilment, influence and wellbeing. The result is the book you are reading today. If you find you are curious to learn more about the rigorous work that laid the foundations of this paradigm once you come to the end of this book, I encourage you to read *BEING*.

Whether you are studying and unsure about your future direction, pursuing a professional career or a trade, starting or nurturing a relationship, raising a family, creating a startup, building or leading an organisation, serving humanity, or whatever it is that fills you with joy and sparks your enthusiasm and ambition, this book is for you. My challenge is for you to take the understanding you gain from this book and be courageous enough to apply it in ways that will not only make a difference for you but also contribute to the betterment of the world. It would be a loss to humanity to miss out on your unique gift.

Introduction

How often are you shocked, blindsided, crushed, misled, ripped off or negatively impacted in some other way by another person's decisions, behaviour or actions, whether it be your business partner, life partner, employee, colleague, boss, elected politician or friend, etc.?

Are you projecting the real you to the people in your life, or are you projecting a fake persona? Do you say your real yeses and noes? Or do you tend to respond to people in the way you believe they want you to or how you think you should because you want to fit in, be accepted, please or be non-confrontational, even at the cost of negating or disregarding your real self? Do you sometimes feel trapped by your 'identity' or 'personality type'? Do you possess what you consider to be flaws in your character that you're not proud of? But you make excuses for them, telling yourself, 'That's just who I am. I was born that way, so there's no point fighting it.' Perhaps you make the same excuses for the so-called 'flaws' in others and assume you have to accept them for who they are because of your perception that human beings are fixed and can't transform.

Do you find yourself setting goals or intentions, but you never seem to hit your targets, no matter how hard you try? Perhaps you are crystal clear on those goals or intentions and know what you need to do to realise them, but for some reason, you keep sabotaging yourself or procrastinating. You have a vision for what you want to achieve and have loads of energy, but you don't know how to channel it to manifest what you really want and care about. You get to the end of each day and wish you had done more. You feel exhausted and dissatisfied that you're still not closing in on your goal. You may have even completed several personal development programs, profiles and personality tests but always come away sensing something is missing. Maybe you've reached the point where you feel like giving up, telling yourself you're just not cut out to achieve that goal. Perhaps you've stopped telling others about your aspirations, even though deep down you still hope and dream that one day you'll have the courage to reinvigorate your original intentions.

Or perhaps people see you as a real go-getter who is proactive, knows precisely what they want in life and who largely fulfils their intentions. You're accomplished, disciplined, and take the most effective actions to achieve your objectives and hit your targets, at least most of the time. Still, you just can't seem to break through beyond your current level, regardless of your efforts or how many self-help books you read, videos you watch, courses you attend, 'gurus' you follow and podcasts you listen to. You feel incomplete and unfulfilled. In your efforts to be effective and live up to the expectations of others, your wellbeing and happiness are being compromised. This realisation hits you like a bolt of lightning. It starts to keep you awake at night because you know you've got what it takes, but there's always something blocking your way, and you just can't put your finger on what that is. So you blindly do what you've always done and remain focused on the areas of your life that are working for you – the things you know you can control – oblivious to the fact that what got you here may not get you where you want to go. But deep down, you wonder why you can't move forward in the areas you genuinely care about.

If you lead an organisation or a team, do you feel you're not being heard or are often misunderstood? Do you lack the influence you know you need to go from good to great and to stop high-performing team members from leaving and finding better opportunities elsewhere, often with the competition? But things keep getting in the way of making the changes you know you need to make. Perhaps you're too busy or don't know where to start.

Imagine if there was a way you could see the blindsides and deceptions coming and, with vision and discernment, avoid them before they strike? Suppose you could revisit your lost goals and rekindle them, even after many years, by uncovering and addressing the hidden roadblocks that were always in the way but which you failed to see? What if there was a way to break through the barriers you've always believed to be unbreakable because they are your 'set identity' or 'personality type'?

What if you could see, with vivid clarity, the unpolished aspects of someone's character when making critical decisions involving them?

Imagine the profound difference this ability would make when choosing your life partner, business partner, next employee or future boss. What about when casting your vote at the polls? How can you see through the facade of each candidate and critically assess the integrity of their Being so you can vote with confidence?

What if you could dive deeply into your core essence and see who and how you are, why you interpret the world the way you do, and why you behave and act a certain way in different situations. What if you could demystify your current worldview and also have a lens to understand the worldviews of others with greater clarity. This clarity could result in you making more effective decisions and taking more effective actions with the people you interact with. Imagine if there was a way to unveil the curtain that prevents you from vividly seeing your intentions, calling and potential. You could then become attuned to the intentions, calling and potential of the people around you. Insights of this kind change everything! They enable you to become a better, more authentic version of yourself, which in turn leads to more effective performance, the ability to engage more fully in life and more powerful ways to interact with others and the world.

Right now, there are people worldwide who have adopted a new framework that methodically zooms in on, breaks down and articulates how we human beings are being in a clear and tangible way. It explains how the way they are being in great part drives their decisions and behaviours and determines the outcomes and consequences they end up producing. This framework enables them to identify the hidden root causes behind whatever is holding them back, allowing them to move forward with renewed vigour, grit and a fresh perspective. Today, they are taking effective actions to achieve their objectives, do what they genuinely care about, express their authentic selves, build successful relationships, achieve wealth and prosperity, and live a life of influence, integrity, wellbeing and fulfilment.

Changing behaviour is only part of the solution

'Change the behaviour, change the outcome' seems to be a dominant way of thinking in a variety of contexts, from parenting and clinical psychology to corporate culture and traditional HR practices. But while changing behaviour is necessary if you want a different outcome, it is only part of the solution. Changing behaviour alone is like watering the individual leaves of a tree without paying attention to the whole tree from the roots up.

Let's say you fear spiders, and there is a giant spider on your bedroom wall. You could get your partner or flatmate, who is not afraid of spiders, to remove it, and the object of your fear – and hence your fear at that moment – would be gone. But what would you do next time you see a spider in your home and you are alone? A more effective way would be to become aware of and learn how to BE with fear-generating situations so that you can respond appropriately as they come.

To put this in a business context, imagine you have an employee who is constantly arriving late to work. You may tell them their behaviour is unacceptable. You may warn them or even put them on a performance review and force a change in their behaviour. But that is not going to change the real reason for repeatedly arriving late to work. Maybe they don't care about the job or they have an unhealthy relationship with commitment and responsibility. Perhaps there is another underlying cause that they are not open and vulnerable enough to share with you. The point is, there are always deeper qualities driving our behaviours. Unless you become aware of these underlying qualities, you will forever be reacting to situations as they arise and applying bandaids rather than being proactive and nipping them in the bud.

The Being Framework™

The Being Framework is a multi-layered paradigm that sits alongside a comprehensive methodology and tools that support us in developing a more congruent and authentic conception of the reality of human beings in the scope of performance, wellbeing, integrity, effectiveness, leadership and fulfilment. By casting light on our underlying qualities, the framework enables us to demystify human beings – ourselves and others – and, in so doing, unravel the reality behind our decisions, behaviours and actions.

Why this framework?

To categorise human beings into groups such as personality types and socio-economic classes suggests we are fixed objects doomed to be dealing with our shortcomings for life. That is not only absurd, it's destructive on every conceivable level. Many disciplines of, or approaches to, mainstream modern psychology – like Personality Type Theory, Behaviourism and Positive Psychology – focus on fixing or refining individual thoughts, feelings and behaviours or, at best, behavioural and cognitive patterns. However, they ignore the deeper, more subtle, yet far more important qualities that drive our behaviours. I set out to define and map those deeper qualities and drivers of our behaviours, resulting in the Being Framework. As human beings, we are not fixed objects; we are not hardwired to remain how we currently are. This means we can change and transform. But to transform, we must first discover who and how we are being beneath the surface – the qualities that drive our behaviours and actions and the ones holding us back.

The Being Framework, as explored in this book and examined in great depth in my book, *BEING,* is a radical approach to applied psychology with its foundations in philosophy, particularly leveraging ontology, epistemology and phenomenology. It breaks down the reality of human beings into readily understood and relatable qualities, which I call Aspects of Being. It's like being given X-ray vision glasses that allow you to see through human beings – yourself and others – to the deeper layers you would otherwise not be able to see, bringing you to a whole new level of awareness. And then you are given effective and practical words and tools to articulate those qualities and begin the journey to facilitate transformation. By breaking down the reality of human beings into readily-digestible chunks and expressing it using a common language, the Being Framework delivers clarity in understanding and facilitates effective communication.

Why now?

In the modern era, we spend considerable time focusing on doing, achieving and having, and how we need to behave and act to get what we want. But we don't consider what is behind our behaviours, what drives them. To become a high achiever, a person of influence, and someone who is authentic and can read others well to avoid, mitigate and manage the pitfalls and challenges of life requires access to the deeper qualities of human beings, ourselves and others; to know human beings. Why others as well as ourselves? Because as human beings, we are social beings. To build an organisation, a business, a relationship, a movement or a team, we need to work and be with other people. Nobody can do it alone. Even renowned entrepreneurs like Steve Jobs, Elon Musk, Melanie Perkins and Jeff Bezos relied on their teams to achieve what they have. Therefore, if you cannot see beneath the facade when you are interviewing candidates to join your organisation or team, seeking a business partner, negotiating a business deal, acquiring a new customer or even dating someone for the first time, etc., you are setting yourself up for failure and disappointment.

Raising awareness of the reality of who and how you (and others) are being

HUMAN BEING casts light on our collective lack of understanding of human beings and how this leads to making ineffective, expensive and damaging decisions in our lives, the source of great pain and suffering, individually and collectively. It will paint a vivid picture of how you are being and how others are being, with the ultimate goal of creating a world in which everyone is a better version of themselves.

This book debunks the myths and shows you a radical and effective way to understand yourself and others. It gives you access to the lens and language to see, decode, assess (without judgement) and articulate the drivers of your behaviours and actions and those of the people around you. It is not about positive thinking or affirmation, and it's not a typical self-help book or a quick-fix recipe for success. It doesn't suggest that opportunities will miraculously fall in your lap if you follow the guidelines. Instead, it draws your attention to the extraordinary power of discovering and honing your well-polished qualities and casting light on and transforming your unpolished or troubled aspects. How you and others are being around the various qualities inherent to us as human beings will spark a transformational process and support you to see clearly when it comes to being with others. It will enable you to know human beings – yourself and others – better than ever before. This will enable you to make more effective decisions, know when to say yes and when to say no (and mean it), fulfil your intentions, achieve your objectives and be true to your authentic self for a life of influence, wealth (however that looks for you), meaning, fulfilment and wellbeing. Put simply, it's about how to BE so you can DO what it takes to HAVE what you care most about in life.

CHAPTER 1

A Lens into Human Beings

There is far more to human beings than just our emotions, thoughts, actions and the surface-level behaviours that are readily visible and accessible to others. And we humans are very capable of hiding what lies within, our deeper qualities, ulterior motives and, most importantly, our authentic selves. We excel at putting up a front, raising our guard, filtering what we say and portraying a fake persona, like a mask we wear depending on the situation. For some, this constant charade consumes them to the point where they no longer know who they really are. This presents problems when attempting to form meaningful personal and professional relationships.

Think of a first date you have been on where your date spends the entire evening working overly hard to portray the best possible image of themselves in the hope of a second date. Imagine if that person managed to maintain that facade and you ended up making a lifelong commitment to them. Eventually, the walls are bound to come down, but what if you are already sharing a life, a mortgage and children by then? Imagine the pain and suffering that would cause. Compare that to a first date where your date was open and honest with you from the start and continued to show you who they really are, warts and all, from that moment forward. This would enable you to decide whether or not you wish to pursue the relationship based on fact, not fiction.

Whether in a personal or professional context, people who are excessively obsessed with their reputation, for example, are likely to exaggerate, lie or deliberately hide the truth. Technology, particularly social media, has dramatically amplified this dynamic. Many people are so committed to selling the persona they have created that they constantly hide behind the mask. In my organisation, I see many startup entrepreneurs trying to scale their business despite not knowing much about business, investment, technology, marketing and all the other elements required to build a successful startup. Often, they try to sell us a persona, not realising that most angel investors – investors who inject capital in the early stages of a startup – don't expect their potential candidates to have much experience in business. An angel investor knows it's the beginning for the first-time entrepreneur, so being genuine and vulnerable enough to seek their advice and feedback around their business concept is seen in a far more positive light than if they were to exaggerate and boast in order to try and win them over. An effective and highly accomplished angel investor like Jason Calacanis, the author of *Angel – How to Invest in Technology Startups*, knows how to read people and build relationships founded on authenticity and vulnerability (two qualities, or Aspects of Being, that we will explore later in the book).

As social beings who have to relate to each other, interact, collaborate and work together for our survival and growth, not only do we face and are impacted by our own troubled parts, but we are also impacted by other people's troubled parts and misdemeanours, whether we like it or not. Since nobody is 'perfect' and we cannot import perfect beings from Mars or other planets, the best option is to train ourselves to understand human beings and decode the reality beneath the facade. The more authentic our awareness and understanding of human beings in general and the particular individuals we are teaming up with, the more effective we are likely to be. This is highly relevant to all the human interactions and relationships in which we typically engage, from being in a partnership in life to partnering with others in business and relating to others at work. And it is even more critical for those of us working towards a significant cause in our quest to lead a life of higher purpose. Before we look into understanding human beings through the Being Framework, let's consider why it is relevant to you and your life, specifically in terms of fulfilling what is important to you.

The Fulfilment Pyramid

The Being Framework enables us to zoom in on the deeper qualities of human beings, drawing attention to the areas that are working effectively and casting light on the troubled or ineffective parts, which I refer to in this book as the 'shadow'. It's like being given a magnifying lens to see yourself and others with sharper clarity than ever before. You may ask, why bother? The answer is because you CARE; we all do to varying degrees. The fact that you are reading this book shows you at least care enough to be curious. Perhaps you are more than just curious and have a sincere intention to expand your awareness of human beings, yourself and others. As shown in the Fulfilment Pyramid diagram, when you care about something, whether it be a cause, another human being or any endeavour you are working towards, it's only natural to want to be fulfilled in that pursuit.

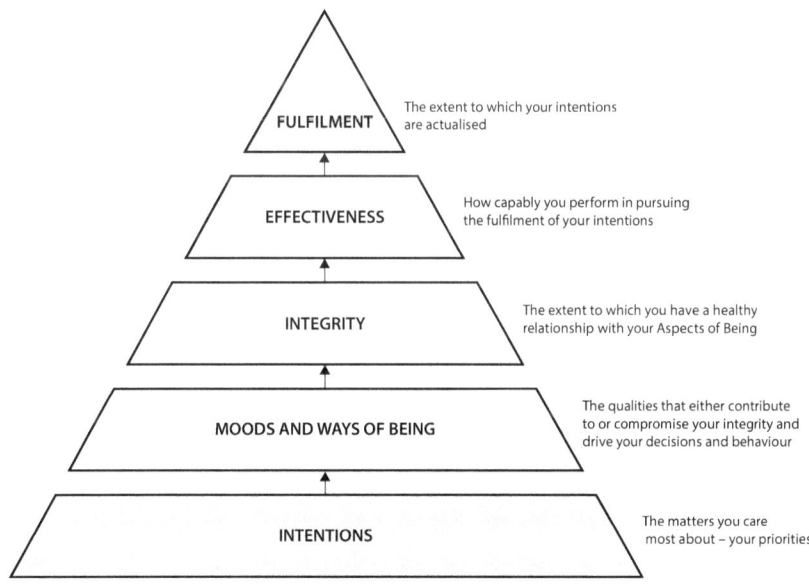

Fulfilment Pyramid

To fulfil the intentions you care deeply about requires you to be effective. And to be effective in your decisions, actions and endeavours, you need to be integrous; all the cogs in the machine – the parts, or Aspects of Being, that shape you into a whole and complete human being – must be working at an optimal level. None of this can happen without awareness. Later, we will learn that awareness, integrity and effectiveness are the top high-level Aspects of Being we acknowledge in the Being Framework.

To recap, we all have matters we care about. And when we care about something (or someone), we want to be fulfilled. To be fulfilled, we need to be effective in our decisions and actions. To be effective, we need to be integrous. And to be integrous, we need authentic awareness of the parts – Aspects of Being – that are getting in the way (the shadow parts). The greater the deviation from integrity or wholeness, the greater the suffering, for yourself and others. Why? Because no matter what stories you tell yourself, the religion you subscribe to, where in the world you live or the culture you were born into, you are here. Your presence, existence, everything you do, everything you create, the way you interpret and express your true self – or Unique Being, as I call it – to the world, and even the things you don't do; it all matters.

The Projection Process

We constantly express ourselves through our thoughts, emotions, feelings, speech, decisions, actions, body language and behaviours. These modes of expression appear on the surface and are therefore readily observable. Yet there are deeper, more subtle qualities that drive those surface-level expressions. In the Being Framework, the reality of this projection process has been modelled in the Projection Process diagram.

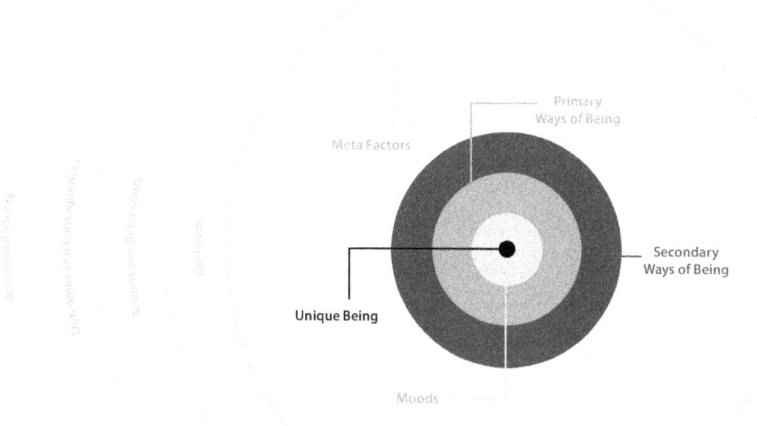

EXISTENCE

The Projection Process

When we are born, we are 'thrown' into the ocean of existence. From that moment on, however, everything we are and whatever we do in life releases another drop of water into that 'ocean', creating a ripple effect, as depicted by the outer circles in the diagram. This is a metaphorical way of articulating that you are constantly expressing yourself, whether or not you are present to that fact, just as a rose expresses itself through its exquisite beauty and scent. This expression of self starts from your Unique Being – what is there for you to express – before passing through your Moods, then your Primary Ways of Being, followed by your Secondary Ways of Being before ultimately being projected as your decisions, actions and behaviours. You could say that your decisions, actions and behaviours are the actualised version of the potential that is within you, waiting to be expressed. Then your decisions, actions and behaviours impact the reality around you. While this may all seem unfamiliar to you at this stage, rest assured we will be walking through each of the layers as you progress through the book.

Consider that you are a node in the network of all that exists (existence). By acknowledging this and taking it seriously, the opportunity to strive to be the leader of your own life by having influence over and being responsible for the decisions and actions you take would become apparent. From your choice of a life partner to your business, professional and lifestyle choices, your priorities – what you care most about – and choices will define your results and accomplishments and, ultimately, how fulfilled you will be in your life.

You are constantly being contributed to and you are also contributing, in one way or another, through your interactions with others. I call this our Paradox of Importance. So while it may seem like your presence in the world is insignificant in the greater scheme of things, who and how you are being and whatever you say and do has an impact. Even a leaf falling from a tree has an impact on the ecosystem, so why wouldn't you have an impact too? While it is inauthentic to consider yourself the epicentre of the universe, it is equally inauthentic to live life from the viewpoint that you don't matter and therefore have no influence. I encourage you to consider that everybody is somebody and we all have the potential to impact how others – at the very least those close to us – experience life. On a greater scale, each of us also has the potential to expand the shared reality out there for larger groups of people, even the whole of humanity.

You are free and autonomous. You are not hardwired to be a certain way. I encourage you to be aware of that and bring it into your intentional consciousness. Acknowledging this will enable you to make more effective decisions and take more effective actions and that will increase the probability that you will prosper and fulfil your intentions, whatever they may be. In short, it will give you more control over your life. Here lies the opportunity for transformation. We will explore the process of transformation in Chapter 5: Transformation Methodology.

Who you are – your Unique Being – is here to be expressed. However, unless you choose powerfully to work on **how** you are, your deeper qualities or Aspects of Being – Meta Factors, Moods, Primary Ways of Being and Secondary Ways of Being as shown in the Projection Process diagram – then it is very unlikely that you are going to be fully expressed and your intentions won't be actualised.

The Being Framework adopts an ontological ('let's get real') approach to understanding human beings. Ontology is the branch of philosophy that studies subjects such as existence, being, becoming, and reality.

In taking an ontological approach, we see a rock-solid fact about human beings: we are ALL self-interested. The very first question we keep asking ourselves is, 'What's in it for me?' And I want to assure you I am not coming from a moral standpoint here. It is what it is; it's neither good nor bad. The fact that we want to know how something will benefit us personally can lead us to care about certain matters in life and neglect others. This defines what we value and our priorities, which differ from one person to another. Yet the fact that we care is something we all have in common. We all have matters we care about. It's how we relate to the quality of care, one of the thirty-one Aspects of Being, that can differ. This is just one example of a quality we have in common as human beings which makes us, at least in part, able to be studied in an objective and scientific way. How you are being determines what you contribute, the extent to which you allow yourself to be contributed to and how much you accomplish in life, which is precisely why you should care.

The fact that each and every person has a unique set of matters they care most about leads to their unique contribution to the world. I call this the projection of your Unique Being. Your Unique Being is where your talents and innate qualities lie. Unless you become aware of and polish your Aspects of Being, your Unique Being (the real you) is at risk of being suppressed and may never be amplified and expressed to the world. This is not just personal; suppression of your Unique Being would be a liability to the whole of humanity! Imagine if Mozart, Beethoven, Celine Dion, Tesla, JK Rowling, Edison and Steve Jobs had not managed to express their Unique Being to the world. Not only did expressing their true selves fulfil their potential at an individual level, but it also provided meaning and context to their lives by sharing their unique contributions and being of service to others. I would like to acknowledge and convey my respect to them.

At this point, you may be thinking that some of the words I am using do not align with the meanings you attribute to those words. Integrity is a classic example. In dictionaries, the word integrity is commonly defined (at least in part) as the quality of being honest and having strong moral principles or something along those lines. It is seen as being honest and virtuous, which is what most people think of when using the word integrity. However, ontologically speaking, integrity is the state of being whole or complete. This is not a definition I have made up. It aligns closely with the definition of integrity defined by both the *Oxford English Dictionary* ('the state of being whole and undivided') and the *Cambridge Dictionary* ('the quality of being whole and complete'). You will likely observe some different distinctions for words used to convey other Aspects of Being in this book too. It is natural to question any meaning that differs from what you are accustomed to. However, because I adopted an ontological approach to my studies, I gave primacy to the meaning/concept I was trying to convey and did my best to choose the most appropriate word for it. Therefore, at times, I may use words differently to how they are conveniently used. Consequently, each Aspect of Being has an ontological distinction, as opposed to a definition, applied to it, with each distinction depicting a high-level and vivid picture of what the framework is referring to. This is an important point to keep in mind as you continue reading this book.

Before I conclude this chapter, it is important to acknowledge that not everyone has the same opportunity to fully express their Unique Being to the world. Think of those who are systematically oppressed, the minority groups impacted by the collective shared and manufactured reality of their time. I refer to this state as 'being a victim of collective psychosis'. Put simply, collective psychosis is what happens when there is a dissociation with reality on a collective scale. In other words, it is the epidemic of madness that occurs when a large proportion of a society loses touch with reality and descends into delusion. In my view, the oppression of some makes it all the more critical to respect our freedom and relatively high level of autonomy as human beings and choose powerfully to tap into and express our Unique Being rather than falling victim to circumstances. I talk more about collective psychosis in my book, *BEING*.

CHAPTER 2

The Being Framework
a radical paradigm to see yourself and others

Three key facts about human beings led to the development of this framework, a framework that will help us better understand ourselves and others. Firstly, an individual's behaviour only partly reveals who and how they really are. Secondly, there are deeper underlying qualities that drive our behaviours and actions. And last but not least, as human beings, we are not fixed objects; we can transform.

Of all the complex entities in the world, human beings are arguably the most complex. In conducting my research, I found that there are abundant resources that help people assess and work on single human qualities, like responsibility, assertiveness, fear and confidence. However, nothing considered who and how we are being holistically, the relationships between each quality, and how those relationships affect our behaviours and actions. I realised that unless we were able to map out the qualities we all share as human beings – and the relationships between those qualities – it would be like trying to complete a giant, extremely complicated jigsaw puzzle while wearing a blindfold.

The Being Framework is an engineered way of looking into our deeper qualities in a tangible, readily-digestible way. While it has a solid philosophical foundation, as discussed in detail in my book, *BEING*, I was committed from the outset to ensuring the framework would bring that philosophy into our daily lives. This commitment is far beyond a vision today, as the framework is increasingly being adopted by individuals, leaders and organisations around the globe. By breaking down the complex puzzle into smaller pieces, the framework supports us to understand and articulate the constituent parts that make up human beings. Furthermore, the framework does not slot people into categories or boxes as some other popular schools of thought and many psychological tests do. Instead, it supports us to understand and discover the missing pieces of the puzzle, making us more self-aware and aware of others.

Many people who have adopted the framework to date have reported that it also supports them to relate to and digest content produced by other thinkers far more effectively. That's because one of the Being Framework's primary objectives is to support us to relate to awareness and thinking, in and of themselves, as opposed to purely introducing a particular belief or opinion. In this way, the framework also encourages and supports authentic and critical thinking.

The Being Framework consists of three core components:

- **The Ontological Model** – In this model, I have mapped out the qualities of human beings linked to our influence, performance and ability to be the leader of our own lives and the relationships that hold true between those qualities.

- **The Transformation Methodology™** – A model and series of processes and principles designed to lead an individual on a transformational journey.

- **The Being Profile®** – The core assessment tool associated with the Being Framework, which accurately measures an individual's relationship with all thirty-one Aspects of Being, providing them with a 'health' score for each one.

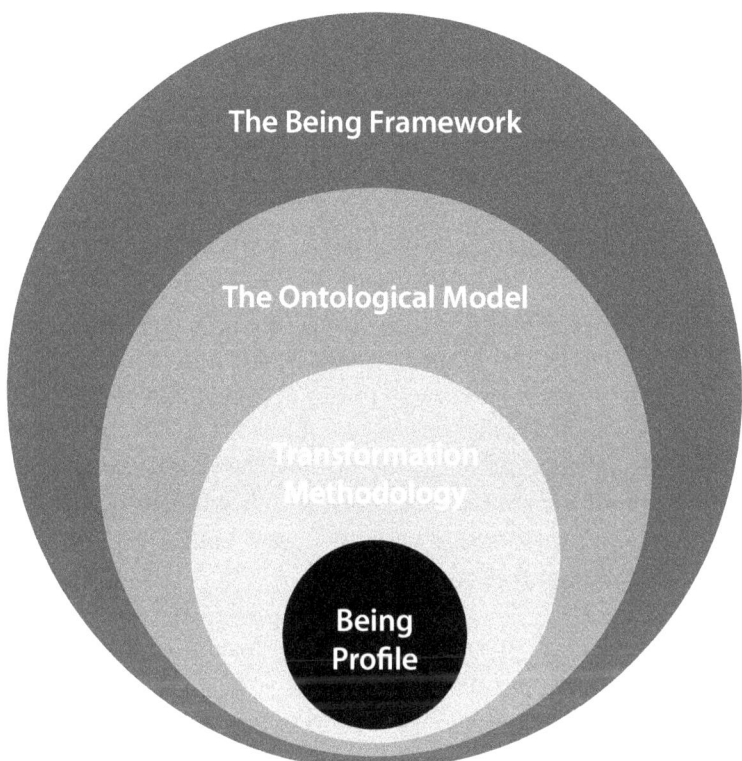

The Being Framework

Let me explain, with a simple example, what I mean in reference to the Ontological Model mapping out the qualities of human beings. Imagine you are presented with the following data: brown, 1988 and Neil. It's hard to make sense of this data because it is nothing more than an array of textual data when presented this way. Now imagine you are presented with the metadata for this array of textual data – the information explaining what each piece of data refers to – for example, name, year of birth and hair colour. This additional information enables you to match the corresponding data to its metadata. From this, you can extrapolate that Neil is a person who was born in 1988 and has brown hair.

The Being Framework Ontological Model presents the metadata for how you, as an instance of the class 'human being', are being. For example, you, like everyone else, have a relationship with awareness, authenticity, fear, care, commitment, etc. Although, objectively, you share all of this with others of the same class, subjectively, you relate differently to each of these attributes. So the ontological model provides the metadata. How you, as an individual, relate to each quality within the model is considered data. Both the metadata and data enable relevant information or knowledge to be extracted about you.

This book focuses on the Ontological Model component of the framework to raise your awareness of the reality of human beings. I will also introduce you to the principles of transformation in Chapter 5: Transformation Methodology. Essentially, the Transformation Methodology is a series of processes and practical exercises geared to support you to work towards a higher degree of awareness and effectiveness in all Aspects of Being, but especially those with which you have an unhealthy relationship and therefore need to work on. The more Aspects of Being you have a healthy relationship with, the higher your degree of integrity (wholeness) and overall effectiveness.

By gaining an insight into the Ontological Model and its thirty-one Aspects of Being as provided in this book, you will see human beings – yourself and others – with greater clarity than ever before. This awareness alone will likely influence your perceptual structure and alter some of your perceptions and the stories you have told yourself about human behaviour and performance in the past. It will empower you to move forward with more confidence, freedom, effectiveness and peace of mind. In addition to enabling you to see human beings in sharp clarity and from a unique perspective for the first time, the Being Framework Ontological Model gives you a means to clearly articulate how you and others are being. Imagine how advantageous that will be next time you're discussing an important matter with your life partner or attempting to get to the bottom of an issue with an employee or colleague at work! Furthermore, by learning the principles of transformation, you will have some simple yet effective tools in your arsenal that will enable you to work on yourself for each Aspect of Being where you find yourself struggling.

Importantly, the Being Framework is a judgement- and values-free paradigm. When I talk about the health of your relationship with an Aspect of Being, there is no right or wrong, positive or negative. It doesn't prescribe how you should be, what you should take as moral or immoral, or actively promote a particular ideology. It is a snapshot of reality, so it is what it is. It will show you that, like a coin, there are always two sides. In the case of our Aspects of Being, there is always a light side and a troubled side (shadow). At times, one will dominate over the other. When the shadow is dominant, it will act as a roadblock, preventing you from achieving wellbeing and integrity and impacting the workability and effectiveness of your performance. Consequently, it may get in the way of you achieving your goals. Addressing the shadow begins with awareness. You can't effectively address a physical ailment if you don't know why it's happening and the underlying reason. That's why diagnosis is the first step in any medical intervention. The same is true when it comes to your Being. It is not until you have gained awareness of your relationship with your Aspects of Being that you can see what's stopping you from hitting your targets or being happy and fulfilled.

Let's now zoom into the Being Framework Ontological Model. The right-hand side of the model, shown overleaf, represents you as a complete human being, at the centre of which lies your Unique Being. You will recognise the image from the Projection Process diagram in Chapter 1: A Lens into Human Beings. As mentioned earlier, this is the real authentic you, the person you are meant to be according to the talents and gifts you were born with and your potential. The next layer is Moods, which in the context of this model are vulnerability, care, anxiety and fear. Between Unique Being and Moods lies Temperament. Temperament seems hard-wired from birth. My studies revealed that our innate temperament influences our Moods, which is why I have included it in the model. The two outer circles are Primary Ways of Being – underlying Ways of Being that are primal to all human beings – and Secondary Ways of Being – Ways of Being that are readily observable in our decisions, behaviours and actions.

Let's now examine Unique Being more closely and consider why it matters. In a nutshell, your Unique Being, to a great extent, determines your innate calling and talents – your 'thing'. We will explore this more when we talk about self-expression, a Primary Way of Being. It is your distinction from others. While existentially we are all from the same root, you are a distinct piece of the puzzle that makes up the masterpiece in its totality and is unique enough not to be readily replaceable by another puzzle piece. Many artists, entrepreneurs, inventors and others tap into their Unique Being. Since it is so scarce, they leverage its power in self-expression, setting up their lives around it, building their careers and even monetising their unique art or service. As long as your uniqueness doesn't fool you into considering yourself to be the epicentre of the universe, leading you to be inauthentic and project a bloated and exaggerated personality and become arrogant, your Unique Being is there to give your life meaning.

Unique Being explains why there can be two identical twins where one is instinctively drawn to sport from a very young age while the other is more interested in creative play from the same age, despite growing up with the same parents in the same environment. Some refer to this part of themselves as their soul or spirit. Essentially, it is you at the deepest possible level. Most of the world's greatest leaders and high achievers know and understand their Unique Being and have aligned their lifestyle and profession to it. If you ignore your innate uniqueness, you will miss out on its immense rewards, and so will the rest of humanity. The Being Framework Ontological Model does not delve too much into

Awareness	Integrity	Effectiveness	
Vulnerability	Care	Anxiety	Fear
Authenticity	Peace of Mind	Empowerment	Compassion
Commitment	Freedom	Contribution	Forgiveness
Responsibility	Self Expression	Love	Courage
Higher Purpose	Presence	Partnership	Gratitude
Resourcefulness	Proactivity	Resilience	Assertiveness
Confidence	Reliability	Accountability	Persistence

The Being Framework Ontological Model Layer

this unique aspect of ourselves, as it seems to be very mysterious and intangible at times. However, it is important to be aware of it, not only within yourself, but also within the people you associate with, from your work colleagues, business partner and employees to your life partner, children, extended family and friends. The most important thing to remember is that the healthier your relationship with your Aspects of Being, the higher the chance that you will discover, realise and actualise your Unique Being.

To the left of the model, you will observe that the thirty-one Aspects of Being are broken down into four layers: Meta Factors, Moods, Primary Ways of Being and Secondary Ways of Being. These will be explained in greater detail in upcoming chapters, but here is a high-level overview of each layer.

Meta Factors are the high-level qualities of awareness, integrity and effectiveness. They are the three factors that influence your performance, power and ability to lead. Awareness has an impact on all Aspects of Being, integrity is impacted by your Primary Ways of Being and Moods, while all Aspects of Being contribute to your effectiveness.

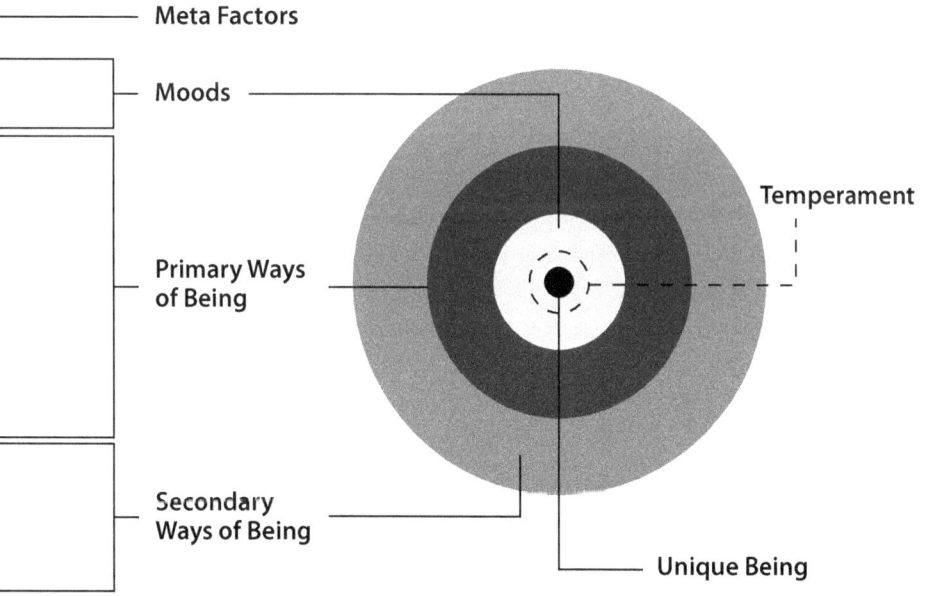

Imagine you are driving a car and are unaware of the motorbike in your blind spot when you're about to overtake the car in front of you. The consequences of your lack of, or unhealthy relationship with, awareness could be catastrophic. Similarly, if you don't see or ignore the rust developing in the roof of your car, you will neglect to have it fixed and end up with a hole that is beyond repair. You can't influence anything you can't see or about which you are unaware. In other words, it is impossible to be intentionally effective in something around which you lack awareness or have misunderstood. Returning to the car analogy, once a hole has developed in the roof, it is no longer whole and complete, meaning it has lost its integrity and is no longer effective.

Moods and their relationships with Primary Ways of Being are like the warning lights on your dashboard that indicate if something is not functioning as it should. At times they will compel you to apply your foot on the accelerator or the brake. Moods are the qualities that set the scene, give context to your participation and are at the heart of what drives you deep down. They are also the channels through which you disclose yourself to the world. The four Moods in the model are fear, anxiety, care and vulnerability. Put simply, the healthier your relationship with these Moods, the more effectively you will disclose yourself to the world.

You attune yourself to the orchestra of all other beings playing the symphony of life through your Moods, which play a significant role in how you experience life. Moods set the context for your action or inaction and, therefore, also for your performance. For example, while some may see it as a negative trait to be vulnerable, it is actually the opposite. To have a healthy relationship with vulnerability means you are open and not prone to putting your guard up when you are excessively concerned about how you are being perceived or thought of in different situations. But when you have an unhealthy relationship with vulnerability, your ability to communicate with others is impaired. The same is true with fear. The healthier your relationship with fear, the less it will prevent you from taking considered risks and moving forward. A healthy relationship with fear also supports you to avoid taking impulsive, overzealous, uncalculated risks.

Primary Ways of Being distinguish the fundamental ways through which you project the true manifestation of who you are and how you experience yourself to be in the world. These primal qualities impact your behaviour, performance and the subsequent results you produce in life. In other words, they determine the way you contribute to your work, engage in relationships, participate in life and also how you experience and expand on the shared reality around you. For example, one of these qualities is authenticity – whether you are being yourself or are in the mode of pretending and filtering your expression of self as well as how sincere and accurate or lenient and fickle you are in shaping your beliefs and opinions. Primary Ways of Being are deep and subtle so they may not be clearly visible in your behaviours and/or the behaviours of others.

Secondary Ways of Being are behavioural factors that bridge the gap between the subtle, deeper parts of you – awareness (a Meta Factor), Moods and Primary Ways of Being – and the outward manifestation of your subsequent decisions, behaviours and actions others can see. An example of a Secondary Way of Being is assertiveness. When you are assertive, you openly and firmly say what is on your mind and needs to be said while taking full responsibility for it, instead of being submissive or aggressive.

Being aware of your relationship with your Aspects of Being enables you to be present to the gaps, blind spots or the matters you are in denial about, and how much more effective, happy and fulfilled you would be if you could shift or transform them. The good news is you can, as you will see from the two scenarios below. These scenarios also show how no Aspect of Being shows up in isolation.

A tangible example of how your Aspects of Being play their role in your life

Imagine you are in an uncomfortable argument with your partner, whether it is your business partner or life partner. When you want to express yourself, your Moods are the first Aspects of Being to set in. For the sake of this discussion, let's say your dominant Mood at the time is anxiety or concern about the future. You ask yourself, 'What if I bring up my genuine complaint or request and he/she leaves me again? And what if it escalates the matter at hand?' This then channels into your Primary Ways of Being – for example, authenticity – causing you to start filtering what you want to communicate. This leads you to package your argument in such a way that you assume it won't create more problems on the surface. With your anxiety Mood occupying the driver's seat, another Primary Way of Being is being impacted: your presence – you are no longer paying full attention to the conversation as your inner voices are taking you away from the matter at hand and, more specifically, what is being communicated by the other person. Two other Primary Ways of Being may also be impacted: self-expression – you feel you are not getting a chance to express what you initially wanted to communicate and may feel you are not being heard – and freedom, in that you may feel restrained and suppressed. Now we move to the Secondary Ways of Being – let's say assertiveness – which has never been your strong suit as you generally have a tendency to be submissive in these types of situations. Failing to communicate your perspective, you hold resentment towards your partner. You are now a victim and start to self-sabotage. I'm sure you know where this is going and that the only outcome of having an unhealthy relationship with these Aspects of Being is suffering, both for yourself and others.

Now imagine you have a healthy and effective relationship with anxiety, authenticity, presence, self-expression, freedom and assertiveness. Let's recreate that scenario. You are arguing with your partner. While you have concerns about the future, you find it important and trust that this conversation needs to take place. You can be with anxiety and the discomfort it brings as you acknowledge it as a necessary part of the relationship. It does not suppress you, so you find no reason to be inauthentic and you are present, in sync and in communication with your partner, politely telling them that you have a complaint and a request. You share it with them assertively and appropriately demand a response. You engage in the conversation and ask for a commitment or give your partner the opportunity to share their point of view authenti-cally and assertively. There may be a need for gentle confrontation with the intention of restoring the integrity of your relationship and, while uncomfortable, you give it what it takes because you are committed to resolving the problem so that the relationship can continue. Even if your partner resists and shuts down, you can appropriately confront them and hold them to account. Naturally, this example depicts the scenario from one side only; the other person's Being in any situation is always as important to be aware of as yours.

The first scenario illustrates an unhealthy relationship with the Aspects of Being in question, while the second illustrates a healthy relationship with the same Aspects of Being. Which scenario would you prefer? The good news is even if you feel as though you are stuck in scenarios like the first one, you can transform using the Transformation Methodology principles explained later. Over time and with practice, you will even be able to catch yourself and shift whenever you start to slip into your old bad habits. Imagine how a scenario like this would look in the workplace. Communication is critical in any professional setting, only on a larger scale in most cases. Can you see from this example how our collective Beings have the potential to make it or break it in the workplace? Collectively, we can create a relatively higher degree of effective communication, which generates trust, or compromise the effectiveness of our communication, diminishing trust. The degree to which we are effective in communication and trust determines workability and flow. In this way, a team's collective Being can dramatically impact the success of projects and either cost the organisation dearly or bring workability and profitability.

In summary, your Being directly impacts your effectiveness, integrity and ultimately your ability to express your true self (Unique Being), fulfil your intentions, achieve your goals and live a life of wellbeing and fulfilment. And the same is true when it comes to the Being of others around you, such as in your relationship, family and organisation. By offering you a lens into how you are being in the world and how you engage with others, the Being Framework empowers you with knowledge that can be applied in all areas of your life.

CHAPTER 3

The Exposure Triangle
shaping your conception of reality

A re you frequently overwhelmed by the constant explosion of data that inundates you on a daily basis or have you learned to ignore irrelevant information? How do you even know what is relevant and what isn't? In other words, how do you discern what to intentionally bring to your consciousness, be present to and care about versus what to ignore, let go, neglect and forgive? The answer will support you to determine your relationship with reality in terms of how you see yourself, others and the world around you. Becoming clear on your intentions and expectations of yourself and others, and casting light on your Being to reveal the shadows – the troubled parts of yourself that need addressing – will facilitate your ability to transform and fulfil your intentions and the objectives you set for yourself in life.

Why is this chapter, which is focused on reality, called The Exposure Triangle? Just as a photographer relies on a camera's aperture, ISO and shutter speed to vividly and clearly capture snapshots of chunks of reality, our ability to check the accuracy, congruence and clarity of our perceptions relies on the health of three key Aspects of Being: awareness, vulnerability and authenticity. These core qualities massively influence our perceptual structure when it comes to seeing – and not just looking at – ourselves and others. I call this the 'Exposure Triangle'. When the configurations and settings on a camera are not adjusted effectively, they produce blurry or distorted pictures. The same is true for us. If our self-image, the persona we project, beliefs, opinions and interpretations of matters in life (our conceptions) are not aligned with reality – if they are blurry or distorted – it is very unlikely that we fulfil the intentions we most care about.

Before we explore the Exposure Triangle analogy further, I would like to bring your awareness to the importance of vision with respect to shaping your conception of reality and making sense of the world and everything in it. I am not referring to vision in the sense of a business vision or goal. I am talking about vision in the literal sense: your ability to see and observe, which shapes your relationship with reality. Why is this important? For the simple reason that if you are oblivious to or choose to ignore reality, you risk spending the majority of your time on matters that will lead you away from growth rather than towards it, causing you to regress instead of thrive. This chapter explains the relationships between the three Aspects of Being that, when combined, either help or hinder us from having a healthy relationship with reality.

We are all born into a culture with a pre-existing language, set of values and accepted codes of conduct, behavioural patterns and ways of thinking. The dominant way of thinking seems to be that we can invent almost anything without first doing a reality check. How do you relate to reality? To answer this question, it's important to first take a step back and consider what reality is. While you may think the answer is obvious, it's actually not that simple because reality is multifaceted. In other words, there are distinctively different meanings we refer to when using the word 'reality'. To be precise, there are three layers of reality. Firstly, there are the absolutes of the world. This refers to the reality that is not open to debate or negotiation because it is dictated to us, such as the laws of the universe, for example, physics, biology, gravity, etc. Secondly, there are man-made inventions, like money and our taxation and banking systems – these are examples of what we might call our 'shared reality'. And thirdly, there are the stories we make up and tell ourselves as individuals. This is our personal reality. To see clearly, it is critical to discern between these layers.

The point is, when it comes to the first-layer reality, there are things to be discovered. It is this first layer of reality – the one to be discovered, not invented – that I tapped into when formulating the Being Framework Ontological Model. For example, when it comes to fear, one of four Moods in the model, no one can argue that they are fearless or don't have a relationship with fear, although some would have us believe that being fearless is possible. Such a view is inauthentic because fear is innately present within all of us at times; it is part of being human. It is courage, a Way of Being, that enables us to step forward despite the presence of fear. It is impossible to be courageous unless fear is present.

While I tapped into first-layer reality to identify the individual Aspects of Being, I created constructs to depict a holistic picture. For example, the term 'Meta Factor', which is a term I came up with, is my third-layer reality construct. When I communicate that construct to others, it becomes our shared reality (second-layer reality). By communicating constructs, we expand the shared reality.

We all choose to have an incongruent conception of reality at times. This happens for various reasons, from the way we were raised and the immediate benefits we think we may receive holding such views to our unwillingness to be open to the truth. Or we may be inauthentic, lenient and lazy in cherry-picking our beliefs and opinions around particular matters at times. Unless we are encouraged to question our pre-existing ways of thinking or develop an inner desire to do so, we tend to accept that this is just the way things are. For instance, we often use words without thinking because we know what they mean, or at least we think we do.

Imagine you are having a conversation with someone and you come across a word that you both understand differently. One of you is convinced it means one thing, while the other has always applied a different definition to the same word. Consequently, you end up in an argument over the meaning. You do an online search for the answer only to discover both of you could be considered right based on the various definitions that come up in your search. The World Wide Web is not the only place where discrepancies arise. If you look up the word courage, for example, using a few commonly referenced dictionaries, don't be surprised if you find a different definition in each one. So, how can we know what's real and what's not if the authors of dictionaries can't even agree on one definition? It's as though they leave it up to us to make a choice. And how can we effectively communicate with others if we don't have the same understanding of words?

As if it's not confusing enough to have various dictionary definitions applied to words, we also pick up meanings from childhood, often carrying them with us throughout life. As a consequence, we tend to rely on our perceptions and assumptions, and these aren't always correct. Imagine if a pharmacist misunderstood an instruction by a doctor on a script for their patient, or a construction manager misconstrued the structural engineering plans when instructing their team on a high-rise project. Both could have dire consequences.

Why am I explaining the different layers of reality and the confusion surrounding words and meanings? Because being aware of the absolutes of the world (the first layer of reality) and being open to letting that information in will enable you to see things the way they really are. My objective when distinguishing courage as an Aspect of Being was to discover its true meaning based on the first layer of reality I described. In this way, we could call courage 'x' and it would still mean the same thing. The same is true for all other Aspects of Being in the Being Framework. For the intellectual sceptics out there who may argue that the meaning of courage is relative, let me clarify further. By courage, I am referring to the quality that manifests when a mother bear senses a perceived threat towards her cubs or knows they are in danger. This transcendent meaning is so primal that it is inherent in our nature. Furthermore, from a transhistorical perspective, the actions and Ways of Being of leaders throughout history testify that courage exists, as demonstrated by their choices to step into danger despite the presence of fear.

Seeing the reality of matters is like taking off a grimy pair of reading glasses and putting them back on after giving them a thorough clean. It is only when our vision is crystal clear that we can discern where to focus our energy. Just as a phone battery has limited capacity, the same is true for our energy. Most people waste an enormous amount of time and energy on areas that hinder their growth because they can't – or won't allow themselves to – see what's really going on with complete clarity. You could say they are delusional. This gets in the way of whatever they want to achieve and therefore prevents them from ever being truly fulfilled. Nobody is immune to this, myself included. The difference is that some of us deem it worthwhile to become aware of our reality so we can work on polishing and transforming those parts of ourselves that hinder us from growth, while others do not.

Relating to parts of reality

If you have ever practised photography, you would recognise the terminology used when I refer to the word 'exposure'. I use this analogy because it depicts how we human beings see matters and relate to the various chunks of reality to which we are present in any given moment.

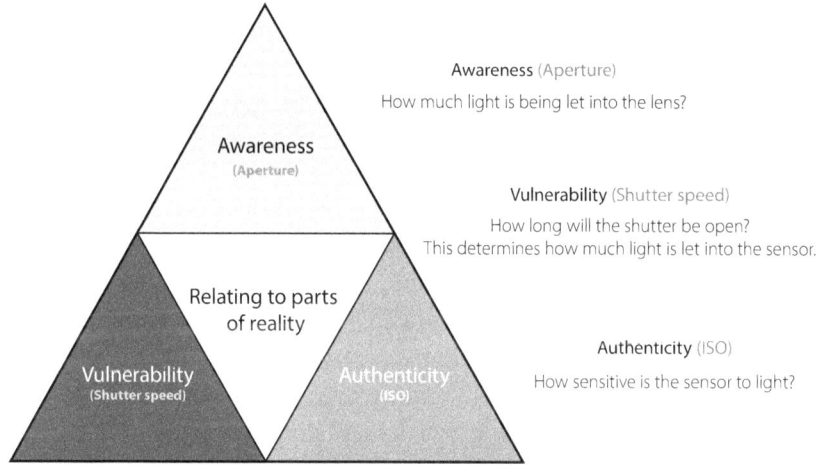

The Exposure Triangle

Just like the aperture on a camera, we develop our awareness (intentional consciousness) based on how much 'light' – or true and authentic knowledge – we let in. The shutter speed is the length of time the shutter is open. The longer the shutter is open, the more light it lets in and the brighter the image. This is about how open you are to the truth, reflecting your vulnerability. The more vulnerable you are, the more at peace you are with your authentic self and the better you will communicate with others. And then there's ISO, which refers to the sensitivity of the camera's sensor. This is about how sensitive we are to the 'light'. In other words, how important is it to you that your beliefs and opinions align with how things really are? This highlights your authenticity. Having a healthy relationship with all three Aspects of Being – awareness, vulnerability and authenticity – is necessary to create a clear, undistorted picture of reality and to have the vision to see with clarity.

Let's look at a tangible example. Imagine you see your doctor to have an annual health check. You undergo a series of tests and the results indicate that your blood pressure, visceral fat levels and cholesterol are dangerously high, putting you at risk of heart disease or a stroke. After quizzing you on your daily habits, the doctor advises that you need to urgently cut back on your consumption of unhealthy foods and alcohol and recommends a program of healthy eating and exercise. In sharing your results and the potential ramifications of doing nothing and continuing on your current course, the doctor has raised your awareness of the situation. However, you choose to turn a blind eye to the results because you feel fine. This points to an unhealthy relationship with awareness because you aren't letting the 'light' (the reality of what your doctor is telling you) in. In other words, you are ignoring the congruent and authentic view provided by the doctor.

What's more, you don't want to miss out on all the festivities you have planned and can't bear the thought of giving up your daily alcohol and sweets. So you decide to act as though nothing is wrong and choose to avert your gaze from what you know to be true and, more importantly, relevant to you and the context of your life. Instead, you tell yourself you'll be fine, indicating an unhealthy relationship with authenticity. You decide to keep your results to yourself, not even sharing them with your partner, once again highlighting a shadow side of authenticity. Your partner, who cares deeply about you, confronts you over the doctor's diagnosis and prognosis, causing you to raise your guard, insisting that it's not important and nowhere near as dire as the report suggests. Your resistance to the facts and your partner's concern indicates an unhealthy relationship with vulnerability.

Six months later, you end up in hospital after suffering a stroke. The point is that reality doesn't care about your views, ignorance, inauthenticity and invulnerability. Had you been aware, authentic and vulnerable, you would have understood the reality check you were being given and heeded the advice of the doctor. In this case, having a stroke may cause certain ongoing limitations, which could impact your job, your finances and your relationship with your partner and children. Switch the scenario to one where you had a healthy relationship with awareness, vulnerability and authenticity and you would have taken the doctor's advice on board, prioritising your time and energy to the things that matter, in this case, the activities designed to restore you to health.

Being aware of the Exposure Triangle will support you to constantly capture snapshots of various chunks of reality as they are presented to you. It's not designed to be a one-off exercise. For example, when it comes to your financial health, there are many perceptions you need to keep refining as you progress through life and your circumstances change so that you can operate from the viewpoint of an aware, vulnerable and authentic person at each stage. If you have an unhealthy relationship with awareness, vulnerability and authenticity, you may be seeing a distorted and blurry reality leading you to delusive conceptions and views. It's just like trying to capture a photograph through a distorted and blurry lens. In short, when we have an unhealthy relationship with awareness, vulnerability and authenticity most of the time, we see the world differently and have a distorted view of reality. This prevents us from operating to our full capacity. It's like sitting in the driver's seat of a car without mirrors. What chance would we have of arriving at our destination without hurting ourselves or others?

At this point you may wonder why I am focusing on these particular Aspects of Being when there are thirty-one in total. My studies, combined with the vast empirical data gathered and collective experience of our community of ontological coaches, highlighted the importance of tackling awareness, vulnerability and authenticity before looking into other Aspects of Being, like responsibility, assertiveness, freedom, confidence, etc. That's because if you are not aiming to be authentic about the things you are about to become aware of (authenticity and awareness) or you have your guard up and are not letting anything in (vulnerability), those missing parts will continue to be blind spots, matters you intentionally ignore and therefore fail to respond to or address. These gaps in your life will lead you away from integrity (wholeness), wellbeing and growth. We will explore awareness, vulnerability and authenticity individually in the coming chapters.

To sum up, there is no direction or understanding of what is going on without vision. Without vision, you will find it extremely difficult, if not impossible, to fulfil your intentions and achieve your potential. You need a healthy relationship with awareness, vulnerability and authenticity to see, discern and access chunks of reality. Without that access, you may never achieve a life of fulfilment and effectiveness. Therefore, addressing how you relate to these Aspects of Being is vital at the beginning of any transformation process. In short, when you have an unhealthy relationship with awareness, vulnerability and authenticity, the result is a distorted conception of reality, including the reality of yourself and others. It's like trying to take a photograph on a professional camera without paying attention to the aperture, shutter speed and ISO settings and expecting a perfect result.

CHAPTER 4

Shadow
casting light on one's Being to reveal the troubled sides

As human beings, we are constantly evolving and changing. I am not just referring to the natural changes that occur as we age. I'm talking about how we are being as individuals, our progress in life and our achievements and growth – or regression – over time. As discussed in the previous chapter, when it comes to first-layer reality, there is a metaphysical law of existence – something is either thriving or perishing. So while we are constantly changing, the direction we take is our choice. We must learn to discern whether we will choose the pathway of regression or growth in relation to all aspects of our lives, from our basic survival to our wealth, health, wisdom, career and relationships.

Consider for a moment how you would compare your current self to the person you were five years ago. What have you achieved over that time? Who and how have you become? What parts of you have you transformed? Have you effectively set the trajectory of how you are choosing to project your Unique Being to the world, whether through art, music, dance, your career, a small business, your organisation, family, relationships, philanthropic pursuits, etc.? Do you believe you are in a better place today than you were back then or have you regressed? Perhaps nothing has changed and you have stagnated. The truth is, every moment that passes, you are moving towards the future you. And every one of those moments that you are not using with awareness to inch closer to fulfilling your intentions and reaching your goals is a loss you will regret sooner or later because you will never get that time back.

Just as regular maintenance is essential to ensure a property's capital value improves over time and repair work must be undertaken when parts of the property break down, your Being requires maintenance, care and polishing too. But to know which parts to work on, you must first become aware of the areas that are taxing you or getting in your way of achieving your goals. I refer to those areas as the shadow. These are the diminished, misaligned or misunderstood parts that draw you away from integrity and wellbeing, and prevent you from being effective, achieving your goals and being fulfilled.

We all have troubled or shadow parts of ourselves – the Aspects of Being with which we have an unhealthy relationship – and, like the shadow cast by the sun, they change in response to whatever life brings our way. By intentionally and regularly casting light on your Being to reveal the shadow and maintaining its integrity over time, you will considerably influence the decisions you make and the actions you take. Ultimately, this will go a long way to determining the future you. This chapter examines the shadow, how to reveal it and why we should care about it.

What is the shadow?

Every Aspect of Being has shadow sides. These shadows prevent us from giving our intentional consciousness to the matters that contribute to our growth. The more we feed the shadows with our intentional consciousness, the more they take us away from integrity and the more we regress rather than grow. By casting light on our Being, we not only get to know the Aspects of Being we have a relatively healthy relationship with – the ones that are contributing to our overall integrity and therefore enabling us to produce our desired results – but also those we don't: our shadow parts.

Just as it is critical to be aware of the Aspects of Being you have a healthy relationship with so you can own them powerfully and hone in on them to enhance your experience of life, it is equally paramount to raise your awareness of your shadow sides: the Aspects of Being where health is diminished. For example, a person who has a healthy relationship with vulnerability – one of the Moods – is not only okay with discovering their shadows; they are thrilled to find yet another area they can own and address before it causes more damage and suffering.

The shadows of the various Aspects of Being come in different forms, meaning it is not just a case of a lack or presence of the quality. That's why we say someone has 'an unhealthy relationship' with an Aspect of Being to convey the shadow instead of saying they lack that quality. For example, it's not just a matter of courage being present or lacking in an individual. Instead, the two common shadows of courage are cowardice on the one hand and recklessness on the other. Cowardice demonstrates an inability to step forward when fear is present. In contrast, recklessness conveys exaggerated courage or bravado, which can be equally dangerous. Let's look at responsibility as another example. One shadow side of responsibility is being a passive victim of the circumstances of life. It's as if life is only happening to you and you can't influence its course. The other shadow side of responsibility is being overly responsible, to the point where you are a control freak and live life from the viewpoint that you are the only primary cause of the matters in your life, which is far removed from reality.

To better understand the shadow, I encourage you to take a step back and accept a fundamental truth about reality, no matter whether it sits in the first or second layer. For any system to have integrity, the constituent parts must come together to shape a whole. Furthermore, for the system to have integrity, each individual part must also have integrity; in other words, all parts that make up the complete system should work at an optimal level. It only takes an unhealthy relationship with one part for the entire system to malfunction. Take a car, for example. If any mechanical part required for the car to function at an optimal level is malfunctioning, the car as a whole entity will not run effectively. The greater the number of malfunctioning parts, the less effectively the car will run. Eventually, it will break down and stop running altogether. While human beings in their totality can't be compared to machines, as a system, our species shares this fundamental law: the optimal performance of the constituent parts leads to integrity and, therefore, the optimal performance of the whole.

Any malfunctioning part will cast a shadow once you shine light on it from the right angle. The shadow cast will manifest, and this can have a snowball effect in terms of the shadow's impact on other parts. If the shadow parts of yourself were to overcome you, it would result in suffering, both for yourself and others. There would be little work-ability in your life and your wellbeing would be compromised. When the shadow takes over, all aspects of your life are impacted, from prosperity and fulfilment to relationships, including your relationship with yourself. You may not be able to tolerate the person you have become to the point where life feels like a burden. And once your experience of life is a burden to you, it's hard to live life with grace. Imagine the impact of the shadow on a collective scale. For example, consider being in a relationship or part of a team where multiple shadows run the show. Can you imagine how toxic things would be? Shadows don't tend to go away on their own. They hang around, grow and manifest until they become all-encompassing if they are ignored and not addressed.

Take the shadow side of authenticity, for instance, a Way of Being we touched on in the last chapter. If you constantly compare yourself to people you believe are superior, you may waste precious time wishing you could be more like them. Jealousy, disappointment in yourself and a lack of empowerment may cause you to focus so much attention on those negative voices in your head that they draw you away from the important matters, the ones that will lead you towards growth. When the shadow side of authenticity is running the show, it may also entice you to forge a fake and bloated persona hoping that others believe the made-up image you are portraying. This may manifest itself as lies and dishonesty, for example. In other words, your inauthenticity – the parts of you that are not authentic, the stories you tell yourself – represent a shadow side of your authenticity.

Becoming intentionally conscious of your troubled sides isn't easy. It's confronting, challenging and can be intensely uncomfortable at times. It takes courage. Most people would prefer to avert their gaze from the shadows or hide them in a closet where they assume they are not visible to anyone, including themselves, rather than face them. Someone who doesn't see the value in being vulnerable, for instance, would avoid being vulnerable by constantly having their guard up and refusing to be open to the ideas and opinions or feedback of others. Instead, they may pretend life is perfect and they have everything in order and under control. This can cause many other issues to arise. The same is true when any other Aspect of Being is troubled, revealing a shadow side.

That's because sometimes our shadow demands things of us that we are not comfortable with, like not remaining loyal and committed in a relationship we are struggling with or maintaining the fake persona we are projecting to the world rather than revealing our authentic self.

If you're not open and humble, you will have no clear sense of what's missing and why you're not getting the results you want or responding appropriately to the things life is bringing you. As a consequence, you may end up believing you are simply a victim of circumstances – that life is happening to you and you have no control, signalling an unhealthy relationship with responsibility, as highlighted in a previous example. This may lead you to give up and 'just go with it' or sabotage yourself to keep feeding that voice in your head that says you are a victim. It may even cause you to blame others for everything that's not going right in your life; what a waste of time and energy that would be.

The shadow is not only a liability – it's an opportunity for growth

The Being Framework supports you to cast light on your Being to reveal the shadow or troubled parts of yourself. It then encourages you to break down each part into smaller, easy-to-understand chunks. By breaking it down, the framework enables you to address each troubled aspect and get to the bottom or root cause of why it's happening, particularly when supported by a Being Profile Accredited Practitioner, which is the recommended approach. Once you have that awareness, you can begin the process of transformation using the Transformation Methodology to facilitate that process, as explained later. This process is also most effective when supported by a coach trained in the methodology.

While the shadow may seem to have negative connotations, those diminished parts are only a liability if you ignore them. If you choose to seize the opportunity to see the gaps and address them through a process of transformation, then the shadow is actually an opportunity for growth. So you should be excited whenever you discover your shadow sides as they highlight your **potential**. Once you identify a bug in a piece of software, for example, you can get it fixed. If you ignore it or are oblivious to it, the bug will likely lead to further problems, which may eventually result in a complete breakdown of your computer system. This could then lead to further ramifications. For example, wouldn't it be better for you to find a bug in your software rather than for a customer to discover it after they have purchased the app you designed? As you can see, by its very nature, the shadow keeps us on our toes. It can motivate, build us up and drive us forward, which is why it is so crucial to bring it to our intentional consciousness rather than ignore it.

In the American fantasy-drama series *Once Upon a Time in Wonderland*, there is a scene in which Alice and Nave come to a river that needs to be crossed. When Nave hesitates, Alice asks him why. To avoid telling her the truth, Nave makes excuses as to why they should not cross the river and suggests they go around it instead. Alice queries the alternative, knowing this would turn a relatively quick exercise into an arduous journey that could potentially take several days. Nave finally admits he is afraid, as he has never learnt to swim. This is the cost of not facing the shadow side of fear. Many of us waste an enormous amount of time and energy 'going around the river' to avoid facing our shadow. Imagine the ramifications in a relationship, personal or business, if both parties avoid and hide their troubled sides.

Many of us often only pay attention to the tip of the iceberg in our endeavours, which blinds us to the potential of transforming the shadow sides of ourselves that we are unaware of because they are hidden beneath the surface. That's the reason most people hit a ceiling and fail to progress further. The high achievers of the world are constantly on a journey of self-discovery and transformation. They are continually transforming from one iteration to the next. They actively seek to uncover the parts within themselves that are not contributing to their integrity, effectiveness and fulfilment, including those buried beneath the surface, the parts that are getting in their way of fulfilling their next venture in life.

Rather than seek to cover up their shadow as many people do, high achievers are thrilled to find the gaps because they reveal precisely where they are out of integrity. In other words, the shadow shows them what is getting in the way of them moving forward or solving a challenge they have been struggling with. Once they find those gaps or misaligned parts, they immediately seize the shadow with both hands and address it responsibly. This proactive and responsible approach to constantly seeking, facing and dealing with the shadow is why high achievers have the courage to take risks, which is a necessary aspect of innovation and disruption.

Imagine if JK Rowling or Columbian novelist Gabriel García Márquez had given up the first time they were knocked back by a publisher rather than facing their fear and approaching others, or if Oprah Winfrey had not believed in herself and persisted after being told she was unfit for television. What if Jeff Bezos had insistently persevered with the Amazon Fire Phone, which proved to be a flop in 2014? Instead, he chose to be open (vulnerable) and allow it to serve as a lesson, resulting in the successful launch of the Amazon Echo and Alexa and spurring on a whole new product line. As Oprah once famously said, 'There is no such thing as failure. Failure is just life trying to move us in another direction.' The same can be said for the shadow.

The ramifications of letting your shadow run the show

Diving into unfamiliar territory and acknowledging and facing your shadow or troubled parts isn't easy. There will always be a level of discomfort associated with it. For example, if you lead a team or run a business with employees, there will be times when you have to tackle certain tasks that push you out of your comfort zone. Examples include reprimanding a team member who is not pulling their weight or is continually arriving late to work, and terminating the employment of a repeat offender. If the thought of doing this makes you want to delegate the task to someone else or pretend the issue isn't happening, that's a sign that the shadow is running the show. It indicates that you struggle with assertiveness, responsibility, vulnerability, courage and fear, to name a few of the Aspects of Being that are letting you down in this situation. So while you may tell yourself ignorance is bliss when it comes to the shadow, nothing could be further from the truth because if you ignore the shadow parts of you, they don't go away. Instead, those troubled parts will continue to operate independently of your intentional consciousness (awareness), causing the shadow to run the show rather than you controlling it. When you are hijacked by your troubled parts, you may feel disarmed and powerless. The shadow could then potentially impact some or even all of your Aspects of Being, infiltrating your emotions, moods, thoughts, decisions and actions. I'm sure I don't need to spell out the potential consequences if this were to happen.

When it comes to knowing human beings, the very first person we all need to be in partnership with is ourselves. Understanding and knowing how to see the shadow within yourself will also help you see it in others, making it an extremely beneficial skill to have when forming relationships, whether you are dating someone, going through the interview process and assessing your potential future boss, hiring someone, or deciding who to partner with in business or in life. While we all have shadow sides, some of us dare to acknowledge them instead of averting our gaze from them, and care enough to take charge, harness them and leverage their power to thrive through transformation rather than letting the shadows take control and rule our lives.

To sum up, in the Being Framework, every Aspect of Being has shadow sides. Having an unhealthy relationship with any of the Aspects of Being shown in the Being Framework Ontological Model reflects a piece of your shadow self. So, when we talk about having a healthy relationship with each quality, we are referring to the light side, and when we refer to an unhealthy relationship, we are referring to a shadow/troubled aspect. The aim is to first raise your awareness of each dysfunctional and unpolished area and then care enough to question it and harness its power in a constructive way, rather than hiding it from yourself and others. In short, a healthy relationship with each Aspect of Being contributes to your overall integrity. In contrast, an unhealthy relationship with each Aspect of Being gives more power to your overall shadow and compromises your overall integrity. The ultimate aim is to transform your relationship with all Aspects of Being, moving towards integrity, wellbeing and effectiveness.

Shadows stem from inauthenticities and are elusive, deceitful and misleading. They represent a digression away from the healthy and authentic way to be with any Aspect of Being. So letting them overtake you will inhibit growth and lead to regression. However, if you leverage its power, the shadow can encourage you to grow and gradually become more fulfilled and accomplished. Over the coming chapters, you will see how the Being Framework brings your attention to the shadow and supports you to articulate those troubled parts, break them down into smaller chunks and relate them to your life and where you struggle or lack fulfilment. With your newfound awareness and clarity, you can address them, ideally using the Transformation Methodology.

Last but not least, this book is committed to supporting you to not only know and see yourself with sharper clarity but also to give you a lens to read others more effectively. So, when it comes to the shadow, it's not just about becoming aware of your shadow sides but also the shadow sides of every other human being you interact with. This has nothing to do with judgement or moral virtue. It's about enabling you with the awareness and discernment to assess others – as opposed to just yourself – and therefore make effective decisions when engaging with other people in all areas of your life. While some people are more polished than others because they have been actively working on and transforming themselves, no human being is without shadows. So as you continue reading, I encourage you to not only apply the learnings to yourself but also to zoom out and see how the content, including any discussion of the shadow, relates to human beings in general.

CHAPTER 5

Transformation Methodology
the dance between awareness and effectiveness

Earlier, we talked about how, as human beings, we are not static objects destined to always be the way we are now. We can and do transform. The Transformation Methodology is a series of processes and principles that lead you on a journey of metamorphosis and show you how to gradually go from where you are now to where you want to be. Integrity fits into this as it enables us to be effective in our endeavours. In fact, one of the major outcomes of integrity is effectiveness. And when we are effective, we can fulfil our intentions. I often refer to this process of transformation as 'the dance between awareness and effectiveness'. Maintaining integrity is a critical step in this 'dance'.

Why transform and not just improve?

Transformation is commonly defined in dictionaries as the act of changing in form, appearance, nature or character; to change a state. It is far more than just improving skills, increasing your knowledge or becoming a slightly better version of your current self. For example, making the transition from employee to entrepreneur requires transformation. This is different from improving yourself by acquiring new skills to climb to the next rung on the corporate ladder. Transformation demands changes in multiple layers of your Being to the point where you achieve a fundamental shift in how you are and who you know yourself to be. I have seen countless people, including many of our clients, transform from employee to successful entrepreneur.

I have also witnessed small family businesses transform into scalable global enterprises that solve humanity's problems and impact many lives.

While the lead-up and preparation to the process of transformation may vary in duration, the actual transformation itself occurs in a moment. It's like becoming a parent, which is instantly transformative, despite several months to years of preparation leading up to the moment when your first child is born. Once a transformation occurs, there is no going back to the way you were before.

The Being Framework Transformation Methodology

As mentioned, transformation occurs the moment you travel from a degree of awareness to a degree of effectiveness. Awareness is always the starting point as you cannot intentionally become effective in something you are unaware of or have misconceptions about.

On the next page is a snapshot of the process involved in the Transformation Methodology. It depicts the dance between awareness and effectiveness through an iterative application process.

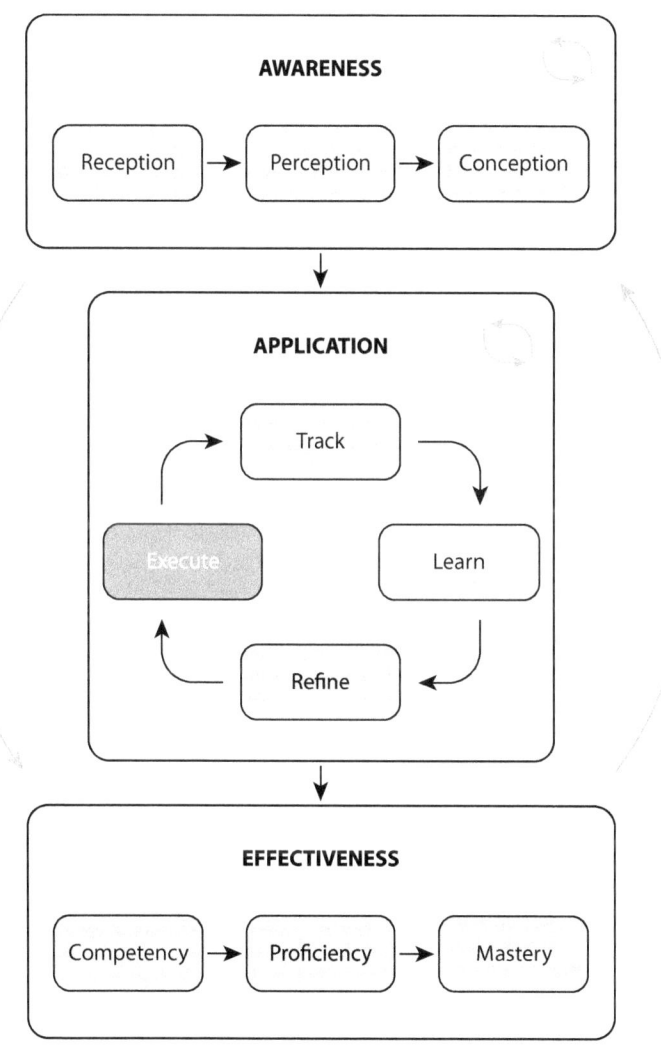

The Transformation Methodology

As you can see from the diagram, the Transformation Methodology is a methodical process of Awareness > Application > Effectiveness. It begins with three degrees of awareness and leads to three degrees of effectiveness via the Application stage, which is an iterative process. While the process is a simple one, that does not mean it is easy. It demands total focus, commitment and sincerity, not just curiosity. Let's now break down the stages of transformation, beginning with awareness.

Awareness

Awareness is a three-stage process: Reception > Perception > Conception. When you receive new information – when you are being informed – you may call it a lightbulb or eureka moment. The moment of awakening when your attention is being drawn to new information – be it an opportunity or an alert – is Reception, the first stage of awareness. There is a degree of vulnerability required in order for you to choose to be present and receptive to the incoming new information. Unless you are open (vulnerable), receptive and present, the new piece of information may pass you by unnoticed.

Once the light has been switched on, you begin to explore a perception of this newly received **information** starting with passing it through your 'authentic awareness filter'. The Perception stage is when you start investigating the information to learn as much as you can about it and verify its validity. It is here where you potentially acquire objective **knowledge** of the newly acquired piece of information. While it is impossible to know absolutely everything about any subject matter, it is important that you do your best to learn as much as you can to ensure your perception is as authentic as possible.

The final stage of awareness is Conception. When you are shaping your conception of any piece of objective knowledge (perception), you relate it back to your own life or to something that matters to you – your subjective understanding. Over time, and with sufficient care about the practical application of the combination of that objective and subjective knowledge, you develop **wisdom**.

So, being receptive means you are ready to let your attention be drawn to a matter and be informed. Then you perceive it, acquiring objective knowledge about the matter. Finally, you relate it back to your life, contextualising the perception in the context of your life and what you choose to care about until it becomes wisdom. To perceive is to know something directly through the senses. To conceive is a mental process whereby you form an opinion or develop an understanding of a matter.

Here is a tangible example that clarifies the three stages of awareness. Imagine you develop a sudden urge to know how the Solar System works. As you begin looking into it, you turn your attention to how the Sun behaves. You become curious and interested to learn more. This is the Reception stage. Then you learn, through a textbook or online search, that the Sun rises from due east. Now you are developing an authentic perception of what the Sun is and how it behaves.

Once you are satisfied with the validity of the information, you internalise the knowledge and slot it into your memory bank until you find an opportunity to draw on it and apply it in a practical way. At this point, your perception of the Sun and how it behaves is still classified as objective knowledge; it's not necessarily going to mean anything to you.

A few months later, you are in conversation with the architect designing your dream home. You are determining the position of the windows in your bedroom to attract the morning sun. This is an example where your objective knowledge that the Sun rises from due east has a particular meaning in the context of something you care about. At this point, you draw on the information about the Sun that is stored in your memory bank with the intention of applying it. By relating the objective knowledge to your life, you now have a conception of it. Not only do you know it, but you understand it because it has a particular meaning in the context of your experience of life.

Now let's say your initial interest in and curiosity to learn about our Solar System has sparked an inquisitiveness to know as much as you can about it. Through consistent learning, application and practice, your conception of the Sun and the Solar System expands, deepens and becomes more authentic. The more you make your conception authentic or congruent with how things are and apply it to your life, the higher the degree of effectiveness you will attain.

Over time, your conception gradually becomes an inherent part of the expression of your self or Unique Being. You gain mastery, which shows up in your decisions and behaviours. At this point, you can say you are effective in that particular endeavour. An actual transformation has occurred at a certain point during that process. You no longer relate to yourself as the person you knew yourself to be. You could replace the Sun and Solar System with any subject matter you wish to know more about. The process of transforming your awareness is the same: Reception > Perception > Conception.

Effectiveness and the Application Process

Just as there are three degrees of awareness, there are also three degrees of effectiveness: Competency > Proficiency > Mastery. To progress through the stages of effectiveness towards mastery, you need to undergo an iterative process of transformation through the Application phase of the Transformation Methodology.

The Application Process is the practical stage of transformation. It is a cyclical, iterative process of Execution > Tracking > Learning > Refinement and then back to Execution again. The idea is to repeat, tweak and make progress with each cycle, ultimately transforming. Here is where you act based on your current conception of a matter, such as your conception of one of your Aspects of Being. Let's use assertiveness, one of the eight Secondary Ways of Being, as an example. The idea is to track, observe and reflect on your decisions, actions and behaviours in relation to assertiveness and the consequences and outcomes of those decisions, behaviours and actions. The assumption is that you would have a clear conception of the ontological distinction of assertiveness and how that relates to your life before commencing the Application Process. The process of transformation takes time, usually over several iterations. However, the moment when the actual transformation takes place happens in a particular moment. That is when you no longer relate to the person you knew yourself to be.

Putting it all together – the Conception Worksheet, a practical tool that facilitates transformation

The Conception Worksheet is a simple tool designed to facilitate the Awareness and Application processes (both iterative processes) and help clarify your thinking around the area you wish to transform. The worksheet will support you to learn more about your relationship with an Aspect of Being, subject matter or any other matters or incidents you are dealing with in life. It will also support you to shape a deeper conception of it, making adjustments as you go. It has a direct link to the Awareness phase as its focus is on helping you shape, refine and deepen your conception of the subject matter or Aspect of Being in question.

The worksheet prompts you to think about a number of things in relation to the Aspect of Being you are focusing on. How does it (e.g. assertiveness) relate to me personally and professionally? How do I relate to the matter in question? For example, am I assertive enough to speak up in a meeting? What's in it for me and why should I care? For example, how will my life and the lives of others around me change for the better if I transform my relationship with assertiveness as a Way of Being?

Over time, you will refine how you are being with the matter in question – in this case, assertiveness – in action. It is a continuous process designed to gradually transcend you to a higher degree of awareness and effectiveness.

Let me give you a brief rundown of how it works. Remember, while we are using assertiveness as an example here, you can apply the same process to any subject matter or aspect of your life.

Conception Worksheet

How does this relate to me? What's in it for me? Why should I care or bother?

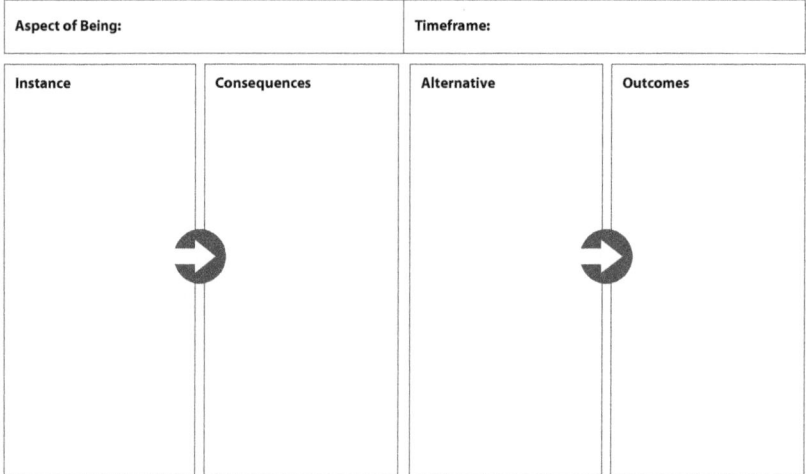

As you can see, the Conception Worksheet is a table consisting of four columns: Instance, Consequences, Alternative and Outcomes. Start by defining two key variables. The first is the Aspect of Being or matter you are aiming to transform your relationship with. The second is time. Like a camera, how far are you willing to zoom in or out? This refers to the period of time on which you are prepared to reflect. When you first commence this exercise, it is recommended that you start by reflecting on a longer period of time, say the past three years. As your effectiveness builds, you will be ready to zoom in more and more by reflecting on an increasingly narrow timeframe. The ultimate goal is to work in real time and have the ability to predict a potential future scenario and be ready to act or respond appropriately. In the case of assertiveness, you would be able to stop yourself from being submissive or aggressive and be assertive instead.

Step 1: Download and print a copy of the Conception Worksheet from engenesis.com/c/being or draw it on a blank sheet of paper.

Step 2: Write down the Aspect of Being you are working on transforming and the timeframe you are focusing on at the top of the form.

Step 3: In column 1, Instance, write down all the instances you can remember over the past three years when you were not being assertive. For example, it could be a time when you were submissive and were afraid to speak up in a meeting or when you failed to back yourself in an argument with a friend or your spouse. It could also be a time when you found yourself being aggressive, controlling or passive-aggressive and mistaking that behaviour for assertiveness. Be vulnerable and specific.

Step 4: In column 2, Consequences, write down the consequences, cost or impact of you choosing not to be assertive on each of those occasions. By this I am referring to the damage, harm and suffering you may have caused for yourself and/or others.

Step 5: In column 3, Alternative, articulate what you could have done differently on each occasion. Write down how you could have been and responded differently based on your current conception of assertiveness. In other words, how would your current conception of the distinction of assertiveness have manifested into a different response, decision or behaviour for each instance back then. Be present to how your current conception of assertiveness is being projected into tangible actions here.

Step 6: In column 4, Outcomes, write down the alternative outcomes that could have transpired had you chosen to be assertive on each occasion. Here you are predicting what would have happened had you been assertive, based on a healthy relationship with assertiveness as a Way of Being.

Repeat this process using a fresh Conception Worksheet and zooming in a little more each time. For instance, consider a one-year period, then six months, then last week, all the way to the present and immediate future.

Let's consider how this exercise looks when we bring it into the present, including its impact on the immediate future. Allocate a specific time to reflect on what happened throughout the day in relation to whichever Aspect of Being you are working on. For the purpose of this example, we will stick with assertiveness. Reflect on and write down when and where you weren't being assertive during the day. As mentioned, not being assertive is either being submissive, aggressive or passive-aggressive.

These are the shadow sides of assertiveness. As you will recall from the previous chapter, your shadows constitute all the unhealthy relationships you have with any of the Aspects of Being, while the light sides represent your healthy relationships and contribute to your overall integrity as well as your effectiveness.

Once you have repeated this daily reflection over a number of days or weeks (however long is necessary), the next step is to change the timing again, making it even more present, right down to a specific moment in time. Now you are in a position where you can catch yourself on the spot at the exact moment when you are about to let yourself down by not being assertive. Perhaps you catch yourself holding back on what you know you need and want to get off your chest to your partner during an argument. Maybe you find yourself hesitating when trying to negotiate a pay rise with your boss, or you can't bring yourself to have an uncomfortable conversation with a team member who is not pulling their weight and letting the rest of the team down and so on.

Instead of letting things unfold in an unhealthy manner, you intercept your imminent lack of assertiveness (being either submissive, aggressive or passive-aggressive) and choose to step up and be assertive in a firm, unambiguous way. In other words, you deliberately choose to be assertive (Execute) in that moment. Write down what happens in the Consequences column. However, if you fail to shift and be assertive in that moment, write down the consequences of that action too. Then follow up with the alternative action you could have taken and the outcomes of that in columns 3 and 4.

Continue to observe when and where you are lacking assertiveness and whether or not you are choosing to interrupt it and why. This is self-monitoring (Track) based on your perception and conception of how not being assertive is holding you back from achieving your goals and fulfilment.

As you have been completing the reflection exercise for some time by this stage and you are committed to transforming and becoming more assertive, you will become adept at identifying whenever your unhealthy relationship with assertiveness is letting you down (Learn). In other words, you no longer let any shadow side of this Way of Being draw you out of integrity and get in the way of delivering the most appropriate and effective response.

You determine what works so you can do more of the same in the future, and what doesn't work so you know what to avoid. You also identify anything missing or redundant so you can add, remove or transform them as required, becoming a more integrous (whole and complete) human being in the process. This is all part of learning. You then change the way you respond (Refine).

Eventually, you will start catching yourself in the moment and choosing to interrupt your lack of assertiveness at will **before** it happens (Execute). All the discoveries you have made and the awareness you have attained, combined with this iterative Application Process, will lead you toward the very moment where you suddenly find yourself being transformed.

I would like to emphasise at this point how critical it is for every iteration of the Conception Worksheet exercise to be completed in writing. While you may be tempted to internally contemplate each response, doing so without clearing them out of your mind and onto paper or into your computer will lead to excessive mental traffic or cognitive overload. Furthermore, writing everything down will enable you to build and maintain a chronology of your growth as you respond to different matters in your life. You will be able to look back on this later to see how far you have come.

Mastering transformation by leveraging the Conception Worksheet and iterative Application Process will lead you to a state I call 'ontological responsiveness'. When you are being responsive, it is the opposite of being reactive. It is when you are no longer someone who acts under the influence of their shadow sides and only catches themselves out on reflection later. Instead, you become quite adept at being able to catch yourself when you are about to be influenced by the shadow, for example, when you realise you are on the verge of being unassertive, inauthentic, irresponsible, uncommitted, etc. This is the state of being responsive (or ontological responsiveness). It's precisely what you should be aiming for in leveraging the power of the Transformation Methodology. When you have achieved mastery – the highest level of effectiveness – you are in a state of ontological responsiveness, at least most of the time; after all, nobody is perfect 100% of the time.

While the Transformation Methodology and its Application stage are more effective when completed under the guidance of a qualified ontological coach, there is nothing stopping you from having a go at it yourself. I encourage you to adopt or at least think about this process as you read the rest of this book and relate each Aspect of Being to your life (conception).

Transformation and its relationship with integrity and the shadow

How does integrity fit into all of this? Becoming aware of the troubled parts of you that are getting in the way of your integrity tells you where the gaps lie. Those gaps represent the Aspects of Being you have an unhealthy relationship with, the ones that are holding you back from being effective (the shadows).

Learning and discovering the impact of your shadows is a continuous process as you undergo transformation. However, developing awareness of and acknowledging the shadow sides of any Aspect of Being is never easy. But that is precisely what you need to do while undergoing a process of transformation in all its iterations. The process is most effective if you can see yourself clearly before you start. This is best achieved by completing a Being Profile, ideally followed by a debrief session with a Being Profile Accredited Practitioner, to highlight the gaps or shadows, which are the areas you need to transform to achieve integrity and a degree of effectiveness. You will be walked through the theory behind the Being Profile and its practical applications in Chapter 10: The Being Profile.

To be effective, the Transformation Methodology requires you to acknowledge the shadow parts of yourself with grace and vulnerability, and give it context by relating it directly back to your life before commencing the process, taking an iterative approach and holding yourself to account until the actual transformation occurs. Once that happens, it's not a signal to stop. It is important to keep applying yourself to maintain your integrity and increase the degree of your effectiveness over time.

Transformation always begins with awareness

Someone with an unhealthy relationship with awareness simply cannot be effective, let alone achieve mastery. For instance, you cannot be effective at building a bridge if you are unaware of the laws of physics. However, the health of your relationship with other factors or qualities within you can also get in the way of your effectiveness, for example, if you have an unhealthy relationship with fear, anxiety, responsibility, commitment or courage, among others. That's where integrity comes in. Wherever there are gaps, integrity (wholeness) suffers. It's like collecting water from a well with a bucket that has holes. That's never going to be effective.

In the context of the Being Framework, your integrity may be compromised because of an unhealthy relationship with one or more of the Ways of Being and Moods identified in the model, from commitment, care and responsibility to confidence, fear and assertiveness to name just a few. This will affect your overall integrity, remembering that we are referring to the actual ontological meaning of integrity here (the state of being whole), not the conventional use of the word. To be an integrous human being, all the cogs in the machine must be in their rightful place and working as they should.

If you have multiple incongruent conceptions or perspectives and you're not open and humble enough to discover why, then you would have no clear sense of the integrity of your Being. You would have no clue about what's missing, what's being diminished, why you're not achieving the results you want and why you're not being responsive or responding appropriately to all the things life is bringing to you. You may even be completely oblivious to those opportunities that are right there in front of you, ripe for the picking. This may lead you to believe that you are a victim of circumstances, that life is happening to you and you've got no control over any of it. We all know someone like this, someone who is always complaining that others have more than they do and that life is unfair. Turning this around begins with awareness. Awareness is always step one.

Summary

The Transformation Methodology is an iterative process. But the actual transformation of your relationship with a particular Aspect of Being happens in a particular moment. That is when you no longer relate to the person you knew yourself to be prior to commencing the journey. Through practice and application, your conception of matters will expand and become more authentic and congruent with how things are or are becoming. This gradual process of moving through the three degrees of awareness combined with the iterative application process leads you to acquire what I call 'effective performance', which is when you are being responsive. Effective performance is very different from just any type of performance, like being a hamster on a wheel. Instead, it is being effective in the sense that you can fulfil your intentions individually, in partnership or in a team. In short, you are constantly in a process of going from a degree of awareness to a degree of effectiveness.

Life is a continual dance between awareness and effectiveness because, deep down, most of us want to grow and expand our boundaries throughout the course of our lives. The sincere intention for growth is a common human experience. And the way we grow is by undergoing a transformational process, dancing between awareness and effectiveness. It is worth repeating that transformation is not a one-off project to be ticked off a list. It is an ongoing, iterative, lifelong process as you progress through life's peaks, troughs and changes.

It's about becoming aware of and present to the gaps or shadows in your Being and sincere – not just curious – about transforming. Once you become aware of the parts that are getting in the way of achieving your objectives and the areas you have a healthy relationship with so you can leverage their power, that's when you can begin the process of transformation to become a more aware, integrous and effective human being. That's the dance between awareness and effectiveness, a dance that constantly changes and evolves and one that you would ideally practise and perfect throughout your life.

From here until the end of the book, we will unpack the Being Framework Ontological Model, the model that enables us to decode human beings – ourselves and others – to provide clarity around who and how we are. We begin at the highest level with the Meta Factors, followed by the Primary Ways of Being and then the Secondary Ways of Being. In the last chapter, you will be introduced to the Being Profile, the tool that measures an individual's thirty-one Aspects of Being.

CHAPTER 6

Meta Factors
the highest level qualities of Being

I n Chapter 2: The Being Framework, you were introduced to the Being Framework Ontological Model. The Meta Factors – awareness, integrity and effectiveness – make up one of its four layers. It sits above the other layers like an overarching umbrella. The Meta Factors are distinct from the other Aspects of Being because they are the three highest-level factors that influence our results, our ability to be the leader of our lives and, ultimately, our fulfilment and wellbeing. Awareness has an impact on all Aspects of Being, integrity is impacted by all Primary Ways of Being and Moods, and all Aspects of Being contribute to our effectiveness. The Meta Factors also have a direct relationship to our ability to transform. Why? Because transformation, as we discussed in Chapter 5: Transformation Methodology, is going from a degree of authentic awareness to a degree of effectiveness such that we generate effective performance.

There is a fundamental relationship between the three Meta Factors. For example, if your conception of money doesn't align with reality, your lack of awareness will prevent you from generating sufficient money and making effective financial decisions. This may negatively impact your financial wellbeing, prosperity and ability to live the life you want. There would no doubt be underlying reasons for this, such as an unhealthy relationship with vulnerability causing you to not be open to discovering the truth (perception) about money. This shadow part within you – the shadow side of vulnerability – erodes your integrity. Any perception that is incongruent with the way things really are will get in your way of achieving a higher degree of awareness. And no one can be intentionally effective in something they are unaware of or about which they have misconceptions. All the parts need to be in place (integrity) to achieve a higher degree of awareness, which in turn will lead to a higher degree of effectiveness. In other words, one's authentic awareness of the constituent parts of a whole – or Aspects of Being in this case – is critical in order for the integrity of that whole (system) to be fulfilled. And, as mentioned earlier, effectiveness and workability are two of the major outcomes of integrity. Given that transformation always begins with awareness, let's begin with this Meta Factor.

CHAPTER 6.1

Awareness

The most important things in life are often invisible unless we bring them into our intentional consciousness or awareness. Awareness leads to vision and the ability to truly see and make sense of the world, including aspects of our lives from the past and present and our ability to be discerning when making decisions. It even enables us to anticipate what might happen in the future and nip in the bud anything that may lead to regret. More specifically, awareness reveals an authentic narrative around our past that leads to responsibility and forgiveness. It illuminates how things are and enables us to influence the present while we still have the chance and prevent the potential for future regret. It even opens our eyes to matters and events that have not yet come to pass, allowing us to predict the potential consequences or outcomes of how we currently are. Here is where awareness, and particularly vision, lead to maturity. And maturity supports us to make more effective decisions about the things we choose to care most about.

Our opinions and beliefs – all our perceptions and conceptions – are largely shaped and influenced by our relationship with awareness (how we relate to knowing and understanding), the stories we tell ourselves and the perspective from which we choose to see things. We tend to be very protective of those beliefs and opinions, even if they aren't aligned with reality and aren't working for us. We human beings can be so delusional that some of us live our entire lives in a world of fantasy! This can lead us to be easily misled and blindsided by others, or ignorant or negligent in the face of what's really going on. Imagine the long-term ramifications if every human being on the planet deliberately avoided and ignored global matters that demand the entire world's attention, or if no one cared enough to generate jobs and contribute to the economy. In the context of this book, an unhealthy relationship with awareness will prevent you from seeing the areas within yourself, others and matters in life that are blocking you from fulfilling your intentions.

When it comes to illuminating the reality beneath the facade of human beings, the subject of this book, the very first person you need to understand and be in partnership with is yourself. And when developing relationships with others, whether dating someone, hiring a new team member, selecting the right business partner and all your dealings with others, it is necessary to have the discernment to be aware of who and how they are being, not to judge, but to assess, to see their qualities beneath the surface. Doing so will give you an insight into what being in a relationship or living or working with that person will be like, including the highs and lows, the latter being particularly important as it is most often in times of challenge that a person's true colours are revealed.

What is awareness from an ontological perspective?

Ontologically speaking, awareness is intentional consciousness. More specifically, it's when you bring your intentional consciousness to certain matters rather than averting your gaze from (ignoring) them. Furthermore, you are not just aware in general, but aware of **something**. Awareness is always directed at something and it has limited capacity. If you let anything draw your attention away from the matters most important to you, then you will eventually run out of capacity because we humans only have so much energy to give. If there are matters that are drawing your intentional consciousness away from the important matters in your life, you will rob yourself of time and energy to direct your awareness towards more productive matters. For example, if you are jealous of someone and those thoughts are consuming you, then you will give your intentional consciousness to comparing yourself to others rather than to the matters that will support you to fulfil your objectives.

In terms of the Being Framework, the awareness Meta Factor refers to your awareness of your Unique Being (aka self-awareness), your temperament, Moods, Primary Ways of Being and Secondary Ways of Being, all the way to your behaviours, decisions and actions. So, it's about bringing your intentional consciousness to the things that matter in your life or that you care about, the matters that are the highest priority for you or that you find most meaningful and inspiring, so you can become intentionally effective in those areas. Being intentionally effective is different from simply being effective out of luck or through rote learning and repeated practice, which is more robotic and lacks awareness. It's the difference between memorising the times tables and understanding the logic and mechanisms behind them.

Imagine finding yourself stuck in a situation that feels like 'Groundhog Day', where you are experiencing a repetitive challenge in your life, day in, day out, but you don't understand why. To remove yourself from this seemingly never-ending cycle, it would help to raise your awareness (intentional consciousness) of all the events, decisions, patterns, Aspects of Being and perceptions that led to this experience. Initially, it may feel like you can't see the forest for the trees. But by directing your attention to the situation and setting your intention to discover more about what is really going on, you will increase your awareness of it, including what led to it. This healthier relationship with awareness will enable you to take action to correct the path, change the outcome and therefore break the dysfunctional cycle.

Your level of awareness increases from the moment you start to see parts of the truth about yourself and others as well as about any matter or concept. Awareness is a critical Aspect of Being that enables you to reach higher levels of satisfaction, build sustainable and thriving relationships and become more effective in life.

Now that we have discussed what awareness is at a high level, let me share with you the Being Framework ontological distinction of awareness.

Awareness

Awareness is the state of being intentionally conscious of your consciousness. It is how you relate to what you know and understand as well as what you don't know and don't understand. *Awareness* is always intentional and directed at something. It is to know and understand yourself, others and the world around you, in particular the impact of the world and others on you and the impact you have on the world and others. *Awareness* is your access to knowing and understanding and is required to fulfil your intentions.

A healthy relationship with *awareness* indicates that you have a clear understanding of your impact on others and on the world around you. You are not easily misled, coerced and/or manipulated. You are both self-aware and aware of how you are perceived by others. You are attentive, alert and rarely surprised or caught off guard. You can find your way forward despite uncertainty or not knowing, and are available to consider feedback, guidance and critique.

An unhealthy relationship with *awareness* indicates that you may choose to ignore or be oblivious to matters and the impact you have on others and the world around you and vice versa. You may often be confused and shocked by matters and how others respond to you and blindsided when they fail to live up to your expectations. You may deliberately choose to ignore what there is to see. Alternatively, you may freeze or find it difficult to progress in the face of uncertainty or not knowing as you are compelled to know everything before making decisions or taking action.

As you can see from the ontological distinction, those with a healthy relationship with awareness have a sound understanding of their impact on others and on the world around them. However, the opposite is true for those with an unhealthy relationship with awareness. How may this impact you? It could cause you to be totally blindsided when your partner announces they are leaving you or bewildered as to why your brilliant business idea fails to get off the ground. You would also tend to see the world either through rose-coloured glasses (overly optimistic) or dark shades (overly pessimistic), sometimes alternating between the two.

Web of perceptions

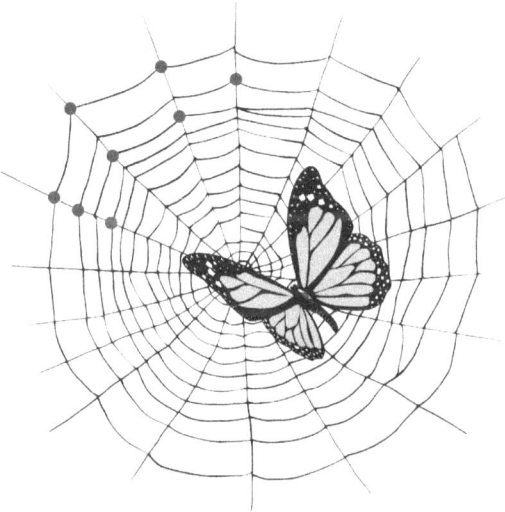

Imagine you have never seen a koala. In that case, you would lack a perception of koalas, let alone have a conception of them. So if you were to see a koala on the ground when out bushwalking, your mind would look for the closest thing that somewhat resembles a koala from the perceptions stored in your memory bank – let's say a wombat. Later, when telling someone what you saw on your walk, you might describe it as 'a wombat with a flat nose and large ears'. You will limit yourself if you form your perception based on that first impression and interpretation without validating the information.

You may wonder, what's the big deal? Let's use an example we can all relate to that explains why it matters: money. In some of the world's financially disadvantaged nations, less than 3% of the population actively invests their money or, more specifically, the income they generate in cash. Their perception is that they need to save money, not invest it, ignoring the fact that money – or currency, to be exact – can rot like tomatoes due to inflation. This becomes their dominant perception and behavioural pattern, which leads to an inability to grow financially as individuals. When the majority of the population adopts the same mindset, it means that collectively as a nation, money isn't being injected back into the economy, and that has its own consequences. My point is that the collective perception of money in those countries is incongruent with the reality of money. Therefore, their economy suffers and, consequently, almost everyone's life suffers. We pay a huge price when we hold invalid perceptions and conceptions, whether individually or collectively.

Whenever we come across something new, it is human nature to choose a perception or potentially form a conception of it. That's why things sometimes occur to two people totally differently. The perceptions we adopt and conceptions we form are influenced by a number of factors, including our cultural and religious background, how we were raised, our education and our political views, among others. By the time we reach adulthood, we have already spun our own 'web of perceptions' and potentially formed conceptions of the world we live in and everything in it. I liken it to a web because if we allow ourselves to, we become caught in the web we have spun ourselves. If we remain stuck in this web of perceptions without venturing out to discover and become aware of how things really are, we limit our potential to become actualised.

The world's high achievers know only too well the cost of holding onto inauthentic opinions, beliefs, perceptions and conceptions that aren't based on reality. They know because they have been burned before and they have the scars to prove it! They've hit enough walls in their careers to know the value of conducting thorough research in order to gain genuine knowledge or simply seeking advice from those who have done it before them. They get the right advisors on their board, engage consultants, hire talented employees and invest in coaches and mentors. They team up with others they intentionally choose with authentic awareness because they know and understand with every fibre of their

Being that they cannot do it alone. So, instead of fiercely holding onto their current opinions and beliefs without grounds, they are open and vulnerable to let them go and learn.

Narrative lens

Everyone loves a good story. We love to hear them and we love to share them with others. However, for some, the stories they tell themselves morph into their own version of reality and they start seeing life through this narrative lens, allowing their fabricated ideas to rule their lives. This is an example of having an unhealthy relationship with awareness. Our consciousness constantly evolves, whether we are committed to being authentic with our perceptions or conceptions, or allow our inauthentic narrative lens and the stories we hear from others to dominate. But I would like to draw your attention to the fact that integrous people and the highest achievers are those who have trained themselves to discern authentic awareness from an inauthentically-evolved consciousness. Awareness is intentional consciousness; it does not come from opinions and beliefs that have been manufactured from external forces or others manipulating you with deceitful ideas. I use the word 'authentic' to emphasise how important the validity of any perception you are about to adopt to form your conception is.

I remember a time in my childhood when my dad was upset and had locked himself in his room because he didn't want me to see him in that emotional state. When I knocked on the door, he turned me away. My immediate reaction was to make up a story about what I must have done to make my dad so angry that he did not want to see me. Obviously, at the time, I didn't think I was making up a story; I thought it was reality. The story manifested into the irrational thought that he didn't love me anymore. The reality of the situation was that he was undergoing financial pressures, which had nothing whatsoever to do with me. The story I had made up in my mind represented my distorted version of reality and that could have ruled my relationship with my dad for the rest of our lives.

We all have a customised narrative lens through which we choose to see life, our environment, people and our experiences. The stories we repeatedly tell ourselves and others due to this narrative lens eventually become our reality. Just as our web of perceptions helps shape our relationship with awareness, so too does our narrative lens, which can easily trap us if we let it. There's nothing wrong with listening to and telling these stories, as long as they are authentic and not distorting your view of how things really are and drawing you away from awareness, integrity and effectiveness.

You can tell any story you want to for the purpose of entertainment, enjoyment, art or culture. But the day you think a story is real is the day you are in trouble. That's the day you conflate the layers of reality by taking a third-layer reality and making it a second-layer reality. Gradually, you may even fool yourself and others into believing that your story sits in the first layer of reality. This is not an uncommon phenomenon; it happens all the time. For example, one person comes up with an idea and invests in promoting it. They entice many others to join forces with them in selling their manufactured idea and they too become swept up in the 'story'. The way Germany's Nazi Party transformed from a small, revolutionary party to the largest elected party in the Reichstag is a good example. One of several factors that helped the Nazis rise to power was propaganda, which they used to boost their leader Hitler's image throughout the late 1920s and early 30s. Another factor was adopting a new framework designed to infiltrate existing social structures and recruit more members and supporters.

Over time, an idea can become so widely accepted that some people start believing it is a transcendent law of existence. When delusion, toxicity and being out of integrity become the norm, we descend into a state of collective psychosis, which you may recall is the epidemic of madness that occurs when a large proportion of society loses touch with reality and descends into delusion. When this happens, we can be readily persuaded to follow others like sheep, including electing and following unstable, malevolent 'leaders' who only act as if they are leaders instead of actually being leaders. Logic, reasoning and human decency don't exist within societies dominated by collective psychosis. Individuals are ethically and spiritually defeated, descending to become unreasonable, irresponsible, erratic, less effective and unreliable beings. In this book, I refer to them as unpolished, ineffective beings who are not of integrity and who have unhealthy relationships with various Aspects of Being.

When I was a teenager, I always wondered why CNN, BBC and other influential news channels put so much effort into their narration. I have since learned that the one who narrates the loudest and the strongest is the one who rules! Therefore, the dominant narrative becomes the stories being listened to and heard the most, influencing our narrative lens, especially the narrative lens of people who are readily influenced. As they bombard us with their stories, they shape the dominant narrative to the point where many listen and follow without question. That is why we have been made to assume that certain types of people are barbaric and uncivilised. It is often not until we meet and get to know these people that we realise those stereotypes have been fabricated and planted in our minds through storytelling to favour the narrators' interests. Such fabricated stories have been used to justify racism, sexism, systematic terrorism and genocide throughout history, resulting in collective psychosis and creating separation within humanity rather than unity and integrity. It is extremely important to be aware of how the dominant narrative came about and its influence on us.

High performers and effective leaders are usually very aware of this circulating, dominant narrative and invest in developing the ability to distinguish truth from imaginary reality. This is yet another key pillar to their awareness and hence effectiveness. Leaders and high achievers of the world also tend to influence the trends and, therefore, the dominant narrative. They are powerful storytellers, opinion makers, trendsetters and style makers as opposed to being followers influenced by an imaginary reality.

You can be overly optimistic and see the world in a romantic, dreamy way, as though you are looking at everything through rose-coloured glasses. Or you can be pessimistic, cynical and negative. However, a person who is committed to being consciously aware, integrous and responsive cares about the reality of every situation, no matter the context. They would never generalise and paint everything with a single brush.

What's your perspective?

Many years ago, I attended a business seminar where the speaker was telling us about the benefits of always thinking like a beginner. To illustrate his point, he held up a cup and asked us to tell him what it was.

Looking around the room, I could see several attendees rolling their eyes and smirking before someone finally stated the seemingly obvious in a bored tone of voice: 'It's a cup'. The presenter then asked, 'What can you do with it?' A woman piped up with a sarcastic grin, 'It's to hold my coffee'.

By this time, people were beginning to get impatient, wondering where this discussion was going. Finally, while still holding the object, the speaker said, 'Let's redefine it, shall we? I would say this is a concave ceramic object with a handle. Now, with that new perspective in mind, let me pose the question to you once more: what can you do with it?' This time, there were various responses from the room, from drinking tea to using it to water a pot plant. My point is, when we are open and think like a beginner, we allow ourselves to see things from other perspectives, not just as we have always seen them. It is worth noting that being open and viewing matters from various perspectives is a key quality possessed by innovators, creative entrepreneurs and artists. While they have their own perspective on a matter, they are also willing to put themselves in the shoes of others when evaluating situations or making decisions. Seeing things from the perspective of others helps them shape a more congruent, well-rounded version of reality.

When a husband and wife are constantly arguing to the point where they are on the brink of separation, other family members may see the matter quite differently. They may see hope where the couple thinks there is none and suggest they seek professional counselling and mediation to help guide each party to see things from the other person's perspective. If two staff members disagree on the direction of a project, their colleagues may see the situation from a completely different angle and, through discussion, help settle the matter so the project can continue without undue delays.

In addition to seeing things from your own perspective as well as another person's perspective and the perspective of others not related to the matter at hand, effective people see things from every angle. They have the ability and willingness to zoom in and out to understand a matter from all angles and views. If I hold a bowl on its side, I will see it as concave, but you will see it as convex. We could argue forever over who is correct, but if we are authentic and vulnerable enough to see the truth of the matter, we will discover that both of us are correct. The reality is that whatever is concave from one side can be convex from the other. Seeing matters from various perspectives encourages empathy and compassion as well as the ability to effectively get to the bottom of a matter.

Vision

In Chapter 3: The Exposure Triangle we talked about how it is only when our vision is crystal clear that we can discern where to focus our energy. Shaping your vision or ability to see begins with a healthy relationship with awareness. Then, if you have the self-expression, presence, courage, authenticity, responsibility, etc. to act on it, you will see it through, no matter what obstacles you encounter along the way. In my experience working with many entrepreneurs, I have come to realise that one of the main reasons they feel they have failed is that they simply gave up too early. They didn't see the end goal clearly enough to give it their all.

Cast your mind back to when you were a child, a time when you were full of potential and the world was your oyster. As you grew up, you got to know who you really are (your Unique Being), including your likes and dislikes and where your talents lie. The question is, did you tap into your calling with awareness or did you ignore it? With vision comes discernment, the ability to choose where to focus your attention and make the right sacrifices. Importantly also, when you have vision, you see beyond what others see on the surface, both within yourself and others. This helps you make the right decisions in all aspects of your life, personal and professional.

In summary, awareness is intentional consciousness. It is the first step towards integrity and effectiveness. Matters that can block your access to awareness are the web of perceptions you spin, your narrative lens or the stories you tell yourself – which end up becoming your own version of reality – and neglecting to see matters from perspectives other than just your own. In terms of understanding human beings, yourself and others, the goal is to become aware of the gaps or dysfunctional parts (shadow) as well as the highly functioning qualities by seeing beyond the surface to the reality that lies within.

CHAPTER 6.2

Integrity

You know when you can sense something isn't quite right, be it in a project, with a device, your car, a relationship or within yourself or someone close to you? You can feel it but can't see it clearly enough to know what's going on and why. Perhaps you feel frustrated and confused about why things aren't working or going the way you believe they should. This is typical of how we feel when integrity, in the sense of being whole and complete, is compromised. 'Having integrity' is a commonly used phrase in reference to this quality. But the quality referred to as integrity in this framework is not something one has. It is a state of Being, a state in which things are in their rightful place and all parts are functioning at an optimal level, which leads the complete system to perform at the highest level possible. In this context, integrity brings about workability and effectiveness. And when we have workability in our lives and are effective, we can fulfil our intentions – those things we most care about.

If you feel like things aren't working as well as they should in your life and that you aren't hitting the targets you set for yourself, you can be certain that there is a lack of integrity in certain aspects of your Being. Identifying and addressing these areas will raise your level of integrity, which in turn will bring contentment, workability, effectiveness and fulfilment.

Now that we have talked about integrity in a broad sense, let's zoom in to examine its constituent parts. Like any other system, we human beings objectively share qualities that contribute to the integrity of our Being. Our integrity constitutes all of our Primary Ways of Being and Moods, the primal qualities that lead us to project the manifestation of ourselves to the world and participate in life. Like any system, it only takes one part of ourselves to malfunction for the rest of the system to be affected. For example, if our kidneys don't function properly, waste products and fluid can build up in the body. This can cause swelling of the ankles, nausea, weakness, poor sleep and shortness of breath. In a similar way, when one aspect of your Being breaks down or is dysfunctional, other parts will suffer. This will impact your integrity and cause the entire system to suffer and, therefore, also your effectiveness and ability to perform at your best.

Away from my main career, I love to cook. My kitchen at home is well stocked with the best tools of the trade and that includes a set of high-quality knives. I realised just how sharp a good kitchen knife is recently when I momentarily lost focus and cut my finger while chopping an onion. The next day, I was constantly reminded of that relatively minor mishap whenever I went to use my injured hand. When we talk about integrity, we refer to it as something whole, something where everything is in its rightful place and working as it should. With reference to the cut on my finger, that small deviation from perfection and wholeness had an impact, albeit minor, on other areas of my life.

Integrity

Integrity is the state of being whole, complete, unbroken, sound and in optimal condition. *Integrity* encompasses all primal Aspects of Being in the same way that the various limbs and organs are the constituent parts of your body. *Integrity* is the prerequisite to being effective and operating at the optimal level of performance and is fundamental to generating trust and workability. *Integrity* brings about ease and flow and is considered 'being well', 'well put together' or the wellness of your Being.

A healthy relationship with *integrity* indicates that you know yourself to be sufficient and mostly experience flow and workability in life. Ease, trust and consistency are present for both you and those around you. You actively address and maintain whatever may impair your *integrity*, particularly qualities that are diminished, misplaced or require refinement or transformation.

An unhealthy relationship with *integrity* indicates that you mostly experience frustration and dysfunction, with recurring problems and unresolved issues. There are many areas in your life you feel the need to fix. Others may experience an absence of workability and consistency around you, hence trust and *effectiveness* are often compromised and brought into question. Alternatively, you may be obsessed with perfection and struggle to be with shortcomings or incompletion. You may avoid pursuing matters unless success is ensured.

Integrity and the shadow

In Chapter 4: Shadow, you were introduced to the shadow. So what's the connection between the shadow and integrity? Essentially, the Ways of Being and Moods with which you have a healthy relationship contribute to the overall integrity of your Being, and those with which you have an unhealthy relationship compromise it and expand and give rise to your overall shadow. In other words, someone who is of integrity is expected to be responsible, committed, authentic, assertive, courageous, etc. among other qualities within the Being Framework. However, someone who is overtaken by their shadow would manifest the opposite. They would be uncommitted, inauthentic, invulnerable, careless, a passive victim of circumstances and so on.

It is important to point out that integrity is not measured as a 0 or 1 binary equation but on a spectrum. That's because it is very unlikely for anyone to be either completely integrous or totally out of integrity 100% of the time. There is always a degree of integrity. That being said, being fully integrous is an ideal towards which we can all aim. Furthermore, integrity is not a static state of Being we reach once and that's it. It is natural to move in and out of overall integrity as we progress through the peaks and troughs of life. The idea is to maintain a relatively high level of overall integrity over time.

When you lack a healthy and effective relationship with any Aspect of Being, it is a reflection of your overall shadow. In other words, an unhealthy relationship with any Aspect of Being highlights the shadow side of that quality. When that involves any of your Primary Ways of Being and Moods, your integrity is directly impacted. To restore integrity, you must delve beneath the behaviours and actions you see on the surface to bring those troubled parts to your intentional consciousness (awareness) and then make it a priority to work on those qualities. The Being Framework articulates and reveals those deep qualities to you. When the framework was first developed, the aim was to break down the integrity of one's Being into smaller chunks so we could pinpoint what was going on beneath the surface. It's like when you go to the doctor and present with certain symptoms. The doctor commonly refers you for a blood test or an X-ray or ultrasound, depending on your symptoms, in an attempt to uncover the root cause of the problem.

We all experience times in our lives when we are greatly impacted by our shadow and, as social beings, the shadow side of others. We may lose a loved one, be betrayed by someone we chose to trust, go through a relationship breakdown, be fired from a job we loved, fail in a business venture and so on. When something like this happens to you, it may feel like you will never recover. It may also make you bitter and ask, 'Why me?' But it is possible to heal your wounds and turn around the parts within you that are dysfunctional. It's up to you to choose to take action and restore your integrity.

Just as a person's Being can fall out of integrity, their lives as a whole can too. This is when we zoom out and look externally rather than internally. When you are being integrous, on the other hand, it means you have set your life up in such a way that it works for you. If your life is set up in such a way that it doesn't serve your values – what you most care about – and intentions, then your life won't be integrous and it is highly unlikely that you will be fulfilled. The same can be said for an entity. For instance, a company is integrous if all the departments work effectively and in harmony to serve the company's overall purpose. When that happens, the whole company thrives. However, it only takes one department to fall out of line for the entire company to suffer and fall out of integrity, and that will get in the way of the company's growth and success.

The more integrous you are internally – in your Being – the higher the probability that you will generate and maintain external integrity. For example, you will be more likely to develop and sustain an integrous team culture in the workplace and an integrous relationship with your life partner, all the way to contributing to the integrity of society or humanity. As mentioned earlier, the solution to all problems of humanity relies upon the integrity of individuals. And the first person you are responsible for and have autonomy over is YOU.

If you are an integrous Being, it's very likely that your life is going the way you hoped it would and that you feel a sense of joy and fulfilment that can only be achieved when everything is in place and working as it should. But the moment you become complacent and lenient about it, that's the time when something will draw you away from integrity. I encourage you to consider life as a constant dance between awareness and effectiveness, knowing that integrity holds the key to that delicate balancing act. Over the coming chapters, we will explore the constituent parts of one's integrity as we delve into other layers of the Being Framework Ontological Model.

CHAPTER 6.3

Effectiveness

When you hear the word effectiveness, do you relate it to performance on a task or in a job? If so, you're certainly not alone. Ontologically speaking, though, effectiveness is the state of being fulfilled in meeting your commitments, intentions and expectations and the extent to which you actualise your ideas, vision and dreams. A rather distinct difference isn't it. Effectiveness is about accomplishing what you most care about. Anyone can perform their duty but lack care around what they are doing. You may tick all the boxes in terms of completing the task on time and in line with the intended outcomes. You may even exceed expectations. But if all this 'performance' is not leading to fulfilment or making progress towards your intended objective, it is not effective performance. Essentially all you are doing is running around aimlessly like a hamster on a wheel. Authentic awareness plays a significant role in achieving effective performance. If you are not authentically aware – of the shadow sides of your Being, for example – it would be virtually impossible to transform and become effective.

Performance is also relative. When we say someone is performing well, we have a benchmark in mind to compare them to. Effectiveness, on the other hand, refers to a probability of achievement or accomplishment. When someone has a proven track record of being effective in various aspects of their life, the probability that they will be effective in life, in general, is high. That's because they would very likely have a healthy relationship with the underlying deeper qualities that bring effectiveness to the table. So, it would be reasonable to describe them as an effective individual. Just as effective performance is distinctly different from how some people traditionally think of performance, it also has nothing to do with being busy. While being busy might make you appear to be effective in terms of your ability to perform multiple tasks, that does not necessarily make you an effective performer. In fact, it is not at all unusual to see people being busy but failing to produce meaningful results.

Establishing the right foundation will determine how effective you will be in life. If your dream is to own and run a profitable global organisation that serves a broad market and has a positive impact on many people's lives, that goal is well within reach if you strive to become a leader who is committed to being effective. The key is to become effective in whatever you care about. Perhaps your goal is to raise your children to become responsible, caring and independent young adults, to run a charitable organisation that serves a group in need that you care deeply about, to graduate with Honours from university, to be the top-performing salesperson on your team, or to run a successful startup business, etc. Whatever you care about and are striving to achieve in your life, no matter how humble, you need to be effective for your intention to be fulfilled.

To be effective, you must first be authentically aware of the gaps or dysfunctional areas (shadows) by looking within and breaking down the Primary Ways of Being and Moods that are contributing to a lack of integrity or wholeness. Raising awareness around those issues will lay the groundwork to bring about the change required to lead you towards effectiveness and effective performance. This discovery process is fundamental to becoming effective in the endeavours you care deeply about, such as a business you may have worked so hard to build from the ground up.

A company director we worked with was dealing with resentment, a shadow side of forgiveness, one of the Primary Ways of Being. Before being exposed to the Being Framework, the director would avert his gaze from the fact that his resentment towards other team members would consume a significant proportion of his attention for weeks, sometimes even months. Instead of dealing with the reality of the organisation's challenges, including responding to the pace of technological disruption and the need for innovation, the director was consumed by resentment. His unhealthy relationship with forgiveness impacted his ability to be assertive, which in turn diminished his effectiveness as a leader and severely impacted the performance of his team. Needless to say, the business's bottom line also suffered.

By working one-on-one with an ontological coach and using the Being Framework to guide their enquiry, particularly in developing the director's conception of the qualities of forgiveness and assertiveness, he brought about substantial personal transformation. This resulted in his ability to relinquish his resentment in a matter of days or sometimes hours.

The result of the director's transformation was that, rather than responding to high-pressure situations with procrastination or victimhood, he effectively directed his energy towards transforming the business. A key outcome of his personal transformation involved the director leading the successful research, planning and launch of an innovative new product. The new product allowed the company to tap into a different market and produce an additional revenue stream in a time of significant disruption and instability within their industry. This is an example of personal transformation laying the grounds for business transformation and effectiveness.

Effectiveness

Effectiveness is the state of being fulfilled in meeting your commitments, intentions and expectations. It is the degree to which you are powerful and accomplished in consistently producing the intended results and outcomes in your endeavours. It is the extent to which you actualise your intentions, vision and dreams.

A healthy relationship with *effectiveness* indicates that you consistently accomplish the results and outcomes you intend to with ease and flow. Your priorities are grounded in reality and you bring workability and success to your relationships and what you are up to in life. Others expect you to fulfil your commitments and consider you to be someone who pursues and produces extraordinary results.

An unhealthy relationship with *effectiveness* indicates that you are frequently challenged, stuck or thwarted in accomplishing what you most care about. You are often powerless, disarmed, overwhelmed and/or distressed. You may be frustrated by your lack of progress and workability and find it difficult to move forward in your endeavours. Others may consider you to be someone who accepts mediocrity and downgrades or minimises expectations while not completing tasks or projects as expected. Alternatively, you may have to win, regardless of the associated consequences or costs. You may be driven to the extent that you let yourself be singularly consumed by your intentions or desires despite any detriment to your health and/or relationships.

Grasping at an illusion

Effectiveness is fundamental to having a quality experience of life. We all care about what we accomplish in life, whether it be wealth, social status, career, family and so on. In my experience and through my observations and studies, I have found that those who care enough to ask for help to achieve effectiveness typically seek a quick fix. This is because they commonly avoid the problem until they start to feel the pain. Then they reach out for help, begging for a shortcut in the form of a series of techniques, or what I refer to as 'DOings'.

Common requests or statements made by those seeking a quick fix include: 'I don't know how to be assertive. How can I get my team to follow my instructions?', 'People on my team keep lying to me. What can I do to stop the lies?', 'I don't think I am confident and assertive enough. What should I do?', 'I feel so stressed but I'm afraid to share my fears with my team because I am the CEO and a leader should never show weakness! What can I do to get rid of my stress?', 'How should I fire this person without hurting his feelings?', 'I am always very responsible and I am carrying enormous guilt for the fact that our revenue KPI is not being met. How can I let go of the guilt as it is affecting everything I do?', 'I don't know how to report to the board. Can you give me some quick tips on how to deliver a polished presentation?', and the list goes on. It's like expecting a prescription for tablets from your doctor if you present with a cold. But at least those people care enough to identify that they have a problem and seek to resolve it.

Those who don't care typically avoid the problem altogether. Instead, they waste time investigating what their competitors or higher-profile people or businesses in their field are doing to see what their own success could look like. They scour social media in an attempt to discover how a particular startup managed to secure four million dollars of seed funding simply by sending a few cold emails. They look into how a competitor is selling a lower quality version of the same product they offer yet makes more revenue, or how another competitor has managed to retain more than 50% of their staff for over a decade. They scroll through a friend's timeline in the hope of understanding why they have been happily married for twenty years, while their own marriage is floundering and so on.

When they interpret the data they have gathered, they only pay attention to the visible aspects of the success achieved, not all the slow, deep preparations they have made over time, such as building a high-performing team, engaging in rounds of R&D or the systems they have created. They also fail to see the passion, love and perseverance they have shown, their polished decision-making processes and the collective qualities of their human potential. And they ignore the opportunities those people and businesses created and took advantage of, and the hard work they put into uncovering and resolving the major causes of their challenges. So essentially, what they are doing is grasping at an illusion.

The 'secret formula' to success

Many people today seek instant gratification, a common desire we will explore further in Chapter 8.7: Higher Purpose. Some also look for the so-called 'secret formula to success'. However, true transformation will never be achieved quickly or by simply learning a series of techniques. Let me share the secret to success with you right now: the secret is that there is no secret! The key is to gradually become aware (truly aware) of the things that you are not yet aware of. This requires you to let go of the current perceptions and opinions you are holding on to that are getting in your way.

Any change on a deep level demands a high degree of two essential ingredients: care and vulnerability. True high performers and leaders care enough to allow their current perceptions to be replaced with knowledge. They are open and vulnerable enough to embrace reality in order to develop their awareness. Failure to embrace reality is like ignoring the fact that the greatest proportion of an iceberg lies hidden beneath the surface. The forces that facilitate such dramatic changes lie within each and every one of us and are almost invisible. They are difficult to find. Too many people only see the tip of the iceberg.

HAVE > DO > BE versus BE > DO > HAVE

There is a common misconception that we must **HAVE** something (more resources, more money and so on) in order to **DO** something that will enable us to **BE** something! For instance, I need to **HAVE** money to take a vacation in Hawaii (**DO**) if I am to **BE** happy/content. The key to creating effectiveness and true transformation in your life, however, is to turn this perspective on its head: **BE** a certain way to **DO** what you need to do in order to **HAVE** the things you desire. This is true whether you are transforming yourself, your small business or a multinational organisation. It's no coincidence that high performers adopt this way of thinking. Indeed, it is the reason they are high performers and achieve the success and wealth they desire. They work on themselves first. Adopting this attitude and approach enables you to take control of any situation, good or bad. It also allows you to take responsibility and see what you should change within yourself before criticising and pointing the finger at others.

While we have a tendency as human beings to focus on what we want, our desires and our accomplishments, the reality is that our achievements are a direct reflection of who we are being at any given point in time. Working on your Being to improve your effectiveness in life isn't easy. It requires you to look inward, to focus on smaller but far more important internal changes, as they will lay the groundwork and foundation for greater and more impactful change over time. The Being Framework Ontological Model facilitates the process of looking within and identifying both the dysfunctional parts (shadow), so you can work on polishing them, and the healthy parts, so you can leverage their power.

There is an enormous difference between grasping at an illusion and immersing yourself in reality. Once you come to realise this, you will not only find it incredibly liberating, but it will also represent the first step towards transforming yourself and being true to your authentic self. Remember, the true meaning of effectiveness is the extent to which your commitments and intentions are being fulfilled in the world. So ask yourself, 'How effective am I? And what could I do to improve my effectiveness, not only in my own life but also for the benefit of others?'

As we come to the end of this chapter on the Meta Factors, it is worth reiterating that it is impossible to become effective at something you are not aware of. At the same time, you cannot be effective at a holistic level if all the cogs in the machine are not working at their optimal level – if you lack integrity. This is why awareness, integrity and effectiveness are Meta Factors that sit at the highest level of the Being Framework

Ontological Model. If you don't have awareness around which parts of you are not working as well as they could, you will have no idea how to become a more integrous human being capable of being effective in the ventures and pursuits you care deeply about.

The dance between awareness and effectiveness is a poetic way of referring to transformation. It is a lifelong process, not a one-off project or a race to mastery. We learned in Chapter 5: Transformation Methodology that we start with a degree of awareness and move towards a degree of effectiveness. And we achieve this by undergoing the iterative Application process, which consists of Execute > Track > Learn > Refine > Execute.

You will recall that there are three degrees of awareness: Reception (awakening) > Perception (knowledge) > Conception (relating knowledge to your life). And there are also three degrees of effectiveness: Competency > Proficiency > Mastery. The minimum level of effectiveness required to fulfil your intentions is Competency and the highest degree is Mastery, which is where you own the field, subject matter or Aspect of Being that you have been working on transforming. Mastery means you are in charge of how an Aspect of Being influences your thoughts, feelings, decisions, actions and behaviours, and demonstrates a healthy relationship with it the majority of the time and in most contexts. It is when you are in a state of ontological responsiveness, meaning you have the ability to pre-empt when you are about to be influenced by the shadow and can prevent it from happening.

As you read the next chapters, where we explore Moods, Primary Ways of Being and Secondary Ways of Being, I encourage you to think about your relationship with each Aspect of Being and then consider how different your life could be if you transformed the qualities you struggle with.

CHAPTER 7

Moods
the drivers that set the scene

Moods are the very first layer in the process of projecting our Unique Being to the world. We disclose ourselves first through our Moods, then through the Primary Ways of Being and finally through the Secondary Ways of Being. These disclosures lead to our thoughts, feelings, decisions, behaviours and actions. As you will discover in this chapter, Moods are critical Aspects of Being because the health of your relationship with them directly impacts your ability to make decisions, take action, be effective and, ultimately, whether you will amplify or suppress the expression of your Unique Being to the world. Let's begin the discussion on Moods by distinguishing the difference between moods (in a conventional sense), emotions and feelings and the relationship between them.

As human beings, we are not only rational beings but also emotional. Emotions have a significant impact on our 'states of mind', or Moods as they are called in this framework. Therefore, it is inauthentic to assume we are just rational beings. Emotions – therefore also moods – play a key role in our lives, particularly in the ways we express ourselves. They contribute to the expression of who and how we are, both with ourselves and others. Being present to our emotions and understanding their nature helps us express them. But what is the connection between our emotions and moods? How do they relate to one another?

Emotions are recognisable and measurable because, at a physiological level, chemicals are released within the body whenever they are triggered. They are undeniably real. However, emotions typically only have a short lifespan. It is only when we make an emotion mean something to us that it becomes what we call 'a feeling'. For example, when a relationship breaks down, a range of emotions may be triggered, from sadness, fear and anxiety to vulnerability, anger and even relief for some. The extent to which those emotions are felt and how they show up in the context of someone's life varies from one person to the next. Where one person may choose to interpret anxiety as a feeling of nervousness, another may interpret it as excitement. This is just one example. As is the case with all Aspects of Being, there is no right or wrong, good or bad, because the Being Framework is a judgement-free paradigm. The important thing to acknowledge is that we all have a choice to make our emotions mean something. When emotions are interpreted as feelings, they become part of our story, our dominant narrative and our personal reality (third-layer).

When we talk about moods, from an ontological perspective in the Being Framework, we are not talking about being moody or emotional in the conventional sense, which traditionally has a negative connotation. I am talking about moods as a fundamental part of being human and in the context of how they can gradually set the dominant state of your mind. Let me explain. When something external or internal triggers us, emotions arise. Those emotions are real when we make them mean something to us. We each have full responsibility over what we make emotions mean to us. Our feelings, on the other hand, greatly influence our moods and, therefore, also our dominant state of mind.

So, emotions arise when you are triggered internally or externally, and they become feelings when you make them mean something to you. You are fully in charge of them. When you repeatedly make your feelings mean something, they internalise themselves into your state of mind and become a dominant mood. Your moods set the scene and context in preparation for your decisions and behaviours. Finally, you act upon them. Let's say you are in a heated argument with your partner and anxiety and vulnerability (two of the Moods within the Being Framework) instantly kick in and set the scene. Those Moods might then impact your authenticity, freedom, self-expression, courage, etc., which could then go on to impact your ability to be assertive.

Primary and Secondary Ways of Being sit between your Moods and your actual behaviours and are the qualities that influence the behaviour you exhibit. The behaviour – your response – connects you to what is happening in the external world. This is how you impact the reality around you, including the environment and other people. Your behaviours either generate your intended results or lead you to consequences for which you are responsible. This continues for as long as you engage in and experience life and plays a significant role in determining the extent to which your intentions are fulfilled. In retrospect, you may be satisfied with an outcome or harbour regret over your actions.

The Being Framework's four Moods

While human beings possess many moods or emotions, the Being Framework incorporates the four Moods that are profoundly connected to the way we participate in life, individually and collectively, from the perspective of performance, influence and fulfilment. These Moods are vulnerability, care, fear and anxiety. This chapter explores these Moods and examines how our relationship with each one impacts our Ways of Being. You will discover how Moods are the drivers or blockages that either enable or limit our effectiveness. They set the scene for our performance and create the context for our decisions and behaviours. When we have a healthy relationship with our Moods, we amplify our expression of self (Unique Being). However, an unhealthy relationship with our Moods has the opposite effect by suppressing our performance and contribution, thus inhibiting our ability to express our Unique Being to the world.

We human beings are, to varying degrees, so concerned about our reputation and how others may perceive our decisions and actions that our fear, anxiety and unhealthy relationship with vulnerability cause us to suppress our expression of self. This prevents us from being authentic, generating trust and doing what we believe in. We may fear failure or being labelled and judged. We may be anxious about the what-ifs or about needing to be assertive with our team and so on.

Imagine you are about to present to an audience and you feel anxious. Some of the questions going through your mind might include, 'What if nobody resonates with what I have to say? What if they find me boring? Imagine if I suddenly get a mental blank, which happens sometimes when anxiety gets the better of me.' These are all normal emotions.

There is nothing wrong with being anxious. But what if instead of letting anxiety about the what-ifs cause you to freeze, you choose to tap into how deeply you care about what you have to share with the audience? This powerful decision would give you the courage to step forward onto the stage despite the presence of anxiety. That would be an indication of your healthy relationship with both care and anxiety.

In another example, let's say an academic cares so much about the research they are involved in that they neglect almost everything else in their life, including their relationship with their family and even their own health. This is an example of caring too much, which demonstrates an unhealthy relationship with care as a Mood. When we are obsessively focused on one thing, forsaking everything else as a result, that is a state of carelessness. This is where many researchers, entrepreneurs, leaders, parents, etc. come unstuck. They allow their mission to consume them at the expense of everything and everyone else, including themselves. At the end of the day, you need to take care of your own wellbeing in order to operate and work towards your mission.

So it's the health of your relationship with each Mood that counts, not the presence or lack thereof. The latter wouldn't make sense because Moods are present in all of us. They are a part of human nature, so the question of whether or not they exist or whether or not you choose to acknowledge them is irrelevant. You will notice that I use the phrase 'health of your relationship' frequently in this book because that is the focus for all Aspects of Being.

The relationship between Moods and contentment

As human beings, our Moods are the first layer through which we disclose who we are to others and ourselves. They are also the dominant means by which we measure our contentment in life. People commonly ask, 'How are you?', 'Are you happy?' or 'Are you okay?' The answer to these questions lies in our Moods. Many people look to their accomplishments to determine their contentment in life. However, they are looking in the wrong place. True contentment comes from having a healthy relationship with all Aspects of Being, starting with awareness and the Moods, and from establishing goals that serve how we want to live our lives. Remember, a healthy relationship with vulnerability, care, fear and anxiety amplifies the expression of self – your Unique Being – whereas an unhealthy relationship with them suppresses it.

Being able to express your true self and being authentic with yourself and others are the keys to contentment. While we all share multiple common aspects as members of the class 'human being', we are also unique as individuals. So how contentment looks is different for each of us. Where one person's goal in life may be to be the best parent they can, another's may be to become an accomplished academic or a successful entrepreneur. Contentment is relative to the individual and the keys to unlocking it are your Moods. More specifically, leveraging the power of your healthy relationships with your Moods and polishing the troubled or unhealthy parts are prerequisites for setting goals, making decisions and taking the appropriate actions to move towards your goals. Those with a healthy, relatively polished relationship with fear, anxiety, vulnerability and care don't let problems ruin or even significantly limit the joy of the journey.

Few people get to see the multiple – and sometimes enormous numbers of – unsuccessful attempts that are behind every successful accomplishment. So it is important to be okay with mistakes and failure, especially when pioneering something new. For example, Thomas Edison failed thousands of times before finally inventing the light bulb. When asked how he managed to persist through so many failed attempts, he responded, 'I have not failed 10,000 times. I have not failed once. I have succeeded in proving that those 10,000 ways will not work. When I have eliminated the ways that will not work, I will find the way that will work'. That's how relating to Moods in a healthy way is the source of power. The end game is personal fulfilment, or fulfilment of your vision or intention if you are working towards a significant cause.

Moods determine your relationship with the present and, more importantly, the future. The good news is they can come to the rescue no matter what foundation was laid early in life. Let me explain. When you were born, you were virtually powerless. You couldn't take care of your basic survival needs, see properly or make sense of the world around you. With limited means of communication, you had no choice but to rely on your parents or carers to correctly decipher your cries and gestures and provide what you needed when you needed it. You were vulnerable and fragile across multiple dimensions: physically, cognitively, emotionally and psychologically. Given how vulnerable we all are at birth, is it any wonder we are anxious and fearful?

As children, we can grow up to become adults who are fearful and anxious about matters we were exposed to through no fault of our own when growing up. We may have been overprotected, delaying our independence and making us fearful or anxious about things we have not yet been exposed to. Or perhaps we weren't given effective boundaries or discipline, leading us to become a victim of our own mistakes and ineffective decisions early in life and so on. Any unresolved matters from our past are commonly carried into adulthood, and these can manifest themselves as troubled parts or the shadow side of us, with Moods being no exception.

Whatever life throws our way, the health of our relationship with our Moods sets the context, influences our decisions and drives our behaviours. For example, when we make critical decisions and act upon them from an unhealthy relationship with anxiety, fear, care or vulnerability, it can lead to procrastination, self-sabotage, victimisation, lies and deceit, abuse and misuse and so on. This results in suffering, misery and an overwhelming lack of fulfilment and satisfaction in life. However, a healthy relationship with those Moods drives us forward and encourages us to actively pursue the endeavours we care deeply about and find worthwhile.

At times, life can be as unpredictable as the weather, and we all need to respond appropriately. For instance, it would be unwise to go surfing during a thunderstorm, drive through floodwaters or overtly pull out a wad of money while walking the streets of a neighbourhood known for its high crime rate. As human beings, we possess a relatively high level of autonomy, making us inherently responsible for making the right choices in life. So, it's about being responsible by responding appropriately to the prevailing conditions.

In summary, Moods impact every one of us more than we may realise and throughout our entire lives. The decisions you make and the actions you take directly reflect the health of your relationship with your Moods. Consequently, these decisions and actions largely determine your results, accomplishments, contentment and fulfilment in life. Moods are critical because they impact the way you express your Ways of Being, such as responsibility, courage, commitment, love, assertiveness and resilience, to name just a few.

There are interrelationships between all Moods and Ways of Being in The Being Framework. The health of your relationship with your Moods indicates the extent to which those Moods will affect your ability to make decisions, take action and perform effectively. If you neglect to leverage your healthy relationship and polish your unhealthy relationship with your Moods, you risk never tapping into your Unique Being, let alone projecting it to others and the world. What a tragedy that would be! This is critical for anyone trying to find their purpose in life. That's why Moods matter so much.

Ask yourself, 'Am I intentional in the way I relate to my fears, anxieties, vulnerabilities and values – the matters I care about? Or do I just let the environment, circumstances or my innate temperament dictate my relationship with my Moods?' In other words, are you the leader of your life, or do you allow yourself to be a victim of circumstances?

Let's now explore each Mood, beginning with vulnerability, perhaps the most powerful of the four and the most misunderstood.

CHAPTER 7.1

Vulnerability

D o you have a tendency to avoid or ignore criticism? Or are you not only open to receiving it, but welcome it? When you are confronted about a mistake you have made, do you try to bluff your way out of it? Or do you willingly own your mistakes? Do you guard your heart against rejection at all times? Or do you have the courage to be resilient in the face of whatever life may bring? Are you comfortable with your weaknesses? Or do you shy away from them? Do you always hold your cards close to your chest? Or are you a 'what you see is what you get' type of person? Being open to criticism, personal weaknesses and being yourself are empowering ways to be. They reflect a healthy relationship with vulnerability. This powerful Mood sets you free because it allows you to learn from the past or your current shortcomings and grow in all aspects of your life, personally and professionally.

Vulnerability is part of the package of being human

> 'What moves me so deeply about this sleeping little prince
> is his loyalty to a flower - the image of a rose shining within
> him like the flame within a lamp, even when he's asleep...
> And I realised he was even more fragile than I had thought.
> Lamps must be protected: a gust of wind can blow them
> out.'

This excerpt from *The Little Prince* metaphorically describes how fragile we are. I have included it here because it highlights the simple fact that we are all vulnerable. It is up to us to choose to acknowledge that fact and act upon it. Without exception, every one of us is susceptible to the perils of life, from natural disasters and diseases to loss and global instability. Our vulnerability naturally leads to anxiety, yet the common approach is that we need to be tough and hold it all together.

We all come into this world almost powerless. So, without exception, we are all vulnerable from birth and our vulnerability extends throughout our entire lives. Your willingness to acknowledge this fact, however, is another matter. We take a risk every time we leave the safety of our home. A person who acknowledges vulnerability as part of the package of being human is authentic. And that in itself has many benefits. It is also beneficial to be aware that, no matter what you do to hide your vulnerabilities from yourself and others in your efforts to impress them – whether it be your potential new boss, future life partner, friend or client – the truth will eventually be revealed. While the facade may remain intact for a while, perhaps on both sides, there comes a point in every relationship – personal or professional – when the masks come off. Unless you prepare for that inevitability, you're both setting yourselves up for failure.

Those who have a healthy relationship with vulnerability acknowledge that they have shadow sides, that they are not perfect. Simply acknowledging that fact is the first step towards polishing and transforming those troubled parts rather than hiding them or pretending they don't exist.

Vulnerability and authenticity are closely connected

There is a close link between vulnerability and authenticity. Polishing our relationship with vulnerability supports us to be authentic. When you are not overly concerned about how others see you, you feel free to be authentic, to be YOU and to see things as they are, not how you wish them to be. It conveys that you have nothing to hide or be ashamed of. You are okay with your imperfections and value constructive criticism. Rather than considering constructive feedback as judgement, you know such feedback allows you to leverage its power to move forward and become a better version of yourself.

Vulnerability and authenticity are both Aspects of Being that generate trust. It is no coincidence that most couples whose relationships endure are both vulnerable and authentic. The same is true for most high achievers in the world. American entrepreneur Jeff Bezos made an interesting remark in an interview that demonstrated his healthy relationship with vulnerability. He said, 'One thing I learned within the first couple of years of starting a company is that inventing and pioneering involves a willingness to be misunderstood for long periods of time.' His comment made me realise that being vulnerable enough to be willing to be misunderstood is a quality many people of influence have in common. Without it, they wouldn't dare move forward. In fact, vulnerability is, to a large extent, why the world's highest achievers are willing to be misunderstood in the pursuit of actualising their vision. They accept the likelihood of being judged for sticking to their guns and being true to themselves, especially when working on a vision greater than themselves that they know will have lasting benefits beyond their immediate interests and lifetime.

Vulnerability is a strength

Our vulnerabilities are qualities to be leveraged, not hidden. Owning your vulnerability enables you to leverage its power, which is an incredibly freeing experience. This may surprise you if, like many people, you are of the view that vulnerability is a weakness. This is quite a common misconception. Many people also think a powerful person is fearless and has everything under control at all times. Some authors, coaches and 'gurus' even promote fearlessness and living an anxiety-free life if you want to be successful. In my capacity as an author and researcher who has studied countless leaders, celebrities and high achievers to date, I can assure you I have never found a single person who fits this description. On the contrary, when someone voluntarily acknowledges their vulnerabilities, it demonstrates their strength and authenticity. They are profoundly aware that there is no such thing as 'the perfect human being' and therefore don't waste their time selling the perfect persona to others. Vulnerable and authentic people are transparent and open; they own their vulnerabilities rather than deny or attempt to hide them. This brings them enormous power when making decisions, generating trust and building relationships.

Therefore, vulnerability is a vital quality to possess for anyone who wants to build a business, a team, a community, an audience, or to find the right business or life partner. A vulnerable person asks for what they need. They are willing to expose their feelings and express what they think. They listen and are present when communicating with others. Being vulnerable has a positive impact on multiple Ways of Being, including self-expression, presence, courage, higher purpose and authenticity. Let's now have a look at the ontological distinction of vulnerability.

Vulnerability

Vulnerability impacts how you relate to the concerns you have with respect to how you are being perceived or thought of in different situations. It is how you are being when confronted or exposed to perceived threats, ridicule, attacks or harm (emotional or physical). *Vulnerability* is not being weak, agreeable or submissive. It is when you embrace your imperfections. It is considered the quality of being with your authentic self without obsessive concern over the impression you make.

A healthy relationship with *vulnerability* indicates that you are open as opposed to guarded or closed in receiving unfamiliar knowledge and feedback. You are willing to reveal your authentic self to others, regardless of what they may think of you or the prevailing circumstances. You may often leverage the power of being vulnerable to generate trust and build relationships. You acknowledge and embrace your imperfections to support your growth and influence. Rather than letting other people's opinions of you hold you back, you learn from them to propel you to wholeness (*integrity*) and fulfilment.

An unhealthy relationship with *vulnerability* indicates that you are likely to defer or avoid taking action or making decisions when you feel they may impair your reputation. You may also avoid or put your guard up in situations where you could expose yourself to ridicule or look foolish. You are more concerned with being seen to do the right things, looking good or impressing others than actually doing the things you know to be right. You may be inclined to sacrifice your authentic self or image to project a fake persona that you consider more acceptable and impressive to others. You tend to take criticism personally. Alternatively, you may attempt to create unrealistic boundaries to maintain a 'safe' distance, avoiding the unknown and refusing to explore new territories. You may be overly controlling of others or your environment.

As human beings, we are all vulnerable, so we'd better be authentic about it

If we acknowledge that, as human beings, we are all vulnerable because there will always be matters beyond our control, the key to not being crushed by that reality is to live life from the viewpoint of authenticity. When we live authentically, we shape our perceptions, opinions, beliefs and self-image in a manner congruent with reality and consistently strive to develop our relationship with our Moods, as they will give us access to the deeper qualities within. Why is this so hard for many people to accept? Because they allow their unhealthy relationship with vulnerability to get in the way of the truth. They do themselves a disservice by keeping their walls up and lying, even to themselves. A person who has a healthy relationship with vulnerability, on the other hand, would voluntarily acknowledge that they are vulnerable and act accordingly.

Let's say you are a software engineer working as part of a software development team. Together, the team has just designed a new piece of software. While testing the software, you notice a bug in the system. You feel frustrated, knowing it has to be fixed and that this may delay tasks to be performed by other team members and, ultimately, the software release date. However, your healthy relationship with vulnerability makes you thrilled that you found the bug in-house before the software was released to customers. Suppose you had an unhealthy relationship with vulnerability. In that case, you might have tried to ignore or hide the bug, hoping nobody else on the team or the customers would notice it, or worse, point the finger at someone else rather than owning the problem.

Being vulnerable means allowing your life or business partner and others to know the real authentic you: your thoughts, feelings, opinions and beliefs, desires, challenges and weaknesses. It can be intimidating to reveal yourself, warts and all, to your partner for fear of being judged or misunderstood. But being vulnerable enough to be willing to be misunderstood or judged is precisely how a genuine connection is achieved. Now I am not suggesting we need to share everything with everyone, including our business or life partner. Vulnerability is more about where our concerns over how others see us get in the way of expressing our authentic selves. It's also about giving others accurate information to make informed decisions about their partnership and interactions with us.

Being vulnerable enables us to be known, accepted, supported and loved for who we are. I have coached many people who struggle to start or stay in a relationship, and the root cause is commonly an unhealthy relationship with vulnerability. Many people fear others will turn against them if they know about their 'weaknesses'. However, your Being – how you are – is not something you can keep completely hidden for too long. You are only fooling yourself if you think others won't see the aspects of yourself that you are trying so hard to keep under wraps. Once you realise that the shadow sides of your Aspects of Being constantly show up in your decisions, actions, speech, body language and behaviour, you will be more inclined to acknowledge them instead of living in pretence.

The power of vulnerability is not limited to partnerships. As a leader, you can use your vulnerability to build trust by allowing your people to see the real you. This tells them that deep down, you are one of them. Like them, you are a human being who is not perfect. In this way, vulnerability generates relatedness. It leads to a willingness to be humble with your assumptions and open to raising your awareness, the key to being effective in areas where you currently lack knowledge or experience. This is also a critical ingredient for innovation when creating something new since it leads to perseverance and resilience when faced with the inevitable backlashes and rejections. For all these reasons, being vulnerable is the opposite of weakness; it is incredibly empowering.

CHAPTER 7.2

Care

When you care about something, you make it a priority in your life. You pay attention to it, are constantly aware of it and value it so much that you dedicate the time and effort required to ensure it thrives. This can be anything from caring for your health and fitness to building a business or career, volunteering for a cause you feel strongly about, or nurturing a relationship.

Think back to a time when you threw all your energy at something, like working on your fitness at the gym, for example. You were motivated and dedicated, so focused on your goal that you planned your week around your gym sessions, never missing one. Months into your schedule, you found yourself making excuses for missing the odd session here and there, telling yourself not to worry, there's always tomorrow. Over time, the sessions missed began to outnumber the ones attended. Then all of a sudden, you found yourself sitting on the couch one evening eating ice cream and bingeing on Netflix, wondering what happened. This example can be replaced with anything you once cared about and gradually let go.

Whatever receives care thrives and whatever is ignored shrinks or perishes. This is a metaphysical law of existence. To put this into context for us as human beings, whatever we care about in life expands, flourishes and grows and whatever we don't care about withers and dies. Care, as a Mood, is the driving force behind this; it literally drives us. However, without intentional awareness, care is a Mood that can gradually slip away, sometimes without us even noticing. As mentioned earlier, we can also care too much, in an obsessive way, which is just as unhealthy as not caring enough. Furthermore, it is inauthentic, unrealistic and equally unhealthy to care about everything. If you make everything a priority, you actually have no priorities at all.

Care and hierarchy of values – what drives our motives and intentions?

Given that we can't care about everything to the same degree at the same time, we need to discern where to focus our care. This discernment links to finding our purpose in life, which we all desire, but which isn't necessarily easy to find. Some people choose to study and expand their minds in their quest to discover their purpose. Others may be faced with a tragedy or be deeply inspired by someone they follow, such as an environmental activist or a philanthropist, and this may lead them to find their purpose. The point is that our purpose, to a large extent, dictates what we care about. And, as mentioned, whatever we direct our care towards thrives and expands. Consequently, we naturally organise what we choose to care about in a hierarchy based on our values. Let's look into the hierarchy of values as the driver of our motives and intentions a little further.

Every human being lives moment by moment, with a set of priorities and values based on the things that are most or least important to us. This set of values in part determines what we pay attention to and drives our decisions and actions in life. The way we choose to act in any given circumstance is largely motivated by whatever is highest on that list of values. In other words, we are intrinsically driven to fulfil whatever we care most about, the things that are most authentically important, meaningful and inspiring to us.

As we move down that list of values, we come to the lower priorities, the things we care least about. Here, our motivation wanes. We tend to procrastinate, hesitate and become easily frustrated when taking action on them because we would rather be focused on the items that are higher on the list. Whether in our personal lives or the workplace, we tend to be extrinsically motivated here. In other words, we commonly need external motivation, such as money, when working on or attending to something lower on our list of values. Importantly, extrinsic motivation is a symptom of us not attending to what we find most worthwhile and meaningful, not a solution for human performance. An external motivation is like a dummy you may temporarily put in the mouth of a baby to pacify her.

The ramifications of an unhealthy relationship with care

As discussed in Chapter 4: Shadow, every Aspect of Being has shadow sides, care being no exception. While you might assume that one shadow of care is carelessness, it is actually indifference. Another is caring too much in an obsessive manner to the point where you neglect other important matters in your life. For example, if looking after your child takes up so much of your time and energy that you neglect your own health and wellbeing, that could backfire and cause you to be less effective in caring for your child. An unhealthy relationship with care can lead to a domino effect of negative outcomes, from broken relationships and dissatisfaction with yourself to depression in more extreme cases.

Have you ever worked for a boss or known a leader who constantly made themselves scarce and unreachable? This is the type of leader who sits in their office and is rarely seen walking the floor and checking in with their people. This commonly happens when a leader feels threatened, misunderstood or isolated, or they may sense a lack of gratitude from their people, leading to disillusionment and indifference. This impacts on many of their Ways of Being, with responsibility, commitment, presence and perseverance being some of the more obvious ones. Eventually, their lack of care may lead them to give up and walk away.

My team and I have seen shadow sides of care in many first time entrepreneurs, particularly the ones who set out with unrealistic expectations of making their fortune in compressed time; the ones where the dominant driver is money, an external motive, rather than care for the people they are meant to serve. When they discover that the road to success is much harder than they anticipated, they commonly stop caring altogether and give up their dream. Is it any wonder there is such a high failure rate among startups?

Why should we own our problems and do something about them rather than take the easier option, which is to avoid them, pretend they don't exist or blame external factors? The answer is because we care. Imagine if the world's top medical researchers and scientists lacked the care to work round the clock to discover the building blocks for the vaccines that now protect the world from a global pandemic. They could have thrown their hands up in the air, saying a vaccine has never before been created and trialled in such a short space of time. Instead, their deep care for human beings fuelled their desire for discovery in record time. If you lead a small business or an organisation or aspire to, your offering should be driven first and foremost by care for your customers and a desire to solve their problems and eradicate their burning pain. Without care, literally nothing of importance can be achieved.

Care

Care impacts how you relate to what matters to you and influences you in such a way that you ensure the matters and people you care about are supported, protected or dealt with in the best manner possible. *Care* leads you to address whatever is necessary to nurture the person or matter and dedicate the appropriate level of time, resources and attention to them. *Care* is considered the epicentre or focal point of Being as, without *care*, nothing of importance can be achieved. When you care about something, you pay attention to it; you value it and it becomes a priority. *Care* influences how likely you are to make decisions or take action based on the level of value you ascribe to that person, relationship or matter.

A healthy relationship with *care* indicates that you have clarity around your value structure – what you value most – enabling you to prioritise matters effectively. You give those matters the requisite consideration and attention to achieve the intended outcome while avoiding damage or minimising risk. This may extend to those areas to which you choose to attach importance, influencing you to make decisions and take relevant action regardless of whether it affects you directly.

An unhealthy relationship with *care* indicates that you may often defer making decisions or avoid taking action in certain areas, particularly outside your sphere of perceived interest. You may be inclined to neglect, pass or abdicate responsibility and be apprehensive about the future. Others may consider you biased or that your judgement is clouded in areas of particular interest to you. Alternatively, you may be distracted, as everything becomes your priority. You may refuse to let go of whatever matters come your way as you are constantly fearful of missing out. Consequently, you may flit from one matter to another, leaving most of them incomplete while forsaking fulfilment.

Care and intentional consciousness

Care is the source of bringing your intentional consciousness (awareness) to something or someone, spending that limited capacity you have and investing your time and energy into the focus of your care so it can grow and thrive. Anyone who has ever worked on creating a vegetable garden would know how much care and attention it takes to ensure it thrives. It gives you a deeper sense of appreciation for the time, care and effort that goes into the produce we buy at the supermarket.

Think of the artisan producer. They care deeply about sourcing locally-grown produce where possible and crafting small batches of their unique product from a recipe that may have been handed down through generations of artisans, tweaking it to ensure it serves their market today and crafting it with love and care. Interestingly, all the successful entrepreneurs I have studied regard the time and effort they put into building their venture as an investment as opposed to an expenditure. They don't see it as a chore. They care so much for their target market that they will happily work long hours day after day to solve their burning pain while potentially creating opportunities for others to join them to share in the rewards of the journey.

Care as a Mood manifests into love, compassion and empathy. It moves us to take action. From an ontological perspective, all Primary Ways of Being have a direct connection to the Moods. So there is a care-courage, care-responsibility, care-compassion relationship and so on. Care is what drives the Way of Being. So in the case of courage, it is care that moves us to step forward, despite the presence of fear. In the case of responsibility, it is care that drives us to be an active agent rather than a passive victim. And the list goes on.

Remember, everything in life either grows and thrives or gradually diminishes until it withers away and dies. Care is particularly profound when it comes to moving forward because when we care about something, we pay attention to it and make it a priority in our lives. Imagine how much could be achieved if care was the driving force towards a cause on a collective scale, such as within an organisation, community, a nation or even globally.

We all have one chance at life. So instead of settling for a life of mediocrity or never finding worthwhile, inspiring and meaningful matters to prioritise, wouldn't it be better to tap into care and live an extraordinary life of fulfilment and contentment? Care is the Mood that gives you access to why you are here, what you should do and how you should be to fulfil your purpose and make a difference. It is a determining factor when it comes to deciding what to say yes or no to. Just be aware, however, that with each yes, you are saying no to other possibilities.

CHAPTER 7.3

Fear and Anxiety

Fear and Anxiety are two separate Moods but they are commonly misunderstood, sometimes to the point of being used interchangeably. For this reason, I have decided to compare and contrast them in the one subchapter. Let's begin with the fundamental difference between fear and anxiety. Fear is always directed at something; there is always a source of our fear: a fear-generating object or situation. It can be literally anything, from spiders, cockroaches and snakes to the fear of flying or the fear of marriage and commitment. If the object of your fear is removed, the emotions go with it, at least in that moment. On the other hand, anxiety is not necessarily directed at anything in particular. It often has to do with something abstract or a matter or event that may or may not happen in the future. It's about feeling anxious about something indeterminate, the what-if scenarios. The anxiety Mood is impacted by anticipation, uncertainty and perceived risks, which may cloud your judgement and cause you to freeze rather than take action if you have an unhealthy relationship with it.

Let's have a look at an example that illustrates the difference and potential link between fear and anxiety. Imagine you have a fear of snakes. As a result of this fear, you may either freeze when faced with a snake or wildly run away in fright. Ironically, both actions could make the situation worse, depending on the species of snake in your path. Your inability to take the appropriate course of action in this situation would indicate an unhealthy relationship with fear and the suppression of self. So fear occurs only when you encounter or experience the thing you are afraid of. A healthy relationship with fear would be demonstrated in your ability to be with your fear and take the appropriate action whenever you encounter the object of your fear, in this case, a snake. It means you can step forward with courage or simply move past the snake so that it cannot harm you, despite the presence of fear, rather than freeze and do nothing or run away in fright.

Now, in the case of anxiety, you may be so worried about the potential to see a snake – the object of your fear – in the bush, that you either decide not to go bushwalking or spend the entire time worrying about seeing a snake. This indicates an unhealthy relationship with anxiety. So you may be fearful, but anxiety brings up the what-ifs, the stories that you make up about things that could happen in the future. With anxiety, it's about being anxious about something that hasn't happened yet – a what-if scenario, a potential future event. Importantly, both fear and anxiety are neither negative nor positive. Everyone experiences both. It's how we deal with fear and anxiety that matters.

Your fear of snakes might cause you to be particularly cautious when going on a bushwalk, wearing protective clothing and boots, etc. and packing a first aid kit in your backpack. But at least you would be prepared to go on a bushwalk, despite knowing you are entering the snake's domain. The fact that you are able to move forward despite the presence of anxiety indicates a healthy relationship with this Mood.

Let's now look at each Mood separately, beginning with fear.

Fear

All living beings experience fear to varying degrees. It is necessary for survival. I'm sure you would have a sense of what fear feels like and what happens to you physically and emotionally when you face the object of your fear. Fear is real. It's not a made-up phenomenon. And, as mentioned, it is neither a negative nor a positive emotion. After all, emotions are just emotions. It is only when we make them mean something that we associate emotions as being positive or negative. Despite what some would have us believe, there is no such thing as being fearless. In fact, if there were such a thing, a fearless person would be a danger to themselves and others. We need fear. It prevents us from taking rash, overly risky actions. It's how we respond to fear that matters. There are times when fear should stop us from moving forward, such as when faced with danger, but other times when we should not let fear hinder us.

Fear

Fear impacts how you relate to perceived dangers or threats in different situations. *Fear* is always related to something particular in the world and has a distinct object or focus for its attention. It is an indication of how you ARE with *fear*, in other words, your propensity and capacity to be with *fear*. *Fear* is often associated with taking an unpleasant experience from the past and projecting it into your future or being confronted with an immediate danger.

A healthy relationship with *fear* indicates that even though you may identify perceived threats, discomfort or danger, you are still able to move forward, make appropriate decisions and take action. Instead of avoiding *fear*, you are prepared and remain powerful and courageous.

An unhealthy relationship with *fear* indicates that you are likely to defer decisions and avoid taking action when confronted or impacted by an object of your *fear*. You are also likely to avoid situations where you have experienced *fear* in the past. Others may consider you to be fearful, weak and someone who backs down, doesn't speak up or take a stand. Alternatively, you may be reckless, inappropriately putting yourself in harm's way, and may avoid managing risk.

It's interesting that some dictionaries define courage as the absence of fear. Ontologically speaking, however, courage needs fear as well as discomfort – a perceived or real threat or concern and worry – to be present. Courage, one of the Primary Ways of Being, is the willingness to step forward despite the presence of fear or concern and worry. So when we have a healthy relationship with fear, it drives us to take action, to be courageous rather than be stopped in our tracks and derailed.

If you have ever felt frozen in the face of fear when you know you should have had the courage to step forward, you would know how debilitating it is. Fear can suppress you. If you let it, fear can literally hold you back from doing something you really want to do, like engaging in a project, starting a business venture or applying for your dream job. When you become familiar with your fear-generating scenarios, you will know how to deal with them next time (to be with your fear). Imagine how empowered you would be if you could transform your relationship with fear. The good news is you can.

The traditional approach adopted by behavioural psychologists when helping someone overcome their fear is to focus on the object of their fear and either try to eradicate it or gradually expose them to it. The Being Framework is different. It encourages you to look at fear holistically.

Let's say you have a fear of public speaking. Rather than attempting to resolve the object of your fear, the Being Framework's ontological approach directs your attention to how to change your relationship with fear itself; to ultimately BE more comfortable with fear, or be comfortable with the discomfort that your fear is causing you. That way, whenever you are confronted with any new fear-generating scenario in the future, you will be able to deal with it effectively. That way, there is no need to see a psychologist every time a new fear-generating scenario shows up in your life and gets in your way.

In the case of the public speaking scenario, you could start by presenting to a small group of people, say no more than ten, and gradually build yourself to a larger group. The point is, your fear of public speaking might always be there, but over time your relationship with it will change to the point where you can deal with your fear and embrace it. This is a very different approach from trying to eradicate your fear of presenting to a huge audience. It's about how you are being in the face of anything that generates fear for you and how you are with fear in general. Why is this important? It's important because there may be thousands of new things that you will develop a fear of in the future. If you work on transforming your relationship with fear, you will know what to do every time fear strikes in the future. Fear will no longer disempower you or have you running to a psychologist for help.

Anxiety

Let's be real. We are all in the face of uncertainty all the time. We face the potential of new pandemics, recessions, natural disasters, crime, corruption, etc. on a large scale and potential problems at home and at work. And that's not even taking our own personal imperfections and weaknesses into account, not to mention the fact that we will all die one day. No wonder we experience anxiety! The question is, why are we not all walking around in a permanent state of anxiety when there is so much at stake and so many things that could happen? This is a question that still baffles the great psychologists and philosophers of the world. The point is, we are all vulnerable, which is why anxiety, like all other Moods, is relevant to all of us. It is inauthentic not to acknowledge that fact.

Fortunately, most of us are able to cope with a level of uncertainty and anxiety about the future. Despite knowing what may lie ahead, the majority of people are still able to move forward. We dance, we sing, we start new relationships even if we've been hurt many times before and we bring new life into an uncertain world.

You will recall from earlier in this subchapter that the key difference between anxiety and fear is that anxiety is about nothing in particular while there is always an object associated with our fear. Anxiety is experienced in the face of the unknown and what may happen in the future.

Anxiety

Anxiety impacts the anticipation, uncertainty, perceived risk or lack of preparedness associated with future situations, circumstances or events. It indicates how worry, nervousness or unease about the future impairs your ability to move forward. *Anxiety* fuels the constant prediction of potential consequences of the decision you are about to make and/or the action you are about to take. *Anxiety*, as a Mood, is clearly distinct from Anxiety Disorder. *Anxiety* can be about 'nothing in particular' and is often indeterminate. It can be experienced in the face of something completely unknown to you, something you do not have a perception or conception of, hence you may be unable to articulate it. It indicates how you are with *anxiety* – your propensity and capacity to be with it.

A healthy relationship with *anxiety* indicates that although certain situations may cause you to experience *anxiety*, you are still able to make appropriate decisions and take effective action. It leads you to be attentive and prepared and considerate of any relevant risks associated with the situation, keeping you on your toes. You may leverage your *anxiety* to achieve the best possible outcome in challenging situations.

An unhealthy relationship with *anxiety* indicates that in uncertain situations, it is likely to cloud your judgement, constrain you and cause you to freeze. Others may consider you as someone who is passive, lacks discernment, procrastinates and defers making decisions. You may have a propensity to frequently anticipate the worst possible outcomes, be overly sceptical and focus on what may go wrong. Alternatively, you may be considered nonchalant and oblivious to or ignore the consequences of your actions or inaction.

Anxiety can appear anywhere, anytime and often in the most unassuming situations, not just when we are alone with our thoughts, as many people assume. It could begin from an overheard conversation at work or at a party, from reading an article about one of your competitors who has just won a prestigious award, or from scrolling through your Instagram feed when it's dominated by the so-called 'ideal' but heavily edited body type. Sometimes, that's all it takes to be suddenly gripped by feelings of inadequacy, which leads to anxiety becoming your dominant state of mind.

Whether or not we like it or want to admit it, we all face situations and thoughts daily that have the potential to make us anxious. For example, any major decision you need to make whereby the outcome is unknown will incur a level of anxiety, but you can't let that get in your way of making a decision. The more responsibilities you have, the more often this will occur. As is the case with fear, it's about how you relate to anxiety that counts. You can either be crushed by anxiety or develop the coping mechanisms to deal with it effectively and not let it get in your way of taking action in the quest to meet your objectives, whatever they may be. Again, it's not about the absence of this Mood; it's about how you relate to it.

If you know certain situations make you anxious, a healthy relationship with anxiety will enable you to be with your anxiety and develop the right coping mechanisms to ensure you are able to move forward. For example, imagine you are about to walk on the stage or upload a video you have created on social media. In your mind, you ask yourself, 'What if people don't like my presentation? How will that impact the brand? Would the share value in my company fall?' However, if you know that the message you have to share is important to your audience and that it will make a positive difference to their lives, then your level of care will overtake anxiety as the dominant Mood and show you the way to step forward with resilience and courage. This is not something that happens overnight. As is the case with fear, it's about polishing and eventually shifting and transforming your relationship with anxiety through consistent practice. Learning to deal with anxiety in different situations like this won't make you immune to anxiety. But it will help you develop the resilience to not let it break you and the courage to regain control and step forward.

A final word on fear and anxiety

Having an unhealthy relationship with fear and/or anxiety has severe consequences. Indeed, the consequences are so much more than just procrastinating, being overwhelmed and lacking effectiveness and accomplishment. It can influence the quality of your experience of life. Why? Because if you are frozen by fear or anxiety, you risk allowing yourself to be taken advantage of or suppressed. People who are present to this realise that it's not about fixing what's happening externally. It's about addressing what lies within.

Conclusion

There is great power in having the ability to discern which Mood is the dominant state of Being at any given time and to learn to be with that accordingly. This is true not only for yourself but also when it comes to being aware of and present to the Moods of people around you, from your partner, spouse and children to your colleagues and staff.

After awareness, our Moods – vulnerability, care, fear and anxiety – are the next layer in the process of projecting your true self (Unique Being) to the world. The health of your relationship with your Moods determines the extent to which you either amplify or suppress this projection through your Ways of Being, which are predominantly expressed through your behaviours, decisions and actions. Over the next two chapters, our focus moves from Moods to our Ways of Being, beginning with the Primary Ways of Being.

CHAPTER 8

Primary Ways of Being
underlying qualities that influence decisions, behaviours and actions

As human beings, we all share certain characteristics. For instance, we are designed to be born with two arms, two legs, two eyes, one heart, a brain and so on. Aside from the physiological attributes we all share, we also have a number of deeper qualities in common. These are our Ways of Being, and I call those that are primal to us human beings our Primary Ways of Being. We all relate to these qualities in one way or another and demonstrate them through our decisions, behaviours and actions throughout our lives. Primary Ways of Being are also studiable, measurable and changeable. The fact that they are changeable is critical. It means how we are is not set in stone or destined to be how we are forever. We can transform our relationship with our Ways of Being if we choose to. While we all possess the same Primary Ways of Being, how we relate to each of them differs. The healthier our relationship with our Primary Ways of Being, the more it feeds into our integrity and effectiveness to become a more polished human being.

Primary Ways of Being distinguish the fundamental ways through which we project the authentic manifestation of who we are deep down and how we experience ourselves to be in the world. The Being Framework Ontological Model identifies sixteen Primary Ways of Being: authenticity, responsibility, freedom, courage, commitment, gratitude, higher purpose, empowerment, presence, peace of mind, compassion, love, contribution, partnership, forgiveness and self-expression. These specific primal qualities were chosen because they are the most critical in terms of workability and effectiveness. They impact our decisions, behaviour, performance and the subsequent results we produce. More specifically, they distinguish the fundamental ways through which we project our Unique Being to the world. They determine how we participate in our work, engage in projects, contribute to society or the team we play in, engage in relationships and life, and how we grow, impact others and experience the reality of the world around us. So, in a broader sense, these qualities also impact our wellbeing and the integrity (completeness) of our lives.

Primary Ways of Being are deep and subtle, so they may not be directly apparent in our behaviours. That's why it is so important to become aware of them and get to know them in more depth. Developing a clear conception of these primal human qualities will enable you to know yourself and others with greater clarity than ever before. Why can't we stick with observing our behaviours and actions alone? For the simple fact that what people say and the way they behave – the readily observable aspects – don't necessarily convey what drives them. It's easy for us human beings to say anything we want to. We can also put on an act or pretend to be someone we are not through our behaviours. Therefore, understanding human beings and having the ability to see through what they say and do on the surface to gauge how someone is being deep down is very beneficial. It will assist you in assessing and evaluating them before entering into a serious engagement with them, be it a partnership, a friendship, taking on a new staff member or subcontractor or entering into a relationship. In short, to determine what drives us, it is necessary to look deeper to learn who and how we are being, as this is what drives our decisions, behaviours, and ultimately, our accomplishments and level of joy and fulfilment in life.

You may be wondering at this point about the difference between Primary and Secondary Ways of Being. The key distinction is that Secondary Ways of Being emerge from underlying Primary Ways of Being. For example, to be resilient (a Secondary Way of Being) requires a relatively healthy relationship with courage, compassion and peace of mind (all Primary Ways of Being). Secondary Ways of Being are also more readily observable, as we tend to project them directly through our decisions and behaviours. They are closer to the surface in the process of our self-expression.

Before we explore each Primary Way of Being over the coming sixteen subchapters, it is important to point out that if you measure yourself in each area, as is possible with the Being Profile (see Chapter 10), you would have a unique combination of 'health' scores. Remember, there is no right or wrong, good or bad. On the contrary, gaining access to these deeper qualities and knowing how you are being, as opposed to how you **think** you are being, acts as a reference or starting point for change. With this in mind, I encourage you to consider the Transformation Methodology and its associated Application process and Conception Worksheet, as discussed earlier. Try applying this methodology when you recognise an unhealthy relationship with any of the Primary Ways of Being. Just choose one to start with and see how your experience of life begins to shift.

I would like to finish this introduction to Primary Ways of Being by reiterating an important point. If, as you read on, you recognise certain qualities within yourself that suggest you have an unhealthy relationship with any of the Primary Ways of Being, regard it as a lightbulb moment of awareness and an opportunity for growth and change. To see the light, we must first face or experience the shadow. For example, if you want to be more authentic, you need to know what it feels like to be inauthentic, including the impact that has on yourself and others which, as you are about to see, can have serious consequences. Who knows, you may discover aspects about yourself over the coming subchapters that explain the roadblocks that have been getting in your way. It may also shed light on why others in your life, from colleagues, leaders and employees to your children, friends and life partner, behave the way they do. You may find that awareness priceless.

CHAPTER 8.1

Authenticity

Have you ever been shocked to discover that the reality of a matter you dealt with was not in line with what you first understood? Have you ever allowed 'whatever' to enter your consciousness of a matter, including the way you understand yourself, before quickly finding that your perception was inaccurate and invalid? Have you ever found yourself in a situation where you leniently allowed yourself to hold a view, belief or opinion which led to a massive dysfunction, unworkability or failure to fulfil your intended result, for example, in building meaningful relationships, expanding a business or advancing your career? Authenticity is how you relate to the reality of matters in life and being consistent with who you say you are for others and who you say you are for yourself. In terms of the former, authenticity is the extent to which you are accurate and rigorous in perceiving what is real and what is not. It is also how sensitive and diligent you are to the validity of the knowledge you perceive and take on.

As discussed in Chapter 3: The Exposure Triangle, how a person relates to parts of reality not only hinges on being vulnerable, open and having epistemic humility, but it also requires us to be authentic in our awareness and understanding of the matters in life. This can include the economy, societal issues, politics, family and domestic affairs, relationships and so on. Gaining authentic awareness includes how we perceive and project ourselves, and this extends to other people and matters in the world. Let's now look more closely at how authenticity applies in terms of how we understand ourselves and project ourselves to others.

Many people around the world are copycats who spend most of their lives crying out for acceptance. They show off or wear masks to appear perfect from every angle, thinking perhaps that if they emulate what their idol or a celebrity they admire is doing, they may be able to replicate their level of success or popularity. What they don't realise is that the person they are copying became successful because they were expressing their authentic self to the world, not trying to conform or copy someone else. It was their uniqueness that attracted so many raving fans. The high achievers of the world are authentic. They make their unique contribution in life by tapping into and projecting their Unique Being. And they know that one of the best ways to gain access to their Unique Being is by being authentic.

Our insatiable quest for approval has become even more prevalent since the introduction of social media, where the desire for likes, shares and positive comments has many people bending over backwards to convey the so-called 'ideal' persona. Despite this, we hear some extol the virtues of being authentic. However, they may be referring to it more as a form of popular culture than what this quality really means. It seems authenticity has become a buzzword for some people, a word that they bounce around without necessarily understanding what it means. Ontologically speaking, authenticity is a Primary Way of Being that means being true to yourself in the way you convey yourself to others and how you see yourself. It's also seeking to ensure your beliefs and opinions are aligned with how things really are. Being inauthentic about reality can have significant consequences. By the end of this subchapter, you will realise that there is more to authenticity than just being yourself.

My studies and data from the Being Profile suggest that very few people genuinely value authenticity and strive to be authentic. Societal conformity is far more common. Therefore, the dominant trend is inauthenticity, which typically leads to a lack of effectiveness, integrity and fulfilment. This leaves high achievers – or 'successful people' as many refer to them – in the minority. While there are many stories about how high achievers achieve their 'fame' and 'good fortune', the reality is that the majority work on polishing their Beings, including authenticity, to perform at the highest level. Each one is original and true to themselves – the person they were born to be – which is far more powerful than pretending to be someone they are not. This is true both for their self-image and for the persona they project to others.

As is the case with all Being Framework ontological distinctions, the following description includes what it means to have a healthy relationship with authenticity and also what an unhealthy relationship looks like. In the latter case, it means you are being inauthentic and a shadow side of authenticity is dominant. If you recognise yourself in the description of an inauthentic person, you are definitely not alone. But remember, having that awareness is a constructive first step to change.

Authenticity

Authenticity is how you relate to the reality of matters in life. It is the extent to which you are accurate and rigorous in perceiving what is real and what is not. It is also how sensitive and diligent you are to the validity of the knowledge you perceive. *Authenticity* is paramount for you to carefully consider that your conception of reality – including your beliefs and opinions – is congruent with how things are. When you are being authentic, you are compelled to express your Unique Being – what is there for you to express – while being consistent with who you say you are for others and who you say you are for yourself. It is the congruence or alignment of your self-image – who you know yourself to be – and your persona – who you choose to project to others.

A healthy relationship with *authenticity* indicates that you take the time to thoughtfully consider your beliefs and opinions, as the validity and accuracy of your conception of matters is important to you. You mostly experience yourself as being true to yourself and others. Others may consider you genuine, distinct and trustworthy, and that your actions are consistent with who and how you are and what you communicate.

An unhealthy relationship with *authenticity* indicates that there may be no solid foundation for your beliefs and opinions and how you choose to examine reality, and you are often lenient and fickle with how you express your views and the truth. You may consider yourself to be fake or an imposter and often question your own abilities. Others may consider you to be someone who lacks sincerity and often acts inconsistently with who you say you are. You are frequently uncomfortable with being yourself and being with yourself. Alternatively, you may be righteous, opinionated, biased or prejudiced, considering your 'truth' to be the only truth, and may be unwilling to give up being 'right'.

The Authenticity Quadrant

I created the Authenticity Quadrant to highlight the four areas we need to understand about ourselves and polish in order to be authentic: Self-image and Beliefs on the left, which are the conversations you have with yourself, and Persona and Opinions on the right, which are the conversations you have with the world/others. In a nutshell, your relationship with your self-image, persona, beliefs and opinions defines how authentic you are.

Self-image	**Persona**
Conversations you have with yourself about yourself	Conversations you have with the world about yourself
Beliefs	**Opinions**
Conversations you have with yourself about the world	Conversations you have with the world about the world

The Authenticity Quadrant

Self-image and persona

When you are alone with your thoughts, perhaps lying in bed after retiring for the day, what does the voice in your head say about yourself? Does it try to convince you that you are not as good as or better than others? Does it make up stories about what you have done throughout the day and how your actions may have been perceived by others? This is your self-image, the conversations you have with yourself about yourself. Put simply, your self-image is who and how you tell yourself you are.

Have you ever beaten yourself up about something you have done, like your performance on a task at work or a presentation you delivered, when in reality, your performance was fine? This is when your self-image is out of sync with reality. It is an example of inauthenticity. To have an exaggerated and over-confident self-image is equally inauthentic. For example, to tell yourself you have the skills to perform CPR when you've never undergone training in it or practised it in real life is not only inauthentic but potentially dangerous. The first scenario can lead to low self-esteem, self-doubt and 'imposter syndrome', all of which can be paralysing, while the second can lead to arrogance and fickleness with how you express yourself. I'm sure you would agree that neither way is healthy.

While self-image refers to the conversations you have with yourself about yourself, persona refers to the conversations you have with others about yourself. It's who you portray yourself to be. Today, the Internet and social media make it easy for us to create fake accounts, modify our images using photo editing tools and filters or convey a persona that makes us seem happier and more accomplished than we actually are. In reality, the opposite is frequently true. While all the likes and comments we receive as a result of creating this fake persona may deliver instant gratification, we all know that this does not get us anywhere or provide fulfilment in the long run.

You may think your fake persona is bringing you happiness and success, but in your solitude, you would know that what people are applauding you for is not the real, authentic you but the fake version of you that you have created. Despite the irony of the situation, it's a common scenario. I once coached a well-known pop singer who struggled to be with himself in his solitude. He was trying to escape the forged reality he had created, which required him to maintain two different personas: one to please his fans and another that was more aligned with his authentic self. He believed he wasn't particularly likeable when he was being authentic and that he would lose his fans the moment they saw the real him. After supporting my client to transform his relationship with authenticity, he no longer felt compelled to create and maintain a fake persona for his fans. In the end, he realised that his fans preferred his authenticity and began engaging with him more regularly. Maintaining the integrity of your authentic self is hard enough, let alone trying to maintain the integrity of a fake persona as well. Imagine trying to keep that up for your entire life!

I am not suggesting that conveying a persona is a bad thing. There are times when we all need to portray ourselves a certain way to fit into society or a role we perform. For instance, a police officer, lawyer or security guard must portray a particular persona at work but can let their guard down and be themselves at home and among friends at a barbecue on the weekend and so on. We all portray a persona at times that may differ from who we are deep down, whether it be in a professional setting or to fit into society. The key is not to let your fake persona take over who you are deep down and that your self-image, persona and the real you are reasonably closely aligned. The more out of alignment they are, as shown in the Authenticity Gap diagram below, the more inauthentic you are being.

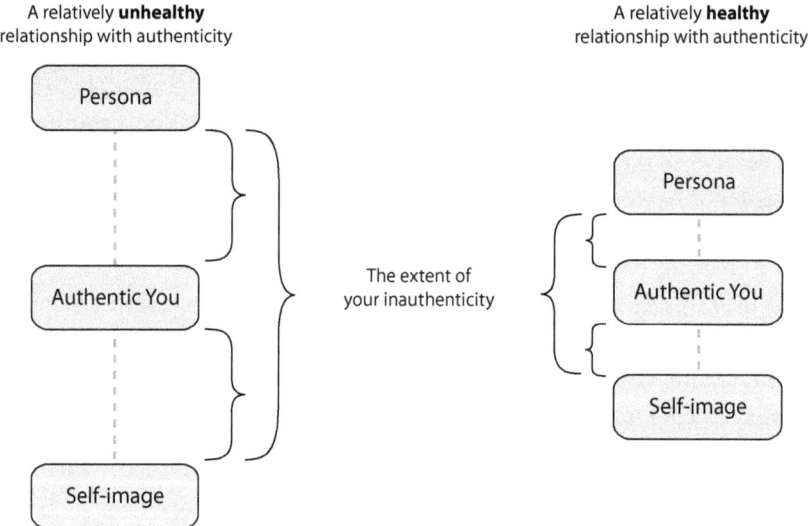

The Authenticity Gap

Imagine someone claiming to be a business coach with little to no knowledge and experience so that they can sell themselves as a professional coach and make a living off unsuspecting clients. Compare that inauthentic person to someone who undergoes the proper training, education and professional development to become a knowledgeable, experienced and effective business coach. The latter enables the coach to be of genuine service to clients, leading to their ability to earn an income from coaching authentically.

Picture what your life would be like if you tried to maintain a fake persona in a personal relationship. The walls would eventually crumble and the mask must come off one day. For many people, that's when their relationship comes to an end because both parties realise that who they fell in love with is not the person sitting across the table from them today. Why would you forsake the chance at real, authentic love by trying to be someone you're not or choosing a partner who is inauthentic?

The same is true in the professional and business world. You may 'fake it till you make it', but will that make you truly happy and fulfilled? And will your success be sustainable? Probably not. And if your goal is to be an entrepreneur, being authentic and serving an authentic need is critical. Why? Because authenticity generates trust and belief in the vision. The saying that a great salesperson can 'sell ice to Eskimos' is a fallacy. A great salesperson would only ever sell a product or service that serves a genuine need.

It doesn't take much to register a business in some countries, which is probably a contributing factor to so many self-proclaimed 'entrepreneurs' being out there. In reality, entrepreneurship is not a label you can simply assign to yourself and hope people will believe it. It's a Way of Being that requires you to immerse yourself in a process of transformation, which doesn't happen overnight. It would be more authentic to let people know you are aiming to become an entrepreneur and then commencing the journey of education and personal and professional evolution, choosing to develop the right persona over time. You would get into the habit of looking for and being present to the genuine needs of your target market and coming up with a solution to solve those needs. You would align with others to deliver the solution. Then, if the market perceives value in what you have created, people will voluntarily exchange money with you for it. And that is how you may start generating an income from your endeavours.

There is a common phenomenon whereby one believes they already are what they wish to become in the future and starts presenting themselves as that future persona before they get there. For example, the day someone decides they want be an entrepreneur is the day they start presenting themselves as one. Projecting a forged and fake persona in this way is what I call 'taking a delusive leap from now to then'. It's like magically teleporting yourself in time from point A to point B and inauthentically daring to sell that fake persona to others. Not only would you fool others into believing you are someone you are not – like an entrepreneur – when you haven't taken the time to learn how to be one, but you would also fool yourself. It's like diving into the deep end of a swimming pool without first learning and practising how to swim. You would miss the preparation, effort and work required to go from the shallow end to the deep end without sinking or needing to cling to the side. Sure, you might manage to keep your head above water for a short time, but that won't work for you in the long run. Your short-term win will be unsustainable. By taking this delusive leap, you ignore all the steps in the middle and will bear the subsequent consequences.

In reality, a persona needs to be developed and aligned with who you are – your authentic self. Doing so takes time. It is perfectly authentic to aim for a goal with the intention of achieving it, but to live as though you have already achieved your intention overnight is inauthentic. In terms of our example, developing an entrepreneurial persona starts when you authentically decide to take the time required to become an entrepreneur. This requires you to undergo a process of transformation, going from a degree of awareness to a degree of effectiveness until you achieve mastery. Attempt to do it inauthentically, however, and you will require skills centred on rhetoric and performance to maintain the fake persona. In short, inauthenticity leads to suffering for yourself and others.

Beliefs and opinions

As discussed earlier and shown in the Authenticity Quadrant, there is more to authenticity than just being yourself by closely aligning your self-image and persona to the real you. It also extends to how you choose to interpret, perceive and conceive the world and everything in it, particularly human beings. We have beliefs – the conversations we have with ourselves about the world – and opinions – the conversations we have with the world about the world. For example, if the conversations you have with the world/others are overly positive, you risk ending up being idealistic, delusional and unrealistic, often expressing romantic, dreamy opinions. Too negative, and you are likely to end up being cynical, sceptical and pessimistic, expressing sarcastic, cutting and acerbic opinions.

A friend of mine once told me how his younger brother had refused to have regular health checks for cancer even though their other sibling and both parents had died from the disease. He deliberately ignored knowing, opting instead to put himself and his family at greater risk. He was not even willing to have a conversation about it. Rather than being authentic and dealing with the reality that he could potentially have the disease, he told himself that if he ignored it, then it didn't exist.

People's conception of money is a classic example where inauthentic beliefs and opinions can lead to poor decision-making. Many people don't have a congruent conception of money. They don't fully understand what money is and how it works. Without a congruent conception of money, you may find that the conversations you have with yourself about money unconsciously play a role in your ability, or inability, to generate wealth and prosperity.

The more balanced and authentic you can be with both positive and negative beliefs and opinions, the more realistic and decisive you will be and the more congruent and accurate your beliefs and opinions. Not caring whether your beliefs and opinions are congruent with reality will have a negative impact on everything from your health and relationships to your prosperity, accomplishments and ultimately, your fulfilment in life. It can lead to a life of misery and regret.

An authentic person is not only consistent with who they know themselves to be for themselves and others, aligning their self-image and persona, but is also concerned with adopting beliefs and opinions as well as seeking perceptions and shaping conceptions that are congruent with reality. The more authentic your conception of reality, the more equipped you are to deal with any matter, including life's inevitable challenges. It will enable you to make more effective decisions and take more effective actions, resulting in an increased probability of hitting your targets. Being inauthentic limits or suppresses your ability to express your uniqueness. The irony is that you are already unique. There is only one real you, not only in your industry, town, city, country and era but in the entire history of humankind. Is that not worth cultivating?

Before we end this subchapter and move on to the next Primary Way of Being, consider how much more you could contribute and how fulfilled your life would be if you transformed your relationship with authenticity. I encourage you to have a go at completing a Conception Worksheet, as explained in Chapter 5: Transformation Methodology, this time with a focus on authenticity. Start by downloading and printing a copy of the Conception Worksheet from engenesis.com/c/being or draw it on a blank sheet of paper. Here's how it could look.

In the first column – Instance – write down all the occasions you can remember over the past three years when you were not being authentic. For example, a time when you pretended to be interested in someone or something when you actually weren't, when you shaped an opinion or belief without due diligence, the time you projected a fake and exaggerated persona with a potential client, or when you lied to your spouse or partner. Be vulnerable and be specific.

In the second column – Consequences – write down the consequences, the cost or impact of choosing not to be authentic on each of those occasions.

In the third column – Alternative – articulate how differently you could have been BEING on each occasion and what you could have done differently.

Finally, in the fourth column – Outcome – write down what the alternative outcome could have been had you chosen to be authentic on each occasion.

After completing this exercise based on a reflection of the last three years, bring the scenario into the present. Allocate a time to reflect on what happened throughout the day in relation to authenticity. Write your insights in a journal or on a new Conception Worksheet, filling in the same four columns and questions you did for the three-year exercise, but now in the present time.

Once you have repeated this daily reflection and journaling over a number of days or weeks (however long is necessary), the next step is to change the timing again, making it even more present, right down to a specific moment in time. Now you are in a position where you can catch yourself on the spot, right when you are about to be inauthentic, say in a meeting at work or in a conversation with your spouse. Instead of letting it happen, you intercept your imminent inauthenticity and choose to be authentic and act upon it (Execute).

Continue to observe when and where you are being inauthentic and whether or not you are choosing to interrupt it and why. This is self-monitoring (Track) based on your perception and conception of how not being authentic holds you back from achieving your goals and fulfilment. You determine what works, so you can do more of the same in future, and what doesn't, so you know what to avoid. You also identify anything missing or redundant, so you can add or remove them as required. This is all part of the Learn stage. You then change the way you respond (Refine). Eventually, you will start catching yourself in the moment and choosing to interrupt your inauthenticity at will before it happens (Execute). Let's look at an example to make this more tangible.

Imagine you are in a meeting and there is an important matter being addressed which requires you to be authentic. For example, you might need to ensure you are providing accurate information so that the decision-makers/stakeholders/participants can rely on you telling it how it is and not hiding or exaggerating the truth. Let's assume your current default is not to be authentic, and by now you are well aware of how this looks. After consistently completing your four columns multiple times, you now have the ability to catch yourself on the spot and turn yourself around in the moment. If you don't succeed in interrupting your inauthenticity in that meeting, you step back and reflect on what happened and what you could have done differently, etc.

When you can catch yourself just as you are about to be inauthentic, which might manifest as inauthentic behaviour like telling a lie or exaggerating an achievement, you can address the matter in real time before it happens. It is at this point that you have transformed your relationship with authenticity. The same process can be adopted to transform your relationship with any other Aspect of Being.

Our inclination as human beings is to assume that the solution to a complex problem should be elaborate. That is not true. There are times when the solution to a complex matter is straightforward. Ironically, that is precisely why the real solution may seem insignificant and is often overlooked. While the Conception Worksheet may seem simple, it is a powerful, thoroughly tested instrument that can support you through the transformation process by enabling you to become more and more responsive over time in any given context. Remember, just because it is a simple process doesn't make it easy. However, rest assured that the more you undergo this process, the easier it will become. With this in mind, as you read the rest of this book, consider completing the Conception Worksheet exercise for any of the Ways of Being you recognise that you struggle with.

CHAPTER 8.2

Responsibility

When you think of the word responsibility, what comes to mind? Do you associate it with duty and obligation, as in who is responsible for completing a task or a project? Or perhaps blame is the first thing you go to, such as who is responsible for creating this mess or who missed the bug in the newly released software? From an ontological perspective, responsibility has little to do with either of those definitions, even though both are correct and used widely in conversation. Those meanings are not what I am referring to here. Responsibility, as a Primary Way of Being, is the willingness to be in charge of your life, no matter what happens and regardless of the source of the problem, and to own your part in a situation and choose to do something about it. Let's begin this conversation on responsibility by considering why it is so important that we honour this Way of Being.

As human beings, we seem to be the only beings on Earth that possess the ability to intentionally and consciously choose and influence an outcome. In fact, most of us have abundant choices in life. We can choose our career path, the organisation we work for, our education pathway, our life partner, whether or not to have children, where to live and so on. Unlike other beings and entities, we don't have to surrender to our nature or whatever life throws our way. Sure, there will always be matters and events beyond our control. We are all impacted by weather events, climate change, global pandemics, financial crises, legislative changes, illness, death and the list goes on. Some of us are also limited in choice based on where we were born, how we were raised, the country we reside in and our culture. However, no matter the circumstances or seriousness of the matter, we all have the freedom to choose how we respond. We can thank our relatively high level of autonomy for our ability to choose, influence, steer the course and not simply let life happen to us and surrender to our fate. We always have options. However, the options available may not always be to our liking.

The fact that we possess the privilege of autonomy is a precious gift, so it is critical that we honour it and use it wisely. Acknowledging our autonomy is both a blessing and a curse because it gives us the freedom to make poor or wise choices in response to life's challenges and opportunities. Our autonomy even provides us with the option to do nothing at all. That's where responsibility comes in. At this point, I would like to encourage you to consider that you are responsible; you are here to respond to the matters in your life. Whether or not you acknowledge that is a different conversation. The world's highest achievers are clear and present to the need to be responsible, regardless of the source of the issue. In other words, whether the issue at hand was caused by them, someone else, a government body or even by unexpected natural disasters, they take the appropriate action in response and persevere.

Responsibility

Responsibility is being the primary cause of the matters in your life, regardless of their source. It is the extent to which you choose to respond rather than react to them. *Responsibility* is distinguished by how you honour the autonomy that you have as a human being and is considered the power to influence the affairs, outcomes and consequences you are faced with. *Responsibility* is not about blaming or determining whose fault it is. Instead, it is to intentionally choose, own, cause and bring about outcomes that matter, work and produce results while also being answerable for the impact and consequences.

A healthy relationship with *responsibility* indicates that you have the power to influence the circumstances you find yourself in and/or cause. Others may consider you capable of appropriately responding to matters, which is a prerequisite to producing and bringing to fruition effective results. You fully accept ownership of both outcomes and consequences and have the capacity to make informed, uncoerced decisions. You are unquestionably the active agent in your life.

An unhealthy relationship with *responsibility* indicates that you may often be stuck, experience a loss of power, and are a victim of circumstances. You frequently experience being disarmed, as though you have no choice in influencing outcomes and there is an inevitability about your future. You may be inclined to self-sabotage and make repetitive complaints without seeking, putting forward and implementing solutions. You frequently make excuses for your lack of accomplishments while abdicating or avoiding consequences. You may be considered ineffective in consistently fulfilling the promises you make and producing intended results. You are a passive victim in your life. Alternatively, you may live life from the viewpoint of being the sole cause of matters and exert your will onto your surroundings and others or be over-responsible and attempt to control all matters all the time. You may also expect that matters should always go your way.

Do you feel as though life just happens to you and there's nothing you can do to change its course? If that's you, then you might be leading a life dominated by anxiety, constantly worried about what's around the corner. Or you might be naive, always hoping and wishing for the best rather than being proactive and taking the necessary action to create your own destiny. At times, you might also feel like a victim or that life is unfair, triggering an endless cycle of struggle, self-sabotage, envy and blame. Or do you believe you can influence most events in your life by the way you choose to respond to them? Ironically, even if you choose to live from the viewpoint that life happens to you and you are a victim of circumstances, the fact that you make this choice is an indication of your autonomy and responsibility. You are the one choosing to interpret reality that way. As a person with a relatively healthy relationship with responsibility, all you need to do is find and pull the tiniest thread to steer the course in your preferred direction. It's your choice, and you are responsible for making it. Even the fact that you give yourself options is a testament to your relatively high level of autonomy as a human being. The more aware and responsible you are in how you respond to what happens in your life, the more things will work out for you. I don't mean in a magical sense or through hopes and wishes, but through the influence you have over your life and your willingness to face the reality of every challenge rather than ignore it or hope it goes away.

We can't control everything

Those who live life from the viewpoint that they are a victim of circumstances and who fail to take charge by responding appropriately to different situations have an unhealthy relationship with responsibility. This is when a shadow side of responsibility is dominant. The same is true for those who regard themselves as fully autonomous and able to control everything. A common term to describe someone like this is a 'control freak'. To think we can control everything that happens in our lives is inauthentic and bordering on delusional. We are all vulnerable to external forces and can only respond to the best of our ability. On the other hand, those who take charge and do whatever it takes to favourably influence an outcome or reduce its severity have a healthy relationship with responsibility.

Imagine you are made redundant because the company you work for is downsizing. The loss of your job is beyond your control. It has nothing to do with anything you have done. In fact, your boss tells you how sorry she is to see you go as your contribution has always been valued. However, she tells you the decision is out of her hands too. While there is nothing you can do to reverse the decision, you have the power to choose how you respond and what you do moving forward. You have two choices. You can play the victim game and wallow at home in self-pity and resentment. Or you can be responsible and take control of the situation by revising your resume and looking for a new job or planning the business you've always had a burning desire to start. While losing your job is beyond your control, choosing to proactively face and deal with the circumstances rather than be crushed by them shows a high level of responsibility. It puts the power back in your court.

Own it, clean up, move on

Another side to responsibility as a Way of Being is owning it when something you were directly or indirectly responsible for goes wrong. Many of us are quick to put our hand up, take the credit and accept the accolades when something goes well. However, when something goes wrong, many will pass the buck, make excuses or attempt to cover up their mistakes.

At times, my coaching clients come to me with an ongoing problem they face in their business, such as employees who are not being honest or suppliers being unreliable. At first glance, the issue may seem to be related to an external force and, therefore, beyond the influence or control of the manager or business owner. However, I usually start by pointing them to the common denominator in these scenarios, which is the person sitting across the table from me. I acknowledge that this is an uncomfortable situation, but it is even more uncomfortable to lose revenue, clients or employees. I am vulnerable enough to openly admit that there are times when I catch myself looking externally when things aren't going the way they should. As soon as I am aware that this is happening, I choose to switch my focus internally to consider the parts of the problem I can own. Acknowledging that you are, at least in part, the cause of what happens to you in life can be a bit confronting at first, but once you do, it puts you firmly in the driver's seat of your life.

Owning a problem is empowering. In fact, taking action is always more empowering than procrastinating or hoping the problem will go away. The latter actually drains your energy and the problem festers. If a glass of water has been tipped over your laptop, it makes no difference who has done it. You must remove the water immediately or face the consequences.

Start by owning your part of the problem. But what if you didn't cause it? I would like to encourage you to consider that there is always at least some part of a problem that you can own. While at face value this may seem as though you are accepting the blame, that isn't the case. By changing your perspective, you will see that owning a part of the problem – even if the problem wasn't directly caused by you – is an opportunity to influence the outcome and consequences. That's how a person with a healthy relationship with responsibility would see it and how every leader should be.

The next step is to clean up without delay, which is about resolving the issue. Last but not least, move on without resentment or blame and forgive all those involved, including yourself. But don't forget. There is always a lesson to be learned from the mistakes we make in life. Let's say you have missed a deadline at work. The first step would be to acknowledge (own) it without making excuses. Then commit to getting it done (clean up), even if it means staying back late or working at home over the weekend. Once the job is complete, move on without shame for the error in your ways or resentment for having to work overtime. The order is always the same – own it, clean up, move on. We will examine how we move on in more detail in Chapter 8.15: Forgiveness.

There is a close relationship between responsibility and a number of other Aspects of Being, but particularly with awareness, authenticity, freedom and vulnerability. An authentic person acknowledges that, as semi-autonomous beings, we have the freedom to choose to take action and steer the course of our lives. Furthermore, an authentic person knows that to respond appropriately to circumstances relies on shaping a congruent conception of reality. Being responsible also drives you to want to know when there is a problem to solve or an opportunity to explore and take advantage of. And it takes a healthy relationship with vulnerability to let your guard down and own your part in a problem.

People talk about their 'rights', particularly in the modern era. Indeed, many people have a sense of entitlement extending from their so-called 'birth rights' to their civil rights. I am not suggesting we shouldn't have rights. However, when a matter requires attention, it won't magically disappear until someone chooses to be responsible and address it, regardless of the source or whether it goes against their rights. The point is you cannot have rights without responsibility. Our autonomy means we are able to respond appropriately to different matters or situations. If we fail to do so, there will be consequences that may impact us all. A leader chooses to be the one who responds to these matters. While that responsibility may sometimes be a burden and cause discomfort, it can also be incredibly rewarding. But just as some may choose to outsource their sanity when it comes to awareness, such as by allowing themselves to be overly influenced by the media, others may choose to outsource responsibility without even first effectively communicating their expectations and coming to an agreement with the other parties because they are so focused on what they believe to be their 'rights'. Consider that whenever you assert your right, there is a responsibility behind it that needs to be taken care of by someone. In other words, your right becomes someone else's responsibility. And, if you are a leader, the buck still rests with you.

While some people today seem to think they have a right to feel safe, supported, comfortable and financially secure, that is not how the world works. Living in that fantasyland paradigm will set you up for a lifetime of disappointment, shock and suffering. There is so much happening in the world that none of us has any direct influence over. That will never change. By choosing to honour your relatively high level of autonomy and be responsible, you are doing the best you can to influence the outcome by steering it in the right direction. Being an active agent rather than a passive victim in the journey of life is one of the keys to happiness, health, prosperity and fulfilment.

CHAPTER 8.3

Freedom

I magine if you could do whatever you wanted to do, whenever you wanted to do it, free from any restrictions. Would you call that freedom? The truth is, freedom is another example of a word that is frequently misused and abused. These days, in particular, freedom is commonly associated with doing something we want to do without restriction or constraints. Most of us are relatively free to exercise our religious practices and rituals, sexual and gender preferences and voice our opinions and beliefs today. However, those choices do not necessarily reflect the meaning of freedom from an ontological perspective and, therefore, don't represent the meaning I am referring to in this book and as part of the Being Framework. In other words, while we may be free in the sense that there may be limited restrictions from authorities within the society in which we live, ontologically speaking, we may not be and/ or feel free on the inside. I am not suggesting there is anything wrong with the common conception of freedom in society or downgrading it in any way. However, the ontological meaning of freedom goes far deeper. The freedom I am referring to here is not something you set out to achieve or obtain. It is a state of Being we intentionally choose for ourselves.

Do you feel free to choose, make your own decisions and forge your own path? Or do you feel suppressed, trapped or coerced, whether it be by your own internal dialogue or by the beliefs, opinions or manipulation of others? Do you frequently feel resigned and give in to others, even though their points of view or actions don't align with your values? Ontologically, freedom comes with choosing and owning a decision and taking full responsibility for the consequences of that decision, even if the outcome is less than desirable. With freedom, you are not trapped, restricted or limited by the attempts of others to manipulate you to fit in with their agendas or external forces. When you are free, you always have options.

Freedom

Freedom is living life from the viewpoint that you always have options. It is your capacity to choose to be, do, say, feel and think whatever you wish without being controlled, coerced, constrained or limited by unwanted external forces while simultaneously accepting any subsequent consequences of your words or actions. You acknowledge that you have the choice to act despite constraints imposed on you while accepting that there are limitations associated with the reality of being a human being.

A healthy relationship with *freedom* indicates that you see options and possibilities available to you and can create opportunities when the need arises. When you are being free, you are not at the mercy of manipulative or distorting forces. Others may experience you as someone who chooses not to be restrained by situations or challenges imposed on them and communicates openly without constraint. You may actively consider self-discipline and self-imposed restrictions to prioritise what you most care about. When you have a healthy relationship with *freedom*, you refuse to succumb easily to the manipulation or domination of others.

An unhealthy relationship with *freedom* indicates that you often experience being held back and suppressed in the face of circumstances in your life due to a lack of options and may feel trapped or coerced. Others may experience that you withhold and are limited in what you can accomplish, contribute and communicate. You may wait for opportunities to be created and offered to you by others or miraculously land in your lap. You may often feel resigned and disarmed and frequently give in to others or external forces. You may feel imprisoned, stuck or frozen by your inner desires, shackled by dysfunctional habits. Alternatively, you may see and consider too many options, which often leads to paralysis. Avoiding self-imposed routines and disciplines may cause you to lack the momentum required to make progress.

The fundamental difference between freedom and responsibility

While we are all vulnerable to external forces beyond our control, a healthy relationship with freedom as a Way of Being empowers us to choose how to respond to those external forces. In this way, freedom is closely related to responsibility. In fact, there is some overlap, which is not uncommon as there are interrelationships between all Aspects of Being. That being said, the connection between responsibility and freedom is a particularly close one. However, they are sufficiently different to warrant being unique Primary Ways of Being in their own right. Our empirical data constantly validates the decision to differentiate them in the framework because many people score considerably differently for these two qualities when completing a Being Profile assessment.

Here's the fundamental difference between the two qualities. Responsibility is living life from the viewpoint that, as a human being, you have autonomy. Therefore, you are to choose powerfully to own that autonomy by being an active agent and responding to matters in life as they arise rather than allowing yourself to be a passive victim of circumstances. Freedom, on the other hand, is centred on **seeing the possibilities** and knowing you have options to choose from with that autonomy. It is when you live life from the viewpoint that you are not fully restrained or constrained by internal and/or external forces. You are present to the fact that you have options. Responsibility is **acting upon your freedom**, choosing powerfully to move forward and select from the available options or even create new possibilities that were not visible to you before.

Consider that prisoners are not physically free. However, they can exercise their freedom and responsibility by choosing to walk in the yard, trade permissible commodities, have visitors and be on their best behaviour. You need only look into the story of Nelson Mandela to appreciate how no one can imprison your thoughts and ideas and what you stand for. The point is, we can be free and responsible, even if we are incarcerated. But we can also be physically free as a bird and yet be imprisoned by our own self-perceived limitations. A healthy relationship with freedom enables us to determine and live by our values without worrying about what others think when driving our priorities in life. Doing so leads us to be more authentic and self-expressive in projecting our Unique Being to the world.

Freedom begins with awareness

In Chapter 6.1: Awareness, you learned that there are three stages of awareness: reception, perception and conception. Every day, we receive information from various sources. Let's say one day you wake to news in the media about something that is happening in the world that you know will have a dramatic impact on your life. An example we can all relate to is the declaration that a virus is a global pandemic. After receiving that news, rather than push it aside and ignore it, you decide to be authentic and vulnerable about it and make the decision to study it objectively and learn all you can about it, exercising due diligence. In this way, your awareness evolves from reception to perception. Your objective studies into the reality of the situation help you develop a congruent perception of the matter.

Next, you relate it back to your life, shaping a conception of how the matter will impact you. This is where freedom and responsibility come in. In terms of responsibility, you know you must respond to what's going on. Freedom enables you to see the possibilities in terms of how to be responsible in relation to the matter at hand. An individual who has a healthy relationship with freedom would think outside the box and see the situation from all angles. They might see multiple options and even some opportunities that could spring from the challenge. Their freedom would empower them to choose (with responsibility) to take action. Freedom is empowering, but it also takes courage, as you need courage to dare to be free. Rather than tackling a challenge head on, too many people trade freedom for comfort and safety, letting others or society decide the path forward for them.

Those who have an unhealthy relationship with freedom can't see the opportunities available to them. It's like they're living life with blinkers and filters on, trapped in their narrative lens, web of perceptions and limited perspectives. As a result, they restrict the possibilities they create for themselves and others. When you can't see the possibilities, how can you act on them? It's why many people are stuck where they are. An unhealthy relationship with freedom quashes hopes and dreams, leading to a life of unfulfillment. If you allow yourself to be overtaken by a shadow side of freedom, you will not dare to participate fully in life, let alone express your Unique Being.

Freedom may at times be seen by some as a burden. Why? Because when you choose freely, you are being responsible and you own the consequences and outcomes of your choices. In the sense of always having options, freedom can also cause analysis paralysis, especially when there are multiple options. To prevent over-thinking and procrastination in these situations, it is often effective to create self-designated boundaries or 'rules' that enable you to be disciplined and stay on the healthy side of freedom.

The paradox of freedom

Freedom lies in being vulnerable and open to possibilities. However, it is important to understand that freedom is not the absence of limits. It's about understanding your limitations and working in accordance with nature or how things are (first-layer reality). So ironically, to be free, you may need to impose certain self-devised constraints. Imagine if you were to consume as much sugar, fat or alcohol as you desire. You may call this freedom, but, in reality, you risk being 'imprisoned' by such behavioural patterns and habits as they can lead to addiction. That is not freedom. It's entrapment by the shadow or your unhealthy relationship with freedom.

Similarly, you are not free when you can be seduced to buy something you don't need. You are not free if you are making a lot of money that you will never get to enjoy or will eventually spend repaying loans. You are not free if you are constantly anxious about your future to the point where your anxiety freezes you. You are not free if you cannot speak from the heart to your loved ones and be vulnerable and self-expressive. You are not free if your opinions and beliefs are constantly shaped by mass media or the opinions and beliefs of others. You are not free if you are entrapped by your forged persona and incongruent self-image (Authenticity Quadrant) or entangled by your inauthentic web of perceptions. You are not free if you cannot think for yourself but merely follow the crowd. You are not free if you are unwilling to see things from another's perspective. All these examples highlight how an unhealthy relationship with freedom may give someone the delusion of freedom when in reality, their freedom is in jeopardy. Being ontologically responsive requires you to impose self-devised constraints on yourself. Doing so demands a healthy relationship with all Aspects of Being, including freedom. An example would be catching yourself out when you are about to lie to your partner and putting the brakes on before the damage is done.

Those who believe they can do whatever they like without regard for the consequences their actions may cause for themselves and/or others will struggle with freedom. If 'freedom' for one person comes at the expense of other people's freedom or their own health and wellbeing, that is not freedom. And if you make unhealthy choices despite knowing the consequences on your health and wellbeing and the damage it can cause in your relationship and professional life, that 'freedom' will lead to suffering. In other words, too much freedom is counterproductive; it will void or limit your freedom. The paradox of freedom is that you cannot have unmitigated freedom! Exercising your freedom demands discipline and the establishment of certain boundaries and limitations. Contrary to what many believe, the presence of limits does not imply the absence of freedom.

Freedom and suffering go hand in hand

There is a great deal of responsibility associated with being free. Why? Because being free means exercising our freedom of choice to make decisions, and there is often a level of pain associated with that. Let me explain. Whenever we make a decision based on our freedom of choice and the outcome is positive, we are happy to take the credit for it. However, not everything goes to plan. Many people worry so much about the potential impact of their decision and what others might think of them that they allow their fear, anxiety about the what-ifs and/or lack of vulnerability to hold them back.

Everything we do in life has consequences, including the choices we make. Even choosing not to act has a consequence. Most of us know what it's like to procrastinate and the ramifications of putting things off.

Let's say you have made a commitment to start saving for a deposit to buy your first home but you keep putting your savings plan on hold and continue to spend frivolously. You are the one who has to deal with the consequences.

In many ways, freedom is a double-edged sword. While you are free as a human being to make whatever decisions you want for yourself, you are also responsible for the consequences. So, freedom comes at a cost. But picture the cost of not being free. Imagine if everyone in society and the world made the decision to have a healthy relationship with freedom as a Way of Being. There would be no crime or corruption because everyone would predict the consequences of their actions and act accordingly. We would live in a world where awareness, integrity and effectiveness are the norms.

Discipline and freedom

Some people think that those who willingly adhere to strict routines and precise timelines are prisoners of their own making. However, the opposite may be true. It all depends on the scenario. There is enormous freedom in powerfully choosing to be disciplined in order to achieve your goals, whether it be to run a business, become a community leader, progress in your career, study, start a family and so on. I practised martial arts for many years and the discipline that was instilled in me has been priceless in terms of freedom and all its associated benefits. I will never forget two pieces of advice I heard when I was young. My Aikido master taught me that I am my own greatest enemy. And a mentor told me 'discipline sets you free'. I often hear both pieces of advice in my head whenever I sense myself hesitating to take control through freedom and responsibility.

Freedom and its manifestations

Ontologically speaking, there is no such thing as different types of freedom. Rather, freedom manifests itself in various aspects of our lives. In other words, your relationship with freedom might manifest itself differently in various contexts. If you zoom out enough, you will see that freedom is not just another manufactured construct or some 'right' we gave ourselves, but a reality, a primal quality relevant to all beings.

It has a transcendent meaning. A bird senses a loss of freedom when caged and a dog can tell when it is chained. You are free whether you acknowledge it or not. If you are in the pursuit of integrity and effectiveness, developing a healthy relationship with freedom matters.

Take freedom of communication, commonly referred to as freedom of speech. This is how we use language to connect, interact and share ideas with others, participate in teams, projects and relationships and express ourselves (self-expression). By this, I am not drawing your attention to just having diversity in perspective and viewpoints, although that is valuable in itself. Instead, I would like to encourage you to consider freedom of communication as a major mechanism by which we relate to the world and everything in it, including ourselves, as part of developing and raising our authentic awareness. So no matter how 'faulty', incomplete, right or wrong our ideas, communicating them and presenting them to others is the way to polish them and become more authentic. That's how we grow and contribute to the growth of others.

Shaping an authentic and congruent conception of chunks of reality requires us to assess and evaluate matters in our lives so that we can respond appropriately. And that is why freedom of communication matters so much; it's the mechanism that facilitates that. Freedom of communication is also the mechanism by which we communicate those conceptions and our narrative of life's experiences to others. It is part of the mechanism that enables us to relate to authentic awareness more effectively, develop our self-image, project our persona, form opinions and beliefs, and communicate them with others.

As we discussed in Chapter 5: Transformation Methodology, awareness, as the starting point for becoming effective in developing a healthy relationship with any of the Aspects of Being, has three stages: Reception, Perception and Conception. Being receptive can be translated to being open, vulnerable, present and free, including being free to communicate and express yourself freely. When you have a healthy relationship with freedom, you are receptive and perceptive. You read the signs being presented to you by matters in life. You freely communicate your ideas to yourself in your solitude and to others, no matter how 'right' or 'wrong' they may appear to be. You are also available and present to the ideas and thoughts presented to you by others, again, no matter how 'right' or 'wrong' they may appear to be. This is how you access various perceptions of a meaning, such as different perceptions of what a relationship, money or happiness is. It's about freely seeing and considering possibilities.

Free communication with others also enables your perceptions of matters to be challenged and confronted, such as if they are outdated, incomplete or one-sided. We all need iterative feedback from others and ourselves – the latter being through reflection and contemplation – in order to refine our conceptions of chunks of reality and act upon our new learnings. We use the Conception Worksheet to work through this process. This is what happens when we undergo a process of transformation using the Transformation Methodology, going through its Awareness and iterative Application stages. That's how we grow. Therefore, being free in communication, or what many refer to as having freedom of speech, is critical to the mechanism that enables growth. Through these discoveries, you allow your existing inauthentic perceptions and conceptions, beliefs and opinions to be shattered. You reconstruct them in new forms and reanimate them through your new decisions and behaviours. This ultimately contributes to you becoming the future you or what I refer to as thriving.

Removing freedom of speech – or freedom of communication as I call it – and self-expression is the absolute worst form of oppression, whether it is imposed by external forces, like authorities and other people, or self-imposed. It removes so much more than just a 'right' we may think we have given ourselves or a social construct. It demolishes the mechanism for our growth. There will be no way forward. Imagine being so oppressed by external forces that you can't speak your mind without risking potentially severe consequences.

Our developed world and civilisations have been radically and brutally challenged over the course of the last decade. In a pseudo-virtuous effort to avoid offending or hurting anyone's feelings, so-called 'emotional safety' or 'trigger-free' zones have been established, such as in the case of political correctness. As a philosopher, I find this quite concerning. It's even more concerning that limiting freedom of communication is being imposed in places like universities, institutions that were traditionally established for the purpose of truth-seeking. In such a culture, many would not dare to challenge the status quo or highlight inauthenticities, misinformation or invalid ideologies and constructs to avoid the risk of causing offence. By oppressing opposing views held by some to protect those we feel are being oppressed, we are ironically oppressing those with the opposing views. Freedom of communication is the last resort that the oppressed would have on either side because it creates the possibility to share their experience, feelings and ideas no matter how 'right' or 'wrong' they may appear to be. It is only through freedom of communication that we can achieve mutual understanding, appreciation and respect.

I am personally happy to be offended and to be given the opportunity to debate and discuss any topic, even if it means allowing my lack of ignorance to become apparent to both myself and others. I am also prepared to offend others by assertively (not aggressively) expressing my views. Just because I may provoke and challenge the views of others does not make me a provocateur. Freedom of communication is the pathway to developing emotional resilience and authentic awareness. All of this applies equally to teams as it does to individuals. Therefore, all leaders should consider encouraging their team members to develop a relatively healthy relationship with freedom and self-expression. Self-expression, another Primary Way of Being, will be explored in more detail later in the chapter.

In conclusion, freedom is a powerful yet subtle Way of Being because it is deep and comes from within. Where others see constraints and limitations, those who have a healthy relationship with freedom see the possibilities and know they have options. Furthermore, those who also have a healthy relationship with responsibility choose to seize those possibilities and decide which option to take. When you are free, nobody can brainwash or manipulate you, even though they may try. Consider also where your opinions and beliefs have been derived and how they have been shaped and adopted. It is naive to think that you are entirely in charge of your views and perceptions. However, you can be free from systematic and strategic forces that do their best to pull your strings. We are all at the mercy of life's challenges and obstacles beyond our control. We must deal with them as they come. Through authenticity, awareness, responsibility and freedom, we can make empowered choices. That is true freedom.

CHAPTER 8.4

Courage

D o you associate courage with being fearless, heroic or being able to confront a dangerous or scary situation without flinching or giving up? If so, you are not alone. Even some of today's renowned thinkers and leadership 'gurus' see courage as fearlessness. However, that could not be further from reality and is an inauthentic view of courage. In reality, courage and fear go hand in hand. More precisely, courage is not the absence of fear. It is the primal quality that enables us to step forward despite the presence of fear, discomfort, hardships, adversities, catastrophes and crises.

Courage is fundamental to each and every one of us and to so many aspects of life. Think back to when you went for your first job interview, first stepped behind the wheel for a driving lesson or went out on a first date. It took courage to do all of those things. Courage is also the central theme to many movies and novels because it's real, it's seen as admirable, a quality to aspire to. But courage is not just for heroes, like the ones we see on the big screen, and it shouldn't be glorified.

Courage is a necessity because life is filled with unpredictability and fear-generating scenarios. We need courage to land a job, open a business, start a relationship, get married or bring a baby into the world, to name just a few examples. We also need courage to be authentic, to dare to let others see who we are deep down, minus the fake persona. With all the perils and uncertainties in the world, we even need courage just to dare to BE – to be alive and contribute to the world rather than crumble in the face of adversities and hardships. Courage is such a critical quality that, along with authenticity, it contributes enormously to being a leader of influence and the leader of your own life. Why? Because without courage, you would never dare to step out of your comfort zone, take risks, assert yourself or say your real yeses and noes.

Courage

Courage is the state of Being that gives rise to the ability to make decisions, move forward and take action when you are uncomfortable, frightened, worried or concerned for your safety and/or the safety of others. *Courage* is not the absence of *fear*; on the contrary, *courage* shows up when *fear* or discomfort is present. *Courage* enables you to continue to be of service and pursue objectives, even when circumstances appear insurmountable, unpleasant or dangerous.

A healthy relationship with *courage* indicates that you are likely to look for ways to move forward, make decisions and take action, even when you are afraid, feel threatened or are challenged. Others may consider you brave-hearted, daring and spirited, and someone who stands up for their values and in defence of others when challenged.

An unhealthy relationship with *courage* indicates you may freeze, shut down or withdraw in the face of difficult circumstances or when you are challenged or frightened. You may be inclined to avoid confrontation and be hesitant to express and assert yourself or deal powerfully with uncomfortable situations while tolerating unwanted circumstances. You may avoid confronting and looking into the reality of matters if they challenge or frighten you. Alternatively, you may be reckless in dealing with dangerous or high-risk situations and be unable to predict the consequences of your bravado. You may also underplay and diminish the impact of how you are being and your actions.

Courage and its relationship with other Aspects of Being

Courage is closely linked to all other Aspects of Being, not just fear. More specifically, it has a direct relationship with all other Primary Ways of Being and Moods and an indirect relationship with all Secondary Ways of Being. For example, it takes courage to be responsible and committed to a cause you believe in, despite pressure from others to conform. It takes courage to let others contribute to you and to partner with others. It takes courage to convey love, compassion and gratitude. Having a healthy relationship with courage and other deeper, primal qualities will be reflected in Secondary Ways of Being like assertiveness, resilience, confidence and persistence.

Think of a leader of an organisation or a successful entrepreneur. The leader often cops criticism from the sidelines for the privileges they may enjoy, such as flying business class, having a beautiful home and luxury model car, or being seated in the front row of an auditorium. However, the critics ignore the immense sacrifices and courage it took to get there. It is the leader who must make the tough decisions and manage high levels of risk to protect the organisation and keep others safe in their jobs. You may observe in this example that courage is also closely linked with care and vulnerability. If the leader of the organisation didn't care, they would have no motive to stand tall and protect their people in challenging times. If they weren't vulnerable, they would be so concerned about the opinions of others that they wouldn't dare to make tough and potentially unpopular decisions.

Of all the Primary Ways of Being, the relationship between courage and all Moods in the Being Framework – care, fear, anxiety and vulnerability – is particularly significant. For example, just as a lioness will confront any danger to protect her cubs, a human being will instinctively do the same to protect their children. However, human beings have evolved beyond purely primal and psychological instincts in that we also choose the matters we care deeply about. This can lead us to draw on courage to step forward for whatever we care deeply about, despite the fear it may generate.

Let's say you are an advocate for change in relation to a matter that is extremely important to you and you are given the opportunity to speak on that issue to a large group of people. However, you are afraid of public speaking and your fear threatens to derail this opportunity that you know could be your one and only chance to be heard. Your care for the cause is so great that courage enables you to step onto the stage and deliver your presentation, despite the presence of fear.

No matter what you are striving to achieve, if you don't care enough about the end goal, you won't have the courage to make it. Based on this example, it may not surprise you to read that insufficient care is one of the main causes of failure among startups. The founders just didn't care enough to be courageous and take the calculated risks every startup inevitably faces along the way.

Those who have an unhealthy relationship with courage may either freeze, shut down or withdraw in the face of fear and uncomfortable situations. Alternatively, they may be reckless, over-confident or take unnecessary and potentially dangerous risks. People can exude confidence, but that does not make them courageous if their confidence is coming from a place of inauthenticity. Being courageous is also not being aggressive. While fear of confrontation that shuts down assertiveness indicates an unhealthy relationship with courage, it is equally unhealthy when someone steps forward with inappropriately directed aggression. That is not courage.

Why do we need courage?

If you are working towards a goal or endeavouring to become effective at anything in life, you can expect the path to be rocky and even treacherous at times along the way. It takes courage to step outside your comfort zone, push through and not give up. Without courage, together with authenticity, you will never be free to express your Unique Being to the world, respond to your calling and take actions that can lead you to accomplish what you most desire in life.

Without courage, you would not dare to assert yourself, making you the shy and passive one at the table of life. As a consequence, your Unique Being would not stand a chance of making an impact on the world, and what an utter tragedy that would be. Let me break it down to help you appreciate the extraordinary significance of courage and authenticity to each and every one of us. It takes courage to limit how much you adjust who you really are, including your words and feelings. It takes courage to say your real yeses and noes, to assert yourself even when you're secretly shaking in your boots. It takes courage to be free to think, be and say who you really are. It takes courage to let go of your inauthentic perceptions, made-up self-image or personas that are incongruent with your Unique Being.

It takes courage to break through your current narrative lens and have the epistemic humility (being open to things you may not know or thought you knew) to pursue truth and reality, even if it comes at the risk of being offensive, confrontational and provocative. It takes courage to be vulnerable, to let down your guard, admit ignorance and open the door to knowledge, knowing it will lead you on the pathway to true wisdom. I take my hat off to those who dare to want to know more and to step into unexplored territories as it takes courage to receive and accept criticism; to take it on the chin, resolve an issue and move forward with your head held high. The courageous persevere in the face of great challenge and adversity while they are also the first to step out of their comfort zone.

It takes courage to dare to transform, to stand out, to be responsible, committed and 'all in, boots and all' despite the what-ifs and pressure from others to conform. It takes courage to honour your calling or higher purpose, putting the concerns of self aside and choosing the pathway of service and the road less travelled over the pathway of ease and comfort. It also takes courage to let others contribute to you, to accept generosity and kindness with humility and grace. To be in partnership with other human beings takes courage; to ignore your cold feet and trust your gut that you've made the right decision to commit to the one you love or your business partner. In any relationship, personal or business, it takes courage to be truly present with another and to convey gratitude or love.

There is always something to be grateful for. When someone comes to you seeking comfort, it takes courage to be compassionate and not to take the easy option and turn a blind eye. It takes courage to be willing to just be with them, even if there is nothing you can do to ease their pain or burden. It takes courage to forgive and it takes courage to be calm in the face of all the challenges and difficulties being bombarded at you in life. After all, it takes courage to dare to be YOU: the real, authentic, one-of-a-kind, beautiful you. In fact, it takes courage to dare to be – to be 'out there in the world'.

CHAPTER 8.5

Commitment

How do you typically feel after making an important commitment, whether it be to a client, your manager, a team member, a group you belong to, or your significant other? Do you feel a sense of anticipation, excitement and keenness to get started? Or do you commonly notice feelings of doubt and anxiety creeping in, your inner voice trying to convince you that you're not good enough and you will fail? Or perhaps you tell yourself and others that you are fully committed to something or someone when, in truth, you are overly relaxed and lenient about your commitment, giving yourself a way out if things get uncomfortable down the track. These are all quite common phenomena when committing to someone or something we care deeply about as there are often significant consequences should things not go as planned.

The word commitment is commonly used and understood to mean a promise to undertake an action, often within a given timeframe, or to make an agreement with someone, such as an agreement to partner with someone in marriage or in business. I am by no means disputing that definition. However, commitment as a Way of Being goes beyond making a commitment. It is how you **relate** to the commitment itself that counts. It's about how lenient and fickle (a shadow side of commitment) or serious and determined you are to fulfil your intentions and promises. It's when a promise or agreement you make is so important to you that you are willing to dedicate a portion of your life in terms of time, freedom and energy – all significant assets – to someone or something. Someone who has a healthy relationship with commitment as a Way of Being is all in when they commit to something or someone and remains engaged and committed until the outcome is achieved or for the duration of the promise to be with another person.

Commitment

Commitment is being dedicated to someone, something, a particular promise or cause that you care more about than anything that may stand in the way. When you are committed, you care wholeheartedly, are considered willing, dependable, trustworthy and loyal. You fulfil and honour the promises you make and appropriately demand the same of others.

A healthy relationship with *commitment* indicates that when you put your mind to something, you are all in and stay engaged until the expected outcome is fulfilled. You prioritise, working consistently and diligently towards the fulfilment of the outcome without giving up. Others may consider you dependable and focused on the things you give your word to.

An unhealthy relationship with *commitment* indicates that you may often struggle to fully invest in and maintain relationships or fulfil your agreements. You frequently procrastinate and may avoid making promises or taking on projects or ventures, even those you consider to be beneficial for you. You may avoid any discomfort associated with fulfilling your promises. Others may be hesitant to count on you or give you significant responsibility, which may be detrimental to your relationships and career. You may often refuse to provide specific and timebound promises, lack clarity and be lenient with your responses, or resort to excuses. Alternatively, you may commit to whatever comes your way, regardless of the workability, and may make unrealistic promises without due consideration.

Commitment is trading your time and freedom for a cause or another being

We live in an era where many people have a sense of entitlement or seem to be satisfied to choose a partner by swiping left or right and breaking up via text message without any closure. Commitment is the opposite of this detached, uncaring, entitled attitude and approach. It is a huge deal that requires sacrifice and unwavering dedication. An Olympic athlete is truly committed to their sport. In order to be that dedicated, they must strictly monitor how they spend their time, the foods they eat, and the other causes and activities they must sacrifice in favour of the sport they are committed to. This contradicts the mainstream way of thinking, such as the 'have it all now' philosophy many subscribe to. If you look at it from the perspective of working on a project, your commitment is literally your time and freedom. You are committing a portion of your life to that project. So it is extremely important to take it seriously. Furthermore, if someone doesn't take responsibility for the things they consider to be their right, someone else will need to take on that responsibility, as discussed in Chapter 8.2: Responsibility.

You can probably gather from the description of commitment so far that it has a fundamental relationship with other Aspects of Being. For instance, the Olympic athlete must care so deeply about their goal that they are willing to dedicate their life to their sport, sacrificing so much along the way. They must be vulnerable enough to accept criticism from their coach and get back on the field for training after a loss. They also need a healthy relationship with fear, anxiety and courage, being able to step forward in front of millions of people worldwide to represent their country and not be anxious about the possibility of losing to the next up-and-comer on the team. These are just a few of the relationships that exist between commitment and other Aspects of Being.

It's how you are BEING WITH commitment that counts

A person who has a healthy relationship with commitment honours their promises one way or another. If something is unworkable and makes it difficult or impossible to fulfil the commitment, they would be open and honest about what needs to change and negotiate a mutually agreeable solution, not jump in and impose their will or drop the ball without any sense of ownership.

Let's say you are leading a team of people at work for a major project. Every team member knows the timeline and understands their individual obligations to contribute to the team as a whole to meet its commitment. You notice that one team member has failed to deliver a task on time, which is holding up the work to be performed by other team members down the line. You speak to the team member in question and they make an excuse for their tardiness rather than owning it and acknowledging that they missed their commitment and putting in extra effort to make up for it, even if it impacts their personal priorities. This is an example of an unhealthy relationship with commitment. They would have demonstrated a healthy relationship with commitment, on the other hand, if they had come to you when they realised they were falling behind and explained the reason – perhaps they had an issue at home or with their health – and talked to you about a workable resolution that would allow the project to get back on track. If the team member then moved forward with the mutually agreed resolution without holding resentment over needing to work extra hours, then their healthy relationship with commitment would be apparent.

The four facets of commitment

There are four facets to commitment as a Way of Being: declaration, expectation, execution and grace. Without all four in place, there is only intention and possibly also action, but not commitment in its entirety. Let's briefly touch on each facet. As implied, a declaration is a verbal or written promise or agreement that clearly states you are committed to a cause and declares that you have 'signed up' for something. For example, when two people get married, they publicly declare their promise to each other. Expectations are established to make the commitment concrete, tangible and measurable, limiting ambiguities and enabling both parties to hold each other to account. At work, this could be a clearly defined scope, start and completion date for a project.

Next is the execution stage, which involves completing the work as expected and agreed to by both parties. It's when you fulfil what you 'signed up for' and get it done as promised, no matter what might get in the way. In the event that you don't honour your agreement, regardless of the circumstances, you should own it, clean up and move on, as discussed in Chapter 8.2: Reponsibility.

Last but not least is grace. This is about honouring a commitment without holding resentment or complaining and making unreasonable demands or excuses when the going gets tough. We can all think of someone who fulfils their commitment but does so begrudgingly and holds onto resentment long afterwards. It's like a parent changing their child's nappy, knowing it is a responsibility and commitment they have chosen to fulfil but carrying resentment every time they do it. Can you think of someone at work who fulfils their commitments but often with an air of resentment? When was the last time you were resentful over fulfilling a commitment? If we are honest with ourselves, we would admit that we all do this to varying degrees at times. Whenever you sense resentment creeping in, you have two choices: hang onto the resentment, which never ends well in the long run, or acknowledge it, drop the negative emotion and move on with grace.

A potential recipe for disaster

When there is an unhealthy relationship with commitment, the outcome can be devastating, and not just for the parties involved. Imagine if an employer failed in their commitment to pay their staff a regular wage and employees could never be certain when their wages would be paid. Not only would the workers suffer, but their families would also suffer if they were unable to pay the rent or mortgage and put food on the table. What if an employee refused to be committed to performing their duties as documented in their job description? That could have serious ramifications for the organisation and its customers. The point is, when you have an unhealthy relationship with commitment, you can't be relied upon or trusted, which is a recipe for disaster in a professional or personal relationship.

I am not suggesting that a commitment must never be broken. That is unrealistic. For example, if someone is in a toxic relationship that causes them to suffer, remaining in that relationship and enduring a life of suffering just because they promised their partner to stay with them for life represents an unhealthy relationship with commitment.

As always, there are two sides to the shadow. Sometimes, we may over-promise and under-deliver or fail to deliver at all, while at other times we may fulfil the commitment, but hold resentment over the promise we made rather than meeting our obligations with grace.

Referring back to the ontological distinction of commitment: 'Commitment is being dedicated to someone, something, a particular promise or cause that you care more about than anything that may stand in the way. When you are committed, you care wholeheartedly, are considered willing, dependable, trustworthy and loyal.' So having a healthy relationship with commitment means that when you put your mind to something, you are all in and stay engaged until the expected outcome is fulfilled.

A healthy relationship with responsibility, care and commitment leads to focus

Having too many priorities is a common phenomenon. After all, there are so many aspects to life. Existence and everything in it, as well as our intentions and actions and the intentions and actions of others, generate matters to which we feel the need to respond immediately or suffer the consequences. Unless we have developed a relatively healthy relationship with responsibility, care and commitment, and zoom in on matters in priority order, we risk living life as though we are a particle floating aimlessly in orbit rather than being in the driver's seat of our lives. While there is nothing fundamentally wrong with living life spontaneously and 'going with the flow', the Being Framework and this book are founded on the philosophy of integrity and effectiveness in order to fulfil one's objectives and purpose in life. This takes focus.

Most of us know at least one person who claims to be committed to solving multiple problems at any given time. However, there is only so much one person can do effectively. We are constantly bombarded with matters that life brings us. Furthermore, when we see a problem, it becomes our problem too. But if you are continually addressing whatever matters come your way and shifting priorities, you are creating a recipe for ineffectiveness and unfulfillment. Just because you can, does not mean you should. As human beings, we can only commit to caring for and focusing on a limited number of matters at a time. When we have too many priorities, we become reactive rather than responsible. The resulting lack of focus draws us away from being able to fulfil our intentions in terms of what we care most about. Overcommitting or being lenient and fickle with your commitments and promises indicates an unhealthy relationship with both care and commitment. Why? Because having too many priorities, caring about everything or committing to too many things means you are not committed and dedicated to anything.

In physics, 'effect of force' refers to a force being distributed over a cross-section of an area. If the area is wide, more force is needed. If it's smaller, less force is required. When hammering a nail into a piece of wood, the blunter the tip of the nail, the broader the cross-section and the greater the effort required. If you don't get it right, the nail might not penetrate the wood, making your effort ineffective. There are many examples of this in nature. If you are attempting to create fire using a magnifying glass, a piece of paper and the Sun's energy, you need to zoom in and zoom out till you find the sweet spot where the light is concentrated and focused on one tiny part of the paper so that a spark can be ignited. Failing to find that sweet spot will mean that even the greatest commitment and effort to get it right is wasted.

Let's put effect of force into a work context. It is very common for inexperienced entrepreneurs who have a relatively unhealthy relationship with commitment – as well as awareness, authenticity, care, responsibility and freedom – to divide their time and energy between too many 'business ventures' or 'projects'. Many will use the excuse that they are working on various endeavours 'in parallel', telling themselves, 'If one works out, then I will take it seriously'. In reality, the opposite is needed: take it seriously and it might work. An effective entrepreneur would put their heart and soul into one business or project at a time to give it the best possible chance of success. Their commitment towards and care for that one endeavour will generate the focus they need to see it through. Focus is a clear manifestation of a healthy relationship with commitment and care. Other Aspects of Being come into play too; however, responsibility, care and commitment are the key determinants when it comes to focus.

In summary, commitment as a Way of Being is more than just making a promise and sticking to it. It's about how you are being with the promises you make and how you relate to commitment in various aspects of your life. Commitment is an empowering Way of Being because, without it, nothing in life would ever be actualised. A high level of commitment leads to conviction, which in turn leads to persistence and reliability, both of which are Secondary Ways of Being.

Imagine the chaos in society or globally if commitment was neglected on a collective scale. What if doctors, nurses and paramedics weren't prepared to literally put their lives and the safety of their families on the line to support patients and test and vaccinate the masses during the height of a global pandemic? Imagine if firefighters weren't committed to fighting fires and protecting people and property, risking their own safety in the process? What if entrepreneurs weren't prepared to work day and night and take enormous risks, initially without monetary gain, to create an innovative solution to a burning pain within humanity, generating jobs and wealth not only for themselves but also for others? Imagine if nobody was prepared to volunteer their time to feed the homeless and destitute or work in an animal shelter to care for and rehome domestic animals in need? It is a blessing that so many people are prepared to trade a significant proportion of their freedom and time for a cause they are passionate about. A healthy relationship with commitment is one of the avenues that enable us to discover and project our Unique Being to the world.

CHAPTER 8.6

Gratitude

Gratitude is a Way of Being that is often overlooked, downplayed or taken for granted. In the business world, it is a quality that many people, especially leaders, regard as a 'soft trait' and is therefore not always taken seriously. In fact, some express their surprise that this quality is included in the Being Framework. Even in our own busy lives, it's easy to get so caught up with the mounting pressures of everyday life that we don't take the time to stop and smell the roses, watch how beautiful a leaf looks as it falls gracefully from a tree or admire a ladybug when it lands on our arm. We miss out when we don't stop long enough to look at and appreciate what's around us.

How often do you inwardly express gratitude for the fact that you have electricity, hot water and the Internet at your disposal, for the friends you have, for the love and support of your family, for the job that allows you to pay the bills, put food on the table and live a comfortable life, for the systems in place that bring more ease and structure to society and so on. The opposite of gratitude is where you feel everyone is obliged to serve you or that your birthright somehow entitles you to everything that existence and others have provided for you. While it may seem a bit exaggerated, there are common political and economic ideologies that are founded on the premise of 'I breathe; therefore, everyone owes me something'. Without gratitude, the first person who will suffer is you, followed by others in your life. It will cost you your happiness, contentment and fulfilment because your thoughts will be dominated by negativity and what you wish you had rather than what is present in your life and the world around you.

There have been many studies conducted into gratitude and the impact this Way of Being has on everything from personal to professional and business relationships. For example, workplace morale, productivity, capacity, willingness to learn and employee turnover are dramatically improved in organisations where the leaders regularly express their gratitude to their staff. Similarly, there are significant benefits when employees convey gratitude and appreciation for the opportunity to earn an income for the contribution they are making to the organisation, as opposed to seeing it as their 'right' to have a job. When it comes to personal relationships, studies have found that individuals who take the time to express gratitude to their partner develop more positive feelings towards the other person and feel more comfortable expressing concerns about the relationship with their significant other. Many other positive benefits were found in studies on gratitude, including improved health and the ability to handle adversities more effectively.

Gratitude begins with a sense of appreciation

Having a sense of appreciation refers to being grateful for everything from the gift of life and the way the planet sustains us to appreciating what we have at an individual level. We all have two choices when it comes to gratitude. We can be grateful and appreciate all that we have, or we can play the victim. Neither option is incorrect. The Being Framework doesn't judge whether gratitude is present or not. It merely explores the reality of this Way of Being, how much impact it has on our emotional state and how closely linked it is to our contentment and fulfilment in life.

Gratitude

Gratitude is being aware of, present to, thankful for and appreciative of what you have or are given and your experience of life and those around you. *Gratitude* is primarily oriented towards what you consider important or valuable. It moves you beyond circumstances, self-focus, worry and suffering. It's about acknowledging and respecting all the contributions and gifts provided to you while not taking them for granted.

A healthy relationship with *gratitude* indicates that you clearly see and appreciate the blessings in life, even when circumstances may suggest otherwise. Others may consider you generous, optimistic and someone who consistently participates in life from a perspective of abundance.

An unhealthy relationship with *gratitude* indicates that you may lose sight of blessings in life and the contribution of others. You may be easily discouraged and disheartened by challenging circumstances. You may also operate from scarcity and struggle to maintain enthusiasm and motivation. You may frequently compare yourself with others, wonder why situations don't go your way or focus on what you don't have, leading to jealousy and envy. Others may consider you ungrateful, entitled, lacking in generosity and someone who frequently complains. You may also be regarded as undermining, negative and as someone who often sees problems before solutions. Alternatively, you may be overly content with whatever life throws at you and lack the ambition to stretch or challenge yourself or others to grow.

By now, you may be starting to see the relationship between various Aspects of Being. Gratitude is closely related to awareness, care, freedom, courage and responsibility, in particular. Being truly present to the chain of events happening around us can spark gratitude and bring great joy. For example, next time you hold a piece of fruit, like a tomato, in your hand, take the time to acknowledge and appreciate its beauty, aroma and taste and what it took to bring that tomato to you. Think about the time, effort and care that went into planting the seeds, and growing and nurturing the plant long before the tomato arrived on the supermarket shelf, ready for you to purchase and eat. The point of this analogy is that awareness and care contribute to our sense of gratitude. And when it comes to human beings, our relatively high level of autonomy encourages us to respond appropriately (responsibility). A sense of gratitude comes when we are free in a sense that we see the possibilities (freedom) and realise how different our experience of life would be in a world without the things we often take for granted.

Gratitude, loss and sacrifice

It is often not until we have lost or had to sacrifice something important to us that we experience a deep sense of gratitude. For example, most farmers would have a different sense of appreciation and gratitude for water as a valuable resource than urban dwellers. As a result, they would be far more conscious of their water consumption and grateful when the rains come after a lengthy dry spell. A farmer would also pay close attention to weather patterns, knowing they only have a relatively small window of opportunity to harvest their crops. They would be exceptionally grateful when it is neither too dry nor too wet during the harvest and would responsibly choose to work long hours and sacrifice time off to harvest their crops while conditions are on their side.

Gratitude is sometimes awakened and amplified by life's adversities. For example, it took a catastrophic bushfire event on Australia's East Coast that choked the atmosphere with thick smoke for many people to realise that the air we breathe is not something to be taken for granted. Sometimes it takes a global pandemic for us to be grateful for having the freedom to see loved ones and visit places without restriction. For some, the diagnosis of a serious illness might cause them to suddenly be grateful for the sheer privilege of being alive and the simple pleasures in life that they might not have been present to before their diagnosis, like feeling the ocean on their skin and the sand between their toes, listening to music, smelling the scent of a rose in full bloom, watching their children play, etc.

Gratitude is a two-way street

After studying high achievers, I observed that they share a deep sense of gratitude. An entrepreneur or business owner who has a healthy relationship with gratitude knows they could not operate their business without their people, acknowledging that they each bring their own unique skill sets and experience to the table. They do not take their people for granted and regularly convey their gratitude for their contribution. They also know their business would not survive without the clients and consumers who voluntarily trade their hard-earned money for the business's products or services.

Employees should also acknowledge and appreciate all the effort and sacrifice that the founders put in to provide them with a secure job. Without gratitude, they would lack a sense of meaning and purpose in their role. And consumers have reasons to be grateful for the products and services created by entrepreneurs and their teams because of how they contribute to improving their lives in some way.

Team members who have a healthy relationship with gratitude are aware that the founders shouldered significant risk when they built the organisation. They are present to many of the moving parts required to serve the organisation's consumers, from capital, talent, knowledge and experience to systems and processes, making it possible to create new jobs and enabling them to build a career, contribute and express themselves. While some of these qualities may not be considered tangible assets from an accounting perspective, it is nonetheless important to be present to them. For instance, many overlook the sheer level of courage it takes to build a company. Those with a healthy relationship with gratitude are present to and grateful for both the tangible and intangible qualities that contributed to building the organisation that employs them.

When founders and their leadership teams have a healthy relationship with gratitude, they are present to and grateful for the contribution of others, from the parents who raised them to their employees and clients. They are grateful to their team members who put in the hard work to become specialists in areas needed by the organisation to create and deliver value to their customers. Even consumers are grateful for the possibilities and value being made available to them. It means they can outsource the thinking, design, innovation, development and delivery of the product they need in exchange for the cash they provide to the organisation. There is always a chain of value. Therefore, gratitude is a must. Extraordinary organisations exemplify the chains of value founded on gratitude, from the leaders and the top talent that join them to their ability to build and grow a community of delighted customers. The fact that those customers willingly and voluntarily exchange their money for the organisation's products and services is largely a testament to gratitude in action.

Is the glass half empty or half full?

Life is full of hurdles, curveballs and challenges. But we all have the power to choose how to handle each situation and not victimise or sabotage ourselves. When businesses were forced to stand people down and shut their doors due to lockdowns during a global pandemic, those that survived found things to be grateful for. Their sense of gratitude gave them the strength to be resourceful, innovate and pivot their business in ways they might never have thought of before that challenge.

For instance, the owner of a yoga school used the closure to not only begin live-streaming classes to students at home, but simultaneously built up a comprehensive library of classes that he could offer to a wider market, even after he was able to welcome students back to his premises. His gratitude for the ability to use his school as a studio and for the technology available to produce quality videos gave him the vision to see what was possible. Today, the online library offers him a new passive income stream that he can market to a global audience. Had the yoga school owner not had a healthy relationship with gratitude, he would have shut the doors of the school without offering his students an alternative to practise at home. He would also not have thought outside the square about new, innovative ways to teach.

If there is no sense of gratitude, the first person who will suffer is you. It will cost you your contentment and happiness because you will be focusing more on the things you don't have or the state of Being you wish you were in rather than being grateful for and nurturing what you have. Thinking that the grass is always greener on the other side only generates suffering, both for you and others. An unhealthy relationship with gratitude causes you to be easily discouraged and disheartened by challenging circumstances in life, most of which are out of your control. You might struggle to maintain enthusiasm and stay motivated, and you might come across as someone who feels the world owes them, who is often part of the problem but not the solution.

Fortunately, as is the case with all Aspects of Being, your relationship with gratitude can be polished and transformed by following the Transformation Methodology guidelines described earlier in the book. Once you transform your relationship with gratitude, you will experience an overwhelming sense of happiness and contentment. You will become more resilient, find little reason to complain and have more realistic expectations of yourself and others. You will also experience better relationships, personally and professionally, especially if both or all parties in the relationship have a healthy relationship with this powerful Way of Being. Gratitude is when you are truly present to the unlimited possibilities at your disposal that enable you to not only survive, but thrive in life.

CHAPTER 8.7

Higher Purpose

These days we have access to almost anything we desire at the click of a mouse or touch of a screen. We can find virtually any information imaginable on the World Wide Web within a fraction of a second, watch whatever content we wish to, listen to our favourite music, read as many books as we like, order a meal and even have alcohol delivered to our door, all without leaving the lounge. While it's pleasing and, in a sense, magical and mesmerising to have all these products and services at our fingertips, it is far removed from reality in a big picture sense. There are many layers beneath the surface that brought them to us. For starters, there are always people and processes running the show. But most people pay little to no attention to that. Although such luxuries bring ease and joy to our lives, they can lead to shortsightedness that limits our ability to be effective in our endeavours. It is also our inclination as human beings to have a 'what's in it for me?' attitude, which can easily slide into an unhealthy obsession with ourselves. This is where higher purpose comes in.

Higher purpose is not something to have. And it's more than just the pursuit of a dream or goal that you value dearly, which is the more common understanding of the term. It's not a quality that can be described with a statement like, 'My higher purpose is xyz'. It is a state of Being, a quality that is partly vision or being visionary and partly going beyond your immediate personal needs, desires, impulses and temptations for the sake of others, which I call inclusive vision. I struggled to come up with the right word(s) to convey the ontological meaning of this primal human quality. In fact, it was the most challenging of all the Aspects of Being to name. Higher purpose was the term I came up with because it conveys a willingness to go beyond yourself and/or going beyond the present time and your desire for immediate gratification. It is also about being generous and participating in life with an abundance ethos.

Higher purpose

Higher purpose is being drawn and compelled towards a future vision or cause greater than your personal concerns and beyond your immediate interests and/or comfort in such a way that it sets your priorities and worldview. It's going beyond yourself and your time without expecting immediate gratification to identify resolutions that will drive you towards that future vision. *Higher purpose* is considered the source of the inspiration and charisma required to effectively influence, inspire and develop others as leaders.

A healthy relationship with *higher purpose* indicates that you draw yourself forward to fulfilling challenges you wouldn't normally take on. You are resolute, willing to delay gratification and have the fortitude to go beyond your own discomfort and self-concern to fulfil your future vision. Others may consider you a charismatic leader who is visionary and committed to something meaningful and worthwhile.

An unhealthy relationship with *higher purpose* indicates that you may be shortsighted, narrow-minded, self-centric or selfish. You are mostly driven to fulfil immediate personal concerns and ambitions. You may be limited and constrained by your personal goals and desire for instant gratification while being oblivious to or ignoring the needs and wants of others. Others may frequently challenge and question your motives as a leader and may not experience inspirational leadership from you. Unable to zoom out and see the bigger picture, you may often get stuck in the present with a fragmented narration of the past and future. Alternatively, you may detach yourself and zoom out too much, being so captivated by and engrossed in your long-term vision that smaller, short-term progression seems insignificant to you. This may lead you to lose sight of and fail to appropriately address more immediate obstacles and barriers.

Let's look at a tangible example of what it looks like when someone has a healthy relationship with higher purpose. Imagine you commute to work by train and each morning you call into the cafe near the train station to purchase your morning coffee. Despite the fact that you are there every morning, the owner never addresses you by name and doesn't remember that your coffee of choice is a latte with one sugar. That's because the cafe owner is simply focused on selling 'x' number of coffees a day and, therefore, each customer is regarded as nothing more than a transaction. The only reason you continue to go to the cafe is that it is the only one at the station.

Now imagine you arrive one Monday morning to find the cafe has been taken over by a new owner. You are greeted warmly, asked for your name and the owner makes a note of the type of coffee you order. Every morning that week, you are welcomed with a smile and a 'Latte with one sugar for you today, John?' confirmation. Over time, the owner introduces new products to the cafe, including a signature blend of roasted coffee and a fresh, healthy breakfast menu. You even start arriving early some days to have breakfast at the cafe because her newly introduced menu options and service are outstanding, and you observe others doing the same.

As the business grows, the owner employs staff who clearly share her values and you notice how well the owner treats them. It's clear the new owner sees her customers and staff – collectively and individually – as assets, not transactions and resources. She is intent on building relationships with them over time, and if that means she sells fewer coffees for the first few months in business than the previous owner did, then so be it. She is there for the long-term and the joy, love, care, compassion, responsibility and commitment, etc., are indicative of her healthy relationship with higher purpose.

My point is, how you relate to people – how you choose to be with them, regardless of whether they are internal (staff) or external (customers) – plays a major role in your accomplishments. When you are working towards a great cause or a grand vision, you have to align yourself with others and build relationships if you want to fulfil your objective, whether it be with your staff, customers, venture partners or, more commonly, with all stakeholders to varying degrees.

Higher purpose and entrepreneurship

As consumers, we are at the end of the supply chain. We have the luxury of choosing not to pay attention to the process it takes to bring a product to the store. Let's once again consider the humble tomato, for example. Tomato farmers spend months nurturing their plants before they bear fruit. And yet it takes seconds for us to purchase tomatoes at the grocery store without any thought for the farmer and the work and care that went into bringing the tomato into our shopping basket.

When I first travelled to Italy, particularly Rome and Florence, I had the opportunity to visit many famous statues, buildings and squares, etc. I remember standing before the Statue of David and my tour guide informing me that Michelangelo spent two years studying the human form in the morgue before commencing his carving. It then took him a further twelve months to complete his famous body of work. Three years of dedication to make just one statue! This is not how most people operate, particularly today. There are also many examples of unique architecture in Italy that took far beyond the average lifespan of a human being at the time to design and construct. No wonder we have the saying, 'Rome wasn't built in a day'! In fact, many of history's most famous artists, architects and builders knew they were unlikely to live long enough to see the end result of their work. My extensive research into high achievers has revealed that they display similar patterns of decision-making and behaviour as those masters in history. This is a far cry from the instant gratification attitude adopted by most people today, particularly our youth.

Have you ever stopped to think how much time, resources, innovation and energy has gone into designing and building the smartphone you use multiple times a day? By only paying attention to the final, relatively perfected product, we don't see – or turn a blind eye to – the thousands of beta versions and prototypes that were created, trialled and failed, the ones that were replaced, rebuilt and upgraded multiple times before they reached the standard we see in front of us now. We also don't see the high employee turnover that occurred in the midst of challenging times and uncertainties, as not everyone on the team was ready to face the unknown, the unthought-of and the new. We fail to see the inauthenticities, lack of commitment and lack of integrity, the betrayals, potential threats and legal battles, the multiple times when the team had to persevere with grit and assertiveness to keep the company going. As you can see, it takes a lot to give rise to a new, innovative idea.

The lure of entrepreneurship is alive and well today, particularly among millennials. Many seem to have a perception of entrepreneurship as the best means to accumulate wealth, have no boss tell them what to do and escape the 9-5 rat race. However, there is a massive gap between how most inexperienced 'entrepreneurs' conceive business-building and what is actually required to create a sustainable, scalable startup that serves a genuine need in the market. For the most part, it would be fair to say that their conception of entrepreneurship is delusional. This is not necessarily their fault. With inadequate literature on the art and science of true entrepreneurship and conflicting definitions and views, the term has become severely bastardised. This has led to a collective distorted reality and high failure rates among startup businesses, venture capitalists and investors, causing the whole startup ecosystem and economy to suffer.

Jean-Baptiste Say, a French economist who first coined the word 'entrepreneur' in about 1800, said, 'the entrepreneur shifts economic resources out of an area of lower and into an area of higher productivity and greater yield.' While many regard entrepreneurs as the ones bearing the brunt of the risks and enjoying most of the rewards, there is far more to it, as articulated in Say's distinction. True entrepreneurship is when the arrangement of economic resources, including people's work, shifts from the area of lower productivity and yield to the area of higher productivity and greater yield. So, unlike the definitions applied to the word 'entrepreneur' by two of the world's most popular dictionaries, the true entrepreneur is less focused on accumulating money than they are on reforming and shaping the currently shared reality by generating jobs and opportunities as well as creating products and services more efficiently and economically. However, not everyone sees it this way.

Some people, including certain high-profile commentators, political activists and influencers, perceive that wealth comes easily to the successful entrepreneur. For example, in an interview at a Martin Luther King Jr rally event, American politician and activist Alexandria Ocasio-Cortez (aka AOC) told the interviewer, who was adopting the role of a hypothetical entrepreneur and billionaire, 'You didn't make those widgets, you sat on a couch while thousands of people were paid modern-day slave wages...No one ever makes a billion dollars; you take a billion dollars'. Not only are such statements offensive and undermine the value and contribution of entrepreneurs to the economy and people's lives, but they are also grossly unfounded and far from reality. Statements like this lead to inauthentic and inaccurate views about the rich and high achievers of the world. They lead some people to think that successful entrepreneurs simply sit back and accumulate wealth while others do the work and that they deserve to be taxed at the highest rate.

In reality, revenue doesn't magically land in anyone's bank account. Revenue is authentically earned when consumers willingly and voluntarily exchange their money for the value they are receiving from the creative thinking and efforts of the entrepreneur. In other words, high achievers achieve their success by taking risks, persevering and dealing with matters far beyond what most people are willing to go through or even see. True entrepreneurs and innovators – who are also consumers like everyone else – are present to the fact that it takes an extraordinary amount of R&D, countless hours of work and extreme risk to bring any of the services many take for granted, like Uber Eats and Netflix, to existence. They have a healthy relationship with higher purpose. So if, as a consumer, you decide to also be the one who comes up with solutions and products that genuinely serve others, a different level of awareness is required. Paying close attention to the matters beneath the surface will be crucial.

The two aspects of higher purpose

The ontological meaning that higher purpose refers to is twofold. Firstly, it is about being visionary. It's about having the vision to see what lies ahead – to predict the future – making this Way of Being strongly linked to awareness and freedom. Secondly, it's about having the willingness, patience, courage and foresight to delay rewards or gratification and take the associated risk – to go beyond your immediate interests, needs, wants and temptations for the purpose of achieving something more worthwhile and meaningful that brings far greater and broader-reaching rewards (inclusive vision). Let's briefly look at each aspect.

1. Vision (being visionary)

We all know the benefits of paying attention to the present moment. However, the mantra 'live in the moment' has been taken too literally by some. An individual who has a healthy relationship with higher purpose does not only live in the moment. They go far beyond the here and now. They are willing to sacrifice immediate benefits, needs and wants for the sake of much greater potential rewards in the future. They know this is risky and that there are uncertainties, but they have the vision to see the bigger picture. Imagine if The Beatles had not operated with this mindset. They would never have persevered after being rejected by at least four respected recording companies. The same is true for JK Rowling, Oprah Winfrey, Jack Ma, Gabriel García Márquez and countless other high achievers who were rejected multiple times before achieving their phenomenal success.

Being visionary also demands sacrifice. If you are pursuing mastery in any field, such as wanting to become a top computer programmer or an Olympic athlete, then you should let go of all other possibilities and commit to your pursuit with laser-beam focus. Making sacrifices in order to focus your energy and attention on one area generates excellence and dramatically increases the probability of achieving mastery and reaching the top of your field. This is when you break mediocrity to the point where you attract people in need of your expertise, resulting in extraordinary personal rewards. You become like a rare diamond, in high demand because supply is extremely limited – someone who is irreplaceable, which is a powerful position to be in.

2. Inclusive vision

Inclusive vision is the willingness to go beyond your own needs and immediate desires and consider the needs and wants of others. Most high achievers are quite clear that they cannot do it alone, no matter how smart, determined and hardworking they are. They have an authentic awareness of human beings' limitations. In aligning themselves with others, they know what each and every key member of their team wants financially, mentally, emotionally and career-wise. They make it a priority to support key individuals on their team to grow and achieve what they want and need. They know that when people on their team are internally motivated, they will be inspired to take ownership of their part in the bigger picture.

The high-achieving leader knows that the collective efforts of many are beyond the arithmetic sum of each individual's contribution. Therefore, they understand the need to aggregate and capitalise on the endeavours of each individual on their team by arranging them in such a way as to generate assets and surplus value (profit). This is easier said than done, which is precisely why high achievers are so scarce in the world. Their scarcity perhaps explains why conspiracy theorists feel the need to make up stories about them to compensate for their own failures or lack of understanding.

There is an art and science to building a successful venture through inclusive vision. It requires ontological responsiveness. It also demands that you have the volition to resist the hardships and hits and remain committed, persistent and resilient, among other key Aspects of Being, even when others aren't as supportive as you'd like them to be. Then it requires care to see it through because working towards a big cause is a lifelong commitment.

Inclusive vision is the opposite of operating in a silo and living life from the viewpoint that we are here to fend for ourselves. For example, while most people are fuelled by a desire to make money or discover opportunities for themselves so they can put bread on the table and pay the bills, an entrepreneur strives to create opportunity, not only for themselves but also so others can benefit. An example of creating opportunity is job creation. As a result, a ripple effect is created, generating personal rewards when the vision is executed in the right way. It's the difference between a person who grows fruit and vegetables for themselves versus a farmer who produces for themselves, their community and others. They take on the responsibilities and hardships to create jobs and recruit and lead people to produce beyond their own needs.

To recap, higher purpose is one of the most important characteristics of high achievers. By higher purpose, I am not referring to a big goal or dream you might have; it is a Way of Being. Many observe the lifestyle and wealth of people like the world's most renowned tech company founders and wish they had what they do. However, what they don't see is the struggle and pain they went through, the times they failed but kept going, the sleepless nights, etc. An individual with higher purpose is someone who cares about matters beyond their own needs and wants and who always takes others into consideration. They have both vision and inclusive vision. They are visionary in terms of their will to achieve greatness and work relentlessly towards their vision, making sacrifices – including the sacrifice of instant gratification – for the sake of better, more meaningful rewards in the future, both for themselves and others.

CHAPTER 8.8

Empowerment

How often do you find yourself saying the words, 'I can't', whether to yourself or to your work colleagues, business partners, employees, life partner, children or friends? Perhaps you tell yourself you're not good enough to apply for that dream job, follow your passion, ask someone you really like on a date or start the business you've always wanted to, despite knowing deep down that the only person standing in your way is you. Maybe you know that a member of your team with great potential is holding back because they don't believe they have what it takes to handle a role for which you know they are more than capable. While I acknowledge that there are multiple variables in life that determine an individual's capacity to do something, empowerment reflects our ability to act powerfully to fulfil a realistic intention to become 'x' or do 'y' regardless of our history or past struggles. Many successful, wealthy individuals come from challenging beginnings.

Empowerment is another word that is commonly misunderstood and to which various definitions have been applied. For example, in the *Oxford English Dictionary*, the word 'empowerment' is defined as 'giving (someone) the authority or power to do something', whereas the *Cambridge Dictionary* defines it as 'the process of gaining freedom and power (ability) to do what you want or to control what happens to you'. It is interesting to observe the difference between these dictionary definitions. The first states that empowerment is giving a person power, which suggests it is a passive state in that we must wait for others to empower us rather than empowering ourselves. The second states that empowerment is gaining freedom and power, which is active. It implies that we consciously choose to gain freedom and power rather than sitting back and waiting for others to empower us. I am not suggesting that we should ignore others and external factors. However, the reality is that they don't 'give' us the power but rather they may influence us so that we can empower ourselves. Therefore, the second definition is more aligned with the ontological distinction of empowerment as shown overleaf.

Two simple yet pivotal words are central to empowerment as a Way of Being – I can. In the Being Framework, empowerment is the opposite of oppression, being stuck or disarmed, a situation in which power is taken away. Without a sense of empowerment, we would not be able to do anything, even the things we take for granted and do without thinking twice. We wouldn't be able to raise children, lead and mentor others, cook a meal, drive a car, etc. We wouldn't even be able to get out of bed! Empowerment can make or break us. Even if you doubt yourself deep down, empowerment is a key quality that drives you to take calculated risks and move forward to tackle new opportunities or ventures in line with your intentions and objectives.

Empowerment

Empowerment is living life from the viewpoint of being able to fulfil your intentions while enabling and inspiring others to fulfil theirs. *Empowerment* is how you relate to your power, capabilities and real or perceived limitations.

A healthy relationship with *empowerment* indicates that you mostly experience being able to take powerful actions towards fulfilling your intentions, purpose and goals while encouraging and inspiring others to fulfil theirs. Others may experience you as someone who takes actions that produce meaningful results in many areas of life and you may inspire them to follow you as your actions also make a significant difference to them.

An unhealthy relationship with *empowerment* indicates that you mostly experience being ineffective or stuck. You may often be unable to act towards fulfilling what matters to you or look beyond the immediate obstacles. You may feel frustration, apathy, resignation or despair. Others may experience you as inconsistent, ineffective, lacking drive or energy and hard work. Alternatively, you may often overestimate your capabilities while acting superior, oblivious to the limitations at hand.

Empowerment is an active and self-generating quality

While we commonly hear and see phrases like 'empowering leaders' and 'empowering you to…', this doesn't mean that you are to sit back and wait for others to give you power. To suggest that power needs to be given is rather contradictory, don't you think? When we say 'empowering leaders' in my organisation, we are drawing a leader's attention and awareness to their potential and the possibilities that might not be visible to them right now. It is far more authentic to consider this view rather than the viewpoint that you actually make someone powerful as if they are an object on the receiving end of your action and not the one in the driver's seat. So, ontologically speaking, empowering someone means you are contributing to their ability to be empowered and supporting them to empower themselves. In other words, empowerment is not something one human being can give to another. It is only possible to inspire and support others to empower themselves and guide them to be present to what it takes to be empowered as well as giving them the space and freedom to be empowered (enabling them).

Let's say you have been offered a promotion at work. You tell your partner about it that evening and express your doubt about your ability to handle the more senior role. Your partner encourages you to go for it based on their authentic understanding of you and your capabilities. In this way, your partner is empowering you. But it is up to you to choose to take their words of encouragement on board and empower yourself to accept the new role because empowerment is an active and self-generating quality. In this way, empowerment is like transformation. A coach can facilitate the transformation process but they cannot transform you. Only you can transform yourself. This example applies to any situation that may cause you to say 'I can't', from expanding an existing business and starting a new venture to getting married or having a baby.

Empowerment and its relationship with other Aspects of Being

Empowerment is closely linked to many other Aspects of Being, but especially freedom (to see the possibilities), courage (to dare to choose to say 'I can' and act upon it), presence (to be present to encouragement from others to go for something when you think you can't), and also awareness, vulnerability and authenticity. You will recall from Chapter 3:

The Exposure Triangle that when you have an unhealthy relationship with awareness, vulnerability and authenticity, the result is a distorted conception of reality, including the reality of yourself and others. Empowerment demands that your conception of how things are is aligned with reality.

For example, there are times when it is more empowering and authentic to say, 'I can't'. Let's say you were born and raised overseas and have dual citizenship, and your goal is to become Prime Minister of Australia, the country in which you now reside. That goal would be unrealistic under the current laws and out of alignment with external man-made/second-layer reality because dual citizens cannot enter Parliament, let alone become Prime Minister. It would be equally irrational if you told yourself you could be an Olympic gymnast at the age of thirty and drop everything to start training if you have never tried gymnastics before, knowing that Olympic level gymnasts begin training and working towards their goal from early childhood. However, in the case of the first example, if you were willing to challenge the status quo, you could legitimately pursue that journey. In that case, you would empower yourself by taking the appropriate actions in an attempt to effect change in the existing laws. After all, since laws and legislations are man-made constructs, they can always be discussed, negotiated and refined for the better.

Let's consider an example that highlights some of the interconnections between empowerment and other Aspects of Being. A friend of mine was once robbed while walking to his car after an evening out with friends. He felt disempowered at the time to prevent the theft from happening. Thinking about it afterwards and admitting he was a victim at the hands of the thieves, my friend realised he needed to learn to protect himself in case he was ever threatened again. This awareness led him to choose powerfully as an active agent – with authority and autonomy (responsibility) – to exercise his freedom to enrol in a martial arts course in order to build his competency and confidence and learn how to protect himself. The more he practised martial arts, the more he knew that if he were ever confronted again, he would have the courage to step forward despite his fear. His initial awareness led to a journey of transformation which ultimately gave him a sense of empowerment.

Empowerment commonly shows up as confidence, which is a Secondary Way of Being. If you attend a job interview empowered, telling yourself, 'I can perform this role. I am the best person for the job', fully aware that your empowerment comes from a place of authenticity and is aligned with reality, you will exude confidence during the interview. In fact, empowerment is a prerequisite to confidence. Unless you are empowered, you won't dare to execute on anything. You wouldn't even go for the job in the first place.

When 'I can't' is the dominant narrative

To discern when to authentically say 'I can' versus 'I can't' requires awareness, authenticity, vulnerability, freedom, presence and courage, among other Aspects of Being. To think you are superhuman and can do everything reflects a shadow side of awareness, authenticity, vulnerability and empowerment, along with responsibility and confidence. Imagine the potential ramifications of telling yourself and others that you can perform cosmetic surgery if you are not suitably qualified. This reflects an unhealthy relationship with empowerment, authenticity and vulnerability, just as being ineffective, stuck, inconsistent and lacking drive when it comes to goals you can achieve also reflects empowerment's shadow.

Inauthentic views on empowerment are expressed all around us. We see them in places like children's books and cartoons all the way to the messages conveyed on the stage or online by some well-known 'gurus' who tell us we can do anything as long as we believe in ourselves. The Being Framework and this book are focused on what it would take to be an effective person of integrity, to become a leader of influence and potentially a high achiever, not how to become superhuman. Unfortunately, many people continually put unrealistic expectations and demands on themselves in pursuit of an unworkable goal or ideal.

As with all other Aspects of Being, it is your relationship with empowerment that counts and there are always two sides of the shadow. On the one hand, someone who has an unhealthy relationship with empowerment often experiences being ineffective or stuck, which could lead to frustration, apathy or despair due to their inability to fulfil their goals. On the other end of the spectrum, individuals who are disempowered,

meaning they have an extremely unhealthy relationship with empowerment – can be dangerous, divisive and manipulative. They may say
or do anything to keep a job, maintain a relationship or protect their
fake persona. Imagine this on a collective scale in society. In the long
run, disempowerment leads to suffering, both for yourself and others.
I resonate with this myself. I know how it feels to be disempowered as
I also experience this from time to time. However, the healthier your
relationship with empowerment, the more effectively and appropriately
you can respond to disempowering situations. I remember a time in
my teenage years when disempowerment hit me quite hard. It was only
through authentic awareness that I realised how my disempowerment
and insecurity could have easily led me to make decisions and take
actions that would have had detrimental consequences and could have
caused harm to myself and others. That realisation was a wake-up call. It
terrified me so much that I made a commitment there and then to avoid
the pathways that could lead to disempowerment.

While traditionally some say power is the source of evil, I assert that
the opposite is also true. In other words, either state can cause a 'good'
or a 'bad' outcome or consequence. Why? Because the outcome or
consequence of how someone uses power to respond to life's matters
depends on their values and intentions. Furthermore, how we perceive
an outcome or consequence of power is in the eye of the beholder. For
instance, a person who lacks power can do as much, if not more, damage
than someone who has immense power. And the more power one has,
the more responsible and autonomous one should be. I would argue
that it's not a lack of power that is the main issue here; it's the health
of our relationship with power that counts. So while power may have
a negative connotation for some, particularly as it can be abused and
misused, power and being empowered are necessary qualities for leaders
of influence, entrepreneurs, high achievers or anyone who wants to fulfil
their intentions, no matter how big or small. You might wonder about
the role of ethics in relation to power. I would answer that conversations
around ethics are vital in this and many other contexts. However, ethics
is a separate topic that sits beyond the scope of this book.

Empowerment when entering uncharted territory

What if you are embarking on something unprecedented, something nobody has ever done before? How can you authentically say 'I can' and be empowered in that situation? The answer is neither black nor white. The dilemma described here is what every entrepreneur, researcher and inventor faces. These pioneers are entering the realms of the unknown, the untrodden path. But true pioneers enter the journey with complete awareness, vulnerability and authenticity. They know they must take a leap of faith, backing their discernment to know the risks worth taking and the ones that aren't. They know they will likely fail many times before they hit the jackpot but have the resilience to bounce back and the persistence to keep going. That's why empowered pioneers are able to say 'I can'.

In summary, true empowerment comes from within and is aligned with reality. It is when you know and, therefore, believe you can realistically achieve something, even if it is something nobody has done before but you believe is possible – the hallmark of an entrepreneur – and draw upon your freedom and autonomy (responsibility) to respond accordingly. It is a Way of Being required for anyone aspiring to be the leader of their own life, to lead others and to achieve a vision, no matter how ambitious or modest.

CHAPTER 8.9

Presence

P resence is a Way of Being that leads you to intentionally and consciously bring your attention to what is going on around you. It is closely linked to awareness, but many other Aspects of Being also have a connection with presence, including responsibility, freedom, authenticity, vulnerability and higher purpose. Once you pay attention to someone or something, a healthy relationship with presence will lead you to connect to that person or being, or develop a clear and congruent conception of an entity. Without presence, your future partner could literally walk right past you without you knowing, an amazing job opportunity could land in your inbox without you reading it or you could find yourself caught in a rip because you failed to pay attention to the signs. As you can see, when you are not present, it can cost you dearly. It can blind you to opportunities and possibilities, reducing your freedom to choose. It can ruin relationships, cause you to feel isolated, limit your growth and potential, and even put your life in danger.

When you read a document or an article, do you tend to flick through the pages and make assumptions as you skim over the words on each page? Or do you intentionally and consciously take the time to really understand and connect with what the author is saying? If the former is true, your assumptions about what the author is saying would likely be based on your own conceptions, perceptions, beliefs and opinions. Think of a function you attended where you met people for the first time. How did it make you feel when a person you had just met barely made eye contact with you as you attempted to strike up a conversation? Or what about the time when you had an important issue to discuss with your partner and their response made it clear that they weren't paying attention to what you were saying. Or the time you had a creative idea to share in a meeting but were ignored because the loudest person in the room dominated the conversation. We can all relate to one or more scenarios like this. The primary objective of this book is to encourage you to zoom in and become aware of the reality of human beings, including yourself. That isn't possible unless you are present and engaged.

Presence

Presence is being so intentionally related to matters and others that you give them your undivided attention and care. It is the authentic relatedness that occurs when all parties experience being fully heard and understood. There is no distance or barrier between you and mutual understanding is fully available.

A healthy relationship with *presence* indicates that you mostly experience being connected, related to, understood and appreciated by others. Others may experience you as open and available to interact and collaborate. You remain in full communication with others with little or no distractions. You may often discern the emotions of others, regardless of what they articulate, and may clearly and accurately sense and interpret their moods. You can also bring your attention and care towards any particular matter you choose to direct your focus to.

An unhealthy relationship with *presence* indicates that you mostly experience being closed, distant and disconnected from others. Others may experience you as quiet, removed or shy and may not understand you well. They may also experience you as hurried, disinterested, distracted and unavailable for interaction and collaboration. You may often experience being misunderstood or not heard while also misinterpreting others' emotions or moods. Alternatively, you may be infatuated or besotted with others and lack discretion or discernment around them.

Presence and BEING WITH others

When it comes to human beings, presence, as a Primary Way of Being, is more than just listening to and connecting with others through communication. It is intentionally listening to them and fully **being with** them. I don't just mean being by their side. 'Being with', in the context of this book, is the state of willingly being aware, present to and connected with others. It is a term derived from philosopher Martin Heidegger's highly regarded book, *Being and Time*, in which he uses the German word 'mitsein' (which translates to 'being with') to articulate an ontological characteristic and need of human beings, which is to be with others of our kind. As social beings, we rely on being with others, from family, friends, teams and our community to movements and organisations. True intimacy with another human being, for example, is impossible unless both parties have a healthy relationship with presence. When this is achieved, there is no distance or barrier between you and each of you feels understood and appreciated. People talk about intimacy, but it is not true intimacy if one or both parties are portraying a fake persona (inauthentic), guarded (invulnerable) or disconnected and disinterested (not being present and lacking in care).

When I first developed the Being Framework, presence was called communication. The reason I changed it is that there is more to presence than just communication, although communication is an important element of it. Most people I work with regard communication as speaking and listening skills. However, you could be an extremely articulate person, yet not be fully present to the person or people with whom you are communicating. That's because many of us have a tendency to predominantly deal with the conversation going on in our own heads rather than focusing on (being present to) what the other person is saying, a behavioural pattern that stems from our relationship with presence as a Way of Being. When we are truly present to another human being, we are intent on fully understanding them, both in what they say and how they are being, taking cues from their non-verbal communication. That's what I mean by **being with** someone.

The consequences of not being present

When we are born, we are all capable of being present. It is a quality to be developed from early childhood, at first with our parents and then continued throughout our lives if we are to master it. Some parents deliberately shelter their children from events happening in the world and how things are at home, including how they are feeling. What they fail to realise is that protecting children from the truth can ironically lead them to become adults who lack awareness and struggle to be present to what is actually going on. It is negligent not to care about being present to and intentionally aware of a matter or another human being. As the leader of your life or an organisation, you would know that negligence has significant consequences. Whatever you neglect will shrink and perish, whereas whatever you choose to be aware of, present to and care for will grow.

I mentioned earlier that, as social beings, we need others, especially if we are working on big projects and contributing towards significant causes. We need to be present to the economic resources available to generate synergy and energy, and in order for us to be able to actualise a dream, we need to be present to the needs and wants of others. This is extremely important. Whether you are in a negotiation with another person, building a relationship or creating a product or service, if you don't know what the other person or your target market wants, expects and cares about, it will be impossible to come up with the right solution. The same is true when attempting to resolve a conflict. If you are not present and genuinely being with the other person and listening to what they have to say, even if you think they are wrong, then how can you possibly produce a mutually agreeable solution?

Focusing on being right and only paying attention to your own internal conversations ironically stops you from hearing what the other person has to say and reaching a workable solution. It can also hold you both back from growth. It is better to give up being right, at least temporarily and in your own mind, so that you can better understand the other person's point of view. Many struggle with this. Taking the time to connect and be with (present to) the other person, even if you believe you are right and they are wrong, will create an opportunity that facilitates open and effective communication and idea sharing. Presence is part of the mechanism we discussed in Chapter 8.3: Freedom that supports us to refine and transform inauthentic conceptions, beliefs and opinions. This is precisely where the potential for growth lies. It also presents an opportunity for transformation, going from what you assume is impossible or are unaware of because it has been sitting in your blindspot to a possibility or blueprint for the future you can work towards and actualise. For this, we can use the iterative process of transformation discussed in Chapter 5: Transformation Methodology.

Many self-proclaimed entrepreneurs come to me and my team with a new product they have built, hoping to secure funding. On the one hand, they claim it's 'the best thing since sliced bread', but on the other hand, they tell us they are struggling to win their first customer and want our help to solve that dilemma. They believe the solution to their problem is to raise funds for marketing. But they have already missed the boat by developing a product they love without being present to what the end users need and want. There is a high level of arrogance and ignorance associated with this approach.

Presence generates trust

Being present is not just about being with others. It's equally about being with yourself. In fact, that is the place to start when working on this Way of Being as it is the key to generating trust and building genuine relationships. If you are not present to yourself, you will never tap into your Unique Being because you won't take the time to listen to your intuition. This will come across as a lack of authenticity. You will also struggle to be present to others. If you are not honest and authentic with yourself, how can you possibly engage in authentic, straight-shooting and open communication with another person, whether it be in business, with an audience or in your personal life? Once you become more present to yourself, don't be surprised if a whole new world opens up to you. Your openness (vulnerability) will be like a magnet; people will be drawn to you, even more so when they realise you are not like most other people who spend more time talking about themselves than listening.

Presence and synchronicity

Have you ever noticed how two people can go through the same situation but experience it completely differently, as though they are out of sync with each other? That's because each creates their own narrative about the experience, causing a breakdown in communication. And if communication breaks down, many other things will break down. As the gap between each party's narrative expands, they may find it increasingly difficult to relate to each other. When this happens, be it in a close personal relationship or with a team member or colleague at work, each party may feel a sense of disconnection and feel misunderstood. The quality that, on the behavioural spectrum, is commonly referred to as 'effective communication' is in part the result of a healthy relationship with presence. To be able to truly connect with others, a healthy relationship with presence is critical.

In many professional and business scenarios, team members' shadow parts are commonly pulling their strings. Consequently, the team collectively lacks integrity and may be run by fear and inauthenticity, etc. When this happens, effective communication and presence will be lacking and this will literally cost the organisation dearly. Like any other Aspect of Being, a lack of presence wastes time, and time is money.

High-performing teams are quick to address the health of their relationship with presence as a collective whenever the team leader senses a lack of effective communication or that team members are out of sync or falling out of integrity. They know that when team members are in sync, they are an effective **team** rather than a group of individuals. And they know that an effective team is more effective than an out-of-sync group of individuals, no matter how professional and qualified each person is. They are also aware that developing synchronicity is not a one-off project and that you cannot technically hire people with built-in synchronicity. It requires a process of building and development – it's not a matter of hunting, but farming. And like a farm, developing team synchronicity requires ongoing maintenance.

Effective team leaders know that if their team is in sync at any given time, there is no guarantee it will remain that way forever. Neglecting this fact is behind many partnership breakups and the breakdown of team integrity. This is where the Being Framework and all its components come to the fore. We start by identifying the areas to look into using the Being Framework Ontological Model. Then we measure the health of our relationship with the various Aspects of Being using the Being Profile. And last but not least, the Transformation Methodology facilitates transformation in the areas dominated by the shadow, ideally under the guidance of trained and experienced coaches.

When there is little synchronicity between two people, presence suffers. This commonly leads to conflict, unconstructive arguments and, ultimately, a breakdown of the relationship. As highlighted, a lack of synchronicity is not limited to personal relationships. It can also prevent teams and organisations from being as productive and reliable as they could be. Whether in a personal, professional or business context, becoming present to what is going on for another person and seeing the world through their perspective and narrative lens allows you to appreciate their points of view, even if you don't agree with them. It is only by being truly present and in communication with others that you can build a picture of how the world and each situation looks to them. Once you have the full picture and you are both on the same page or in sync with each other, you can decide whether to agree, disagree or remain neutral. Too many people jump in with their points of view without taking the time to be in sync with the other person. As discussed, a lack of synchronicity is a major cause of relationship breakdowns and workplace dysfunctionality.

Presence and its connection to other Aspects of Being

By now, it won't surprise you to know that being present requires a healthy relationship with a number of other Aspects of Being. It requires the care to want to **be with** the other person and take the time to listen to them. It demands vulnerability, resisting the temptation to interrupt and impress them and also not to take offence or make excuses. It requires self-expression and freedom, particularly freedom of communication, the gateway to presence and effective communication. For one person to be present to another person, freedom of communication and self-expression should be valued, no matter how 'right' or 'wrong' the thoughts and ideas being shared. For example, when someone feels coerced into being politically correct all the time, their actual views may be kept hidden and undiscussed. However, if those hidden views are strongly held, they will still influence their decisions and behaviours. Imagine if an organisation's HR Manager had racist views beneath a politically-correct exterior. They would likely be influenced by their views, including when hiring new talent.

Presence also demands courage, gratitude and the commitment to be all in and fully of service. It requires both parties to be authentic, to be willing to remove the mask and build a true connection. It's easy to see why employers list communication skills as one of the essential attributes they are looking for in a new team member. But while most employers focus on the skills, they are really looking for someone who is open, willing to listen and learn. That takes more than just someone who can articulate themselves well verbally and in writing. A hearing-impaired person could have a healthier relationship with presence than an experienced, highly engaging and articulate public speaker. Presence is far beyond a 'skill' we possess. It is a Way of Being that directly influences the way we connect, communicate and collaborate with others.

In summary, presence is a Way of Being that is commonly misunderstood. Ontologically speaking, presence is being fully and intentionally connected and in communication with others. It is the authentic communication that occurs when all parties experience being fully related to and understood. When two people are present to each other, there is little to no distance or barrier between them, and mutual understanding is fully available. So if you are too busy dealing with your own immediate problems, signalling an unhealthy relationship with higher purpose, and are continually allowing the hidden conversations in the back of your head to dominate, you are neither connected nor are you being present. Failing to be present can have detrimental effects on everything from your chances of fulfilling your career aspirations or building a successful business and team to developing and maintaining long-lasting relationships.

CHAPTER 8.10

Peace of Mind

Ask anyone what they want in life and you will find that one of the most common responses is peace of mind. Conventionally, peace of mind is seen as the state one achieves from leading a life free of fear, anxiety, worry and stress; a life of calmness, zen and inner peace. But in reality, that state of mind exists only fleetingly and sporadically. Those who think it is possible to achieve it indefinitely are living in fantasyland, no matter how much yoga, tai chi, meditation and other calming disciplines they practise or which religion or school of thought they follow. Why? Because peace of mind is elusive unless it is given regular care and attention. To do so requires integrity – a polished being – including having a healthy relationship with peace of mind as a Way of Being itself. There is no question that we all need more peace of mind in our lives, particularly in today's modern era where we are bombarded with 'noise' from various external forces. That's where peace of mind as a Way of Being is so beneficial. And by now, it won't surprise you to discover that the meaning to which this Primary Way of Being refers is significantly different to the conventional meaning to which many subscribe.

There are no guarantees in life. From the moment we are born, we are vulnerable to life's threats and dangers. Fortunately, nature has hardwired us to have the capability to respond appropriately when we are in danger. While we no longer face the kinds of dangers on a day-to-day basis that our ancestors did, we have retained the fight or flight response that protects us. However, these days it can be triggered by relatively minor things like having an argument, being stuck in traffic when running late for an appointment, technology issues and even the internal conversations that keep us awake at night when alone with our thoughts. To avoid over-the-top responses to non-life-threatening events, we need to learn to manage our fears, anger and anxiety in a more appropriate way. Rather than pretending that fear, anxiety, pain and other perceived negative threats can be obliterated from our lives, peace of mind is a quality that enables us to manage the unavoidable hardships and uncertainties in life and remain focused and on track. But that is only the case for those who have a healthy relationship with this elusive Way of Being. As is the case with all Aspects of Being, the health of our relationship with peace of mind needs to be regularly polished to maintain it.

Peace of mind

Peace of mind is the quality that supports you to remain calm, focused and think clearly, regardless of your situation, circumstances and any feelings of worry, nervousness or unease. It is an inner fortitude that withstands the turmoil around you and supports you in discerning and deciding before taking action.

A healthy relationship with *peace of mind* indicates that you mostly experience that things are handled and you are able to deal with life and circumstances around you, particularly when things may appear chaotic. You clearly distinguish appropriate priorities and remain focused under pressure. Others may experience you as calm, sensible and clear-headed in dealing with life's challenges.

An unhealthy relationship with *peace of mind* indicates that you often experience worry, have troubled thoughts and are distressed when things are not working out as well as you would like them to. Others may see you as frequently distracted, confused, stressed, overwhelmed, stuck or struggling to deal with life's challenges. You may often be consumed by internal dialogue or mental traffic and overwhelmed to the point where you cannot effectively deal with matters at hand. Alternatively, you may choose to be too relaxed while lacking concern for important matters. You may remove yourself from the matters of life, deliberately disassociating yourself from reality and the world around you, often resorting to a fabricated peaceful state. You may rely on substances, practices or techniques to distance or numb yourself from discomfort rather than tackle it head on.

Peace of mind is a quality that is hard to define. The closest word to describe it would be calmness. It is a subtle quality that is closely linked to other Aspects of Being, with awareness, fear, anxiety and courage being the most obvious. Unless you have a healthy relationship with fear, anxiety and courage – and the awareness to know when you don't – peace of mind will not be achieved.

Let's consider an example. Imagine you've been asked to audition for a role in a major theatre production, working alongside some well-known actors, including one of your idols. Landing the role would be a dream come true for you. You've spent a significant portion of your life getting ready for this very moment. You are given the script to rehearse and told that you will be auditioning on a closed set for the producer and director. You arrive early, excited because you've done the research and put in the hard work. You're ready to wow them with your performance, grateful that you only have to perform in front of two people. Your name is called to head side stage and, as you wait to be called onto the stage, you observe that a small group of people, including the stars of the production, are present in the audience with the producer and director. Suddenly you feel anxious and begin to question your preparation. This leads to some doubt and questions in your mind like, 'Did I do enough? What if my idol's presence makes me so nervous that I forget my lines or stumble over my words?' How important do you think it would be to regain your peace of mind before stepping onto the stage? I'm sure you can think of many examples like this where a lack of peace of mind would make things extra challenging and could lead to a less than desirable outcome.

The need to be realistic when it comes to peace of mind

As mentioned, peace of mind is not a state of mind that any of us can expect to maintain constantly. It can be elusive. After all, to expect to live life feeling cool, calm and collected at all times is unrealistic. As discussed in Chapter 8.2: Responsibility, we are here in this world to experience life with all the situations and possibilities it brings us or that we cause ourselves. Regardless of the source, we are to respond to those matters appropriately. And the main way we respond is through our feelings, thoughts, decisions and behaviours. Let me explain further.

No matter who you are, how much money you have or how happy you are, you will face challenges in life. It's how you react and respond to those challenges that counts. Regardless of the source, the matters in life that confront you can cause anxiety, fear, pressure, stress, joy, sadness and so on. While such situations might challenge your peace of mind, it is your responsibility to be ontologically responsive when they show up. In the context of peace of mind, this means remaining calm and doing your best to avoid or at least limit unnecessary mental traffic to avoid cognitive overload. To do so requires a healthy relationship with care in particular, in the sense that you intentionally choose to give your attention to certain matters – the ones you care most about – and not to others. After all, as discussed in Chapter 7.2: Care, it is not feasible to prioritise everything at once. Being ontologically responsive in challenging situations – for instance, remaining calm under pressure – contributes to your peace of mind. It's how effective people operate.

When faced with a challenging situation, two people could deal with it completely differently. One could panic and be completely crushed and frozen by their thoughts and emotions, indicating an unhealthy relationship with peace of mind (or one shadow side of it), while the other (the effective individual) remains calm and focused, able to prioritise the best steps moving forward. The way different individuals deal with and manage adversities, such as global pandemics and natural disasters, is a classic example of a healthy versus unhealthy relationship with peace of mind. The other side of peace of mind's shadow is when we are being careless towards matters that are happening around us and in the world, opting to do nothing at all. That is just as damaging as being frozen in the face of a challenge.

There will always be challenges, adversities and, at times, catastrophes and crises in life. Let's just acknowledge that here and now. Think about a personal or business challenge that you have encountered in your life. How did you handle it? Did you think about all the what-ifs and become so consumed by anxiety about the future that you were incapable of managing the situation? Or did you focus on the present moment and calmly get on with what you needed to do? Peace of mind is not something we can have and hold onto. It can often be fleeting. But we can all learn to cultivate peace of mind and allow it to grow into a healthy Way of Being through awareness, practice and maintenance. When you choose to surrender to the reality of life and manage the outcomes rather than pretend everything is perfect all the time, you will be rewarded with peace of mind.

CHAPTER 8.11

Compassion

As social beings, we are never alone in our suffering, although it may feel as though we are at the time. Even collectively, there are systems in place to ensure we can access support in times of need. While those systems may be far from ideal, the fact that we have created them shows our compassion for our fellow human beings and that we are at least capable of putting ourselves in the shoes of those less fortunate. Imagine a world without compassion. It almost doesn't bear thinking about. Compassion is a quality that is greatly misunderstood. Some mistake sympathy for compassion, while others may compare this Primary Way of Being to empathy. Although there are some similarities, sympathy and empathy do not necessarily lead to being compassionate.

Let's look more closely at the difference between compassion, sympathy and empathy. Compassion is not having sympathy or pity for someone. When we feel guilty, sad or bad about someone else's predicament, that does not necessarily lead us to do something constructive to help them. Compassion is also not just about having empathy or putting yourself in someone else's shoes. While empathy is an extremely important quality to possess since it moves us out of the 'I' perspective to see a situation from other points of view, compassion goes a step further.

As discussed previously, all Moods have a connection with every Primary Way of Being, and care is no exception. However, nowhere is the expression of care more evident than through compassion, as well as love and forgiveness, which we will discuss in upcoming subchapters. Compassion is when you care so much for another human being that you feel compelled to **be with** them in their suffering and take action to support them. This is different from fixing the problem on their behalf, which is not supporting them. People who have a healthy relationship with compassion take the appropriate action to help alleviate someone's suffering instead of feeling sympathy, pity or imagining how they must feel from a distance. They deeply understand what the other person is going through to the point where they are moved to take action and are willing to do something about it in an effort to influence the situation or at least support them in their suffering. However, this does not mean that they are drawn into the other person's narrative of pain, suffering or grief. That would indicate an unhealthy relationship with this Way of Being.

Compassion

Compassion is the quality that compels you to intervene when someone is in pain or suffering and is a clear manifestation and demonstration of your care for others and humanity. It is the capacity to be with the suffering of another. *Compassion* is not sympathy or pity and is also beyond a feeling of empathy for another who is suffering as it moves and motivates you to support them, irrespective of your own discomfort or concerns.

A healthy relationship with *compassion* indicates that you mostly experience yourself as someone who will take appropriate action beyond words or platitudes and intervene when you are present to another's suffering, misery or misfortune. Others may consider you to be someone who is prepared to share and be with the discomfort or pain experienced by another.

An unhealthy relationship with *compassion* indicates that you are often unperturbed, numb or anaesthetised when others are suffering and frequently avoid being in their presence or fully contemplating their circumstances. Others may consider you cold, overly stoic or unfeeling and may not confide in you when challenged or experiencing difficulty in their lives. You may deliberately avert your attention, remove yourself from or avoid situations that bring you into close proximity or contact with someone who is suffering. Alternatively, you may impose your support on others without permission and wish to be seen as the rescuer. You may also become so embroiled in another's misfortune that you create other dramas and draw attention to yourself.

Compassion begins with you

When we think of compassion, it is a natural assumption that it is always directed outward.

While that is true for the most part, you can't be compassionate towards others if you can't be compassionate with yourself. In fact, this is the place to start if you struggle to be with others in their time of need. Start by bringing your intentional consciousness to your own wounds and troubled parts (shadow). It is only when we are able to convey compassion, care, love and forgiveness to ourselves that we can pay it forward. Transformation begins with care and compassion towards oneself, followed by care and compassion for others. That's the significance of compassion. It is also worth noting that it takes vulnerability to be open and willing to receive compassion from others and courage to be compassionate with others.

It is important to understand that you can't be compassionate towards everyone and everything. You need to be selective about where and with whom you choose to channel your compassion because we only have a limited number of hours each day and our capacity to give and support is not unlimited. If you try to take on too much, you may as well do nothing at all because your efforts, no matter how well-intended, will be ineffective.

Compassion in the workplace

Compassion is a Way of Being that is as important in the business world as it is in a personal context because it builds strong and lasting relationships with people, including colleagues, staff, business partners and customers. Despite its significance and value, compassion is commonly considered a 'soft skill' and therefore not taken seriously by many leaders. But nothing could be further from the truth. No matter the size of the organisation or the industry it serves, every business and workplace is made up of a group of human beings working together, ideally in teams, towards a common goal. Importantly, a major factor that distinguishes a group of individuals working together and a team is the presence of care and its major manifestations of love, compassion and forgiveness.

Given that we are all vulnerable to life's inevitable challenges and hardships, there will be times when somebody at work is suffering and needs support. As a leader, not only is compassion towards a team member the right thing to do from the perspective of care for another human being, but it is also the best way to keep things running as smoothly as possible in the workplace. It is equally important for team members to be compassionate towards their team leader. After all, just because they are the team leader does not make them infallible. Like everyone else on the team, leaders are human. They experience fear, anxiety and so on, and will benefit from compassion and understanding from the team during challenging times.

Let's say you run a tech company and you notice that a member on your development team is not performing as well as they normally do. He is making a number of errors and the time required for others to resolve his mistakes is causing a delay in the project timeline. This could have serious consequences on the company's bottom line and reputation. You call him into your office for a chat and give him the space and freedom to open up to you. He lets you know that he is struggling with some personal issues at home and this is causing him to lose focus at work. A leader lacking in compassion would brush off the team member's issues and turn the conversation around to the challenges their mistakes and downtime are causing the company. A leader who has a healthy relationship with compassion, on the other hand, would support their team member because, whether or not they like it, their team member is suffering and that is not going to magically disappear. This isn't just about being virtuous or doing the right thing from a moral standpoint. It is counterproductive to not be present to a team member's suffering because the impact will be far greater than the time it takes the leader to support them.

If you are a team leader, you might argue that it is the team member's responsibility to sort out their own issues and wonder why you should get involved. While you are correct in assuming that it is not your place to fix the issue, it is inauthentic not to acknowledge that there is something going on in the team member's life. As I said, this has little to do with morals and virtue. It's about acknowledging that whatever issue someone is dealing with can disempower them on the job.

A leader simply can't afford to ignore that and hope the situation will resolve itself. Ignorance or negligence in these situations will have severe consequences, including causing suffering for you as the team leader. In other words, unless you are being compassionate, a team member's personal problem could become a major issue for you.

In a situation like this, consider asking if there is anything you can offer your team member that might make a difference. At the same time, assertively communicate any matters that are not negotiable because not attending to them would have severe consequences for the rest of the team and organisation. While this might seem a bit harsh, the reality is that we all deal with a level of challenge or hardship in our lives at times and the world doesn't stop while we sort out our issues. When dealing with a personal hardship, it may feel as though you are alone in your suffering, but that is far from the truth. Everyone is going through something. It is important to acknowledge that. So we all need to perform to a degree despite the presence of our suffering. To live life from the viewpoint that we should only have to perform effectively when everything is going smoothly in our lives is not only inauthentic but also delusional.

There is a practical element to compassion that can't be ignored. If a team member is being impacted by an issue at home that is impacting their effectiveness at work, many others on the team will suffer too. A compassionate leader will take the time to listen and ask their team member what they can do to support them, not only to ease their burden but also to ensure the project can get back on track as quickly as possible. This could mean a temporary reshuffle of duties performed by others on the team or perhaps getting a temp on board to give the team member time to sort things out at home. These acts of compassion will make a world of difference to them and let them know you are there for them. Furthermore, their perception of you as a caring, compassionate leader will positively impact the way they relate to you and the organisation. This, in part, would make you a leader worth following and working for.

To sum up, compassion is not sympathy, pity or just empathy (feeling for someone). It is also not regarded as nothing more than a series of soft skills or moral virtues in this judgement-free framework. Morals and virtue aside, we simply can't afford not to care and have compassion.

Compassion is one of the most tangible manifestations of your care. And remember, the first person you need to be compassionate with is yourself if you want to authentically and responsibly support others. As social beings, we all need others. And there will be times when people you are with are in trouble and need your support. There may also be times when the tables are turned and you are the one needing the compassion of others to support you. So being compassionate is not a 'nice to have', warm and fuzzy skill. It is a critical Way of Being and an absolute non-negotiable in life, including in business or when working towards a cause or vision.

CHAPTER 8.12

Love

One of the most common questions I am asked when introducing people to the Being Framework, particularly if they are leaders or entrepreneurs, is 'What's love got to do with it?' Many switch off, their eyes literally glazing over when this deeply powerful Way of Being is first discussed. The truth is, love is the heart and soul of the entire framework. Without it, this framework would not even exist as I would not have had the commitment, perseverance and vision to make such a contribution to humanity. I am not talking about romantic love or passion here. I am referring to the reality of love from an ontological perspective as the ultimate manifestation of care and the highest level of **being with** or being connected to others and oneself. However, of all the Aspects of Being in the Framework, love was the most challenging to articulate because, let's face it, love has to be the most overloaded, misused and abused word on the planet. This subchapter highlights that love is neither the 'soft trait' many people think it is nor does it just relate to love in a romantic context. I also explain why love is an essential quality for everyone to have a healthy relationship with and in all contexts – personal, professional and business – if they want to perform effectively.

I understand why some people are confused when they first see love as a Primary Way of Being in the Being Framework Ontological Model. It might not seem as tangible as Aspects of Being like authenticity, responsibility, assertiveness and confidence. Many see qualities like compassion and love as being irrelevant to them beyond their personal lives. However, just as care, compassion and forgiveness are critical qualities to possess in business, so is love. Let me explain. It is in times of challenge and crisis – when people are at their most fragile – that love comes to the fore. It is a quality that encourages us to have each other's back, care deeply about the organisation we work for and its vision, values and customers, and have a desire to excel. While compassion is the expression of care in the context of dealing with a specific pain or suffering, love can manifest itself without the presence of pain or suffering. As seen in the ontological distinction overleaf, it can even come across as being unkind when concern for someone is expressed in a firm or stern manner, commonly referred to as 'tough love'.

Love

Love is living life from the viewpoint of being closely and/or intimately connected and is the highest possible level of being with another person and/or oneself. *Love* is the ultimate manifestation of *care* and is not an abstract concept or something you know about or only understand from a distance. *Love* has a quality of *care* that transcends personal interests. It is a quality that may not always be considered kindness, as affectionate concern may also be expressed in a firm, stern or uncomfortable manner, particularly to nurture in a way that is both supportive and preserves the dignity of the other person over time.

A healthy relationship with *love* indicates that you mostly experience both caring and being cared for by others, a true sense of connectedness. Others experience your *care*, warmth and genuine affection towards them. You are free to convey affection and *care* without fear of judgement or concern over the need to comply. You are courageous and can endure prejudice, judgement, rejection and the discomfort of being disliked by those you love.

An unhealthy relationship with *love* indicates that you mostly experience an absence of *care*, warmth and affection in your life. You may feel numb, apathetic or anaesthetised to the *love* and *care* of others. *Love* may be experienced as relational or only with certain individuals, and your relationships are often transactional. You may not experience loving others or being loved by them and may feel lonely, isolated or disconnected and resigned about relationships. Alternatively, you may be transactional in your relationships and use affection to leverage or win favour. Or you may see others from an overly optimistic, dreamy and romantic perspective, seeing their intentions, motives and behaviours through rose-tinted glasses while being excessively protective of them.

Love is considered to be the ultimate level of connection with another being. As social beings, we perform at our best when we are with others. Failing to acknowledge this is inauthentic. That's why, in a business context, we achieve far more in teams than we do alone. Those who are willing to surrender to this part of their nature – namely care and its major and most visible manifestations of love, compassion and forgiveness – would never undervalue or neglect it. As social beings who have a need for interaction with one another, we all require care and its manifestations for us to **be with** each other and develop relationships in all contexts, including personal, business, community-based and professional situations. For example, a business partnership is essentially a relationship with an agreed scope and vision of working towards a common intention or objective. It is not dissimilar to a marriage between two people, as marriage is a partnership founded on similar principles. It is worth noting that partnership as a Way of Being is related to love, but is significantly different enough – as you will observe in Chapter 8.14: Partnership – to warrant being articulated and measured separately.

Love and passion

Passion is another one of those grossly overused and misunderstood words. We hear people tell us how passionate they are about a cause or what they love to do and our newsfeed is bombarded with articles on the importance of passion in leadership and entrepreneurship. However, passion, which is defined as an extreme interest in or desire to do something, is only part of the story when it comes to love as a Way of Being. It's no coincidence that passion is part of the word 'compassion'. Just as compassion and love are two of the most tangible manifestations of care, so too is passion. But love is more than just how you relate to something or someone, no matter how strong the connection. It's when you give something, someone or yourself your full and undivided attention and you are all in without expecting immediate rewards.

Let's look at an example to paint a clearer picture. Imagine you care deeply about environmental sustainability and the global warming conversation. You apply for a role with a small not-for-profit startup that is doing brilliant work in that space and, after researching the founders, you observe that they share your values. During the interview, which is going well, the conversation turns to remuneration and you discover that their offer is significantly lower than the wage other companies are offering people with your qualifications and experience. However, the founders explain that as a startup, that is all they can afford at this time, and your instinct tells you they are not taking advantage of you. Knowing you have the freedom to make your own choice, you decide you would rather sacrifice money for love because you care deeply about what this organisation stands for and know it will give you the opportunity to make a difference and project your Unique Being to the world.

Love demands sacrifice and is driven from the top

Think of any startup and how long it takes for most founders to achieve success. They work longer hours than most for virtually no money and most produce multiple iterations of whatever product or service they are building, failing time and time again before they finally break through. How do you think it is possible for them to persist? The answer, to a great extent, is love. They are so present to the burning pain they are working to solve and the value they are bringing to their identified target market that they are willing to make enormous sacrifices to achieve it. Love is the key to discovering and articulating their WHY.

Entrepreneurs who are focused on the money first are most commonly the ones who fail. Is it any wonder the failure rate among startups is so high? In my entire career working with startups and leaders, I have never seen a business thrive without a healthy dose of care manifested as love by the founders and their leadership team and then infiltrated throughout the organisation. For care to be manifested as compassion and love in an organisation, it must be driven down from the top.

'Love what you do' may seem like a well-worn cliche. But many renowned leaders have been known to communicate those words with conviction because they believe in them so strongly, Steve Jobs being a notable example. If you don't love what you do, how will you persevere when the going gets tough? A purely rational person would surely give up! Love and care for the vision and the solutions you are working towards delivering are the qualities that will keep you going. I would add that there is more to it than just loving what you do. It's also about loving and being connected to those you are serving, the people whose pain and problems you are so present to that you are driven to care enough to prioritise their needs. This deep connection or love will lead you to align other people – such as your team – to the vision, take risks, get out of your comfort zone, put in the necessary time, effort and capital investment, and leverage your creativity to come up with solutions that will serve those people in need. So it is not just about loving what you do; it's also about loving the people you seek to serve.

Most startups and business owners who predominantly focus on the accumulation of money, rather than loving what they do and focusing on giving and serving first, have very little chance of making it through the inevitable tough times, which is why most fail. Your connectedness and love will be challenged, perhaps many times along the way. The key is to maintain your integrity around the qualities aligned with care, including love. This is not just critical for entrepreneurs; it is relevant in almost all contexts. Every successful, lasting relationship, effective partnership and team has gone through their share of challenges and knows there will be more to come. Those who have a healthy relationship with care and its manifestations, particularly love, will persevere and stand the test of time.

When love as a Way of Being is diminished in a business, one of the main consequences is that professional and customer relationships end up being purely transactional. Just as compassion is required for a group of individuals to form a cohesive team, the same is true for love. In other words, for a group of individuals – no matter how qualified and effective on their own – to work together as a high-performing team, compassion and love must be present. Businesses that achieve sustainable success and relatively low staff turnover hire people who are aligned with the vision before they come on board. The owners also know that loyal, long-term customers are true assets to the business and worth nurturing.

The ramifications of an unhealthy relationship with love

Identifying and acknowledging the troubled parts (shadow) of ourselves isn't easy, let alone working to transform them. Many people struggle to identify the shadow sides of themselves and go to great lengths to hide these aspects and even lie to themselves to pretend the shadow doesn't exist. While it takes awareness, vulnerability and authenticity to acknowledge the shadow, it takes courage to face it and responsibility and empowerment to do something about it. Sometimes, the access to these Ways of Being is care and its primary manifestations of compassion and love, especially the latter. Love will draw you closer to the heart of the matter and will guide you on the path towards action and change. The alternative is to let an unhealthy relationship with love suppress you. An unhealthy relationship with this Way of Being can manifest itself in one of two ways: an absence of care, warmth and affection, or obsession or over-dependence. As you can imagine, both can have unpleasant consequences.

Unless you identify and acknowledge the shadow and make change a priority, how can you possibly do whatever it takes to step forward when faced with uncertainties or dealing with matters that seem irrational at face value? Why would anyone choose to work for no or little monetary gain or go through the significant risks and unknowns associated with building a business from scratch? Why would anyone bring a child into a world faced with uncertainties or marry knowing the divorce rate is so high? The dominant quality that enables us to step forward and be all in, even when the odds are not in our favour, is love.

In conclusion, most of the things we value in life don't come easy and there are always going to be potholes and speed humps to navigate. From raising children and developing a lifelong relationship to building a business and pursuing your chosen career, it all comes with challenges. But if care and love are present, the rewards make the path a little less rocky and the hardships worthwhile. Someone who has an unhealthy relationship with love might easily give up when they strike challenges. Another person might be exceedingly obsessive about something or overly dependent on someone. A lack of love for oneself is also the reason why so many feel the need to create a fake persona, which prevents them from being authentic and expressing their Unique Being to the world. Love is the key to creating the willingness to want to change that life of deceit. We all have the power to choose to let love come to the rescue. Importantly, love has nothing to do with morals or measuring up to an ideal or anyone else's expectations in the context of this framework. It's about being true to yourself and acknowledging that as a social being, you are here to **be with** others as opposed to being alone, particularly if your objective is to lead a fulfilled and effective life and contribute to others.

CHAPTER 8.13

Contribution

W hether or not you are consciously aware of it, you are constantly being contributed to by others, directly or indirectly. This includes everyone from your parents, partner, extended family and friends to your employer or employees, peers, the waitstaff at your favourite restaurant, other taxpayers, the government, all the way to the great inventors and innovators who contributed their ideas so that we may all benefit from them. It's easy to take it all for granted. On the flip side, you are also here to make your mark on the world, to contribute so that others may benefit from your talents, skills, experience, qualifications or whatever you have within you to project to the world (your Unique Being).

Tapping into and expressing your Unique Being is the primary objective of the Being Framework and this book. It's about understanding that who you are is distinct from how you are (your Being) and knowing that you are not hardwired to be the way you are now because you can transform. As discussed earlier, polishing and transforming your Being – your Aspects of Being, to be exact – enables you to amplify your expression of self. That in itself can become your major contribution to humanity, no matter which vehicle you choose to do it through, be it through business, as an employee or public servant, family and raising the next generation, art and so on. In short, contribution as a Way of Being is living life from the viewpoint of service and creating and delivering value to others because you care.

A person with a healthy relationship with contribution actively seeks opportunities to serve and add value while also knowing that it is through their contribution that their interests will also be met. This is not being selfish; it is being real. As long as you have an effective structure in place in terms of the way you serve others, people will voluntarily exchange money or other benefits for the value you are providing them.

So whenever someone who has a relatively healthy relationship with contribution engages in a relationship, business partnership, task or project, they are there to serve and contribute in the most effective way they can. And they are also willingly available to have others support them.

Imagine two people moving a solid timber table from one room to another. If one person gives up, the burden is on the other party to do the heavy lifting. This example metaphorically describes how we live our lives, from building a business or career and a home to creating a family and attaining an education, etc. Naturally, there will be times when one party must carry more of the burden than the other. After all, we are not machines and are there to support one another during challenging times. But imagine a world in which most people were of the belief that we are here to live off the generosity of others and the welfare system and acted on that belief. It would be a world dominated by greed, selfishness and idleness. The key point is that we all have certain qualities, skills and expertise, and we are here to be responsible and manifest them as our contribution rather than living off the generosity of society. At the end of the day, contribution brings workability to a relationship, a family, a team, an organisation, a community, a society, etc.

Contribution

Contribution is when you are available to support and compelled to be of service to others to achieve what they are committed to and are also willingly available for others to support and serve you. It is an outward manifestation and expression of your care for others and humanity.

A healthy relationship with *contribution* indicates that you mostly experience being compelled to make a difference to other people and are open, receptive and comfortable in allowing others to make a difference to you. You experience satisfaction and fulfilment from being a contribution as well as being contributed to. Others may experience you as being intentionally supportive of them and what they are committed to.

An unhealthy relationship with *contribution* indicates that you mainly deal with challenges and breakdowns on your own. Others may experience you as unreceptive, disinterested or unavailable for support. You may lack the willingness to participate and add value to others, particularly if you know there is no immediate benefit for you. Your sphere of influence and impact on the world often occurs as narrow and limited. You may experience being unappreciated or consider that what you have to offer is of little value. You may also be resigned and cynical towards other people and question their motives. Alternatively, you may interfere instead of influence and give advice when it is neither asked for nor required. You may also pester others for help without due consideration of the impact on them.

How willing are you to be contributed to?

Serving others comes naturally to most of us. It is a primal Way of Being. But it's not necessarily the same story when it comes to having others contribute to us. Many struggle to see contribution this way. Perhaps they think that being contributed to may remove their so-called 'independence' or make it appear as though they are unable to handle the workload. Maybe they worry that the outcome will be inferior in terms of quality or that the other party will do a better job and make them look bad. There can be many underlying reasons for this, one of the main ones being an unhealthy relationship with vulnerability, not being open and willing to be contributed to. To adopt this view in life is unworkable. For starters, the notion of needing to maintain your independence is inauthentic. As social beings, we are dependent on others whether we like it or not. The high achievers of the world are extremely effective at delegation and outsourcing. They know they need to engage and partner with people who are smarter than they are in various aspects of their business. And they, in turn, know they are contributing to others by offering them opportunities and trading their expertise for capital.

So a healthy relationship with contribution is reciprocal and has two sides. It means you are equally willing to contribute as you are being contributed to by others. No matter what you are building or striving to achieve in life, it is highly unlikely that you will achieve it on your own. You may argue that as a sole proprietor, you don't need the contribution of others to get your work done for clients. But what about all those times when you are working on a project with a tight deadline and your spouse or life partner assists you by taking care of the household chores and parenting duties that you normally share so you can focus on your work? That's an indication of their healthy relationship with contribution. Ideally, you would do the same for them. And if you have hit your ceiling, but the demand from clients for your service is on the rise, the only way to grow is to build a team of people or partner with others who can contribute by bringing their unique skill sets to the table. In turn, you would be contributing to those individuals by offering them the opportunity of regular paid work.

How do you want to make your mark?

Have you ever taken the time to ask yourself how you want to make your mark on the world? As is the case with every Way of Being, awareness is always the first step – firstly, to become consciously aware of the importance of this Way of Being and secondly, to choose how to make your contribution. Start by zooming out and becoming present to your unique talents, qualities and the matters you care about, acknowledging that you are here to express them in a tangible manner. This will become your unique contribution to humanity, the way you leave your mark on the world. It may be that you have the skills, qualifications, expertise and passion to make a powerful contribution to medical science. Or perhaps the app you are developing will solve a burning pain for a portion of the population. Maybe your contribution is to volunteer in a homeless shelter or to become a teacher. However you wish to contribute, viewing life from the perspective of service is very different from regarding the work you do as merely a means to fund your lifestyle.

Many employees expect to be paid just for turning up to work, having minimal care for the contribution they make to the team and organisation. At the same time, there are employers who are focused wholly and solely on the company profits with little regard for their contribution to customers and staff. Both states are unworkable because they convey a distinct lack of care. And eventually, people will see through the facade. Employers will quickly discover an employee who doesn't care about the contribution they are making. It will be evident in their attitude and effectiveness on the job. And team members will grow tired of working with a leader who has no regard for them and may choose to leave and seek work with an organisation in which staff are valued.

The point is, we contribute and make our mark because we **care**. You may be able to see at this point that contribution is closely related to care, compassion and love. Unless you have a healthy relationship with care, compassion and love, you will not be available to contribute. Some tech entrepreneurs prospered during the early stages of the global pandemic in 2020, while others struggled financially. By caring enough to adapt their offering to serve people in a time of need with compassion and love, the successful entrepreneurs thrived through contribution.

You don't need to be tech-savvy to find an opportunity to serve others. Anyone can create opportunities to contribute as long as they focus on what they care about, what the market needs and wants and what they are good at.

The Contribution Quadrant

I created the Contribution Quadrant to highlight the four ways we can all choose to contribute in life or be contributed to. These quadrants apply equally in virtually any context, professional or personal.

1.	**Care about** *and* **Effective at**	**3.**	**Don't care about** *but* **Effective at**
2.	**Care about** *but* **Not effective at (yet)**	**4.**	**Don't care about** *and* **Not effective at**

The Contribution Quadrant

Let's say you want to run a dog-minding business because you are passionate about dogs. However, while you have owned dogs yourself, you have never looked after other people's dogs. What's more, you have never run a business. In that case, you would sit in Quadrant 2. You care about the contribution you want to make – looking after dogs as a business owner – but are not yet effective at it. Ideally, this authentic awareness would prompt you to invest the time and effort to learn how to run a business and perhaps volunteer for the local pet resort to learn more about caring for various dog breeds.

Considering another example, most of us know someone who sits in Quadrant 3. They are effective at what they do but have little interest in it, leading to a life lacking in meaning and fulfilment. An example is someone who has a job simply to pay the bills but has no interest in building a fulfilling career or serving others. Imagine a world filled with people in Quadrant 3 or 4 of the Contribution Quadrant. I'm sure I don't need to articulate the consequences.

Collectively, it is in our best interests for us all to be engaged in roles that we both care about AND are effective at (or working towards effectiveness). If you own a business, the most powerful way to choose to contribute is to shape your business and offering around the areas you care most about. Then focus on employing people who also care about your offering and the people your business serves, and who are either effective at what you need them to do or willing to become effective. Even if they are not yet skilled in what you need them to do, when there is care and love, the skills will be readily learned.

When it comes to contribution, caring makes a world of difference. Authentically contributing and allowing yourself to be contributed to is at the heart of the Being Framework. More specifically, your Being (a combination of all Aspects of Being) shapes the contributions you end up making and your participation in life. Last but not least, consider that your contribution is not limited to your lifetime. For instance, when you raise children or mentor young people, your contribution lasts far beyond you and your time; it shapes future generations. When you write a book or create any piece of art, your contribution may live on indefinitely. In this way, contribution has a clear link to higher purpose – going beyond yourself and your time.

CHAPTER 8.14

Partnership

S o far in this book, we have discussed the importance of aligning ourselves with others many times, particularly when we explored the qualities of compassion and love. You would also appreciate by this point that if you are working towards a significant cause or endeavour, you can't expect to do it alone. As a Way of Being, partnership takes being with another human being – in business or in your personal life – to the next level. It is the closest form of relationship you can build. While logic tells us that one plus one always equals two, when two people who each have a healthy relationship with partnership come together, the outcome is far greater than the sum of the individual parts. More specifically, what you can achieve together in a partnership is far more than you could ever hope to achieve on your own. Why? Because you make a deliberate choice to empower each other.

What do we mean by partnership?

When you form a partnership with another human being, whether it be in your personal life or in business, you generate a 'mutual being'. It is as though two people become one and you see yourselves as inseparable. I am not suggesting you lose your individuality in a partnership. On the contrary, each person brings their own unique talents and skill sets to the table, which is their contribution. In fact, complementary skills and talents generally result in a far more powerful collaboration than if you were to partner with someone just like you. It's not dissimilar to bringing a diverse range of ingredients together to create a delicious meal.

The way to look at it is that each person is an entity and the partnership between them is a new entity that develops its own characteristics over time as the relationship grows and deepens. It's like growing a hybrid fruit tree that generates a new type of fruit when cared for and nurtured while the original trees also continue to grow and flourish. Let me explain further.

In any relationship, there are at least two people involved – Person A and Person B. The partnership or relationship they create is a separate entity. So there are actually three entities in the relationship – Person A, Person B and the partnership they have created (Relationship AB). The priority in any successful partnership is the relationship as the third entity, not the individuals. If two people who enter a partnership only focus on their own personal growth, benefits and interests and take out more than they contribute, the partnership will eventually shrink and perish. However, there comes a time in every effective partnership when the relationship grows so much that, metaphorically speaking, it transitions from a small lake into an active spring that each party can safely remove 'water' from without the risk of it running dry. For this to happen, each individual needs to bring their best to the relationship, allowing parts of themselves to merge into the third entity.

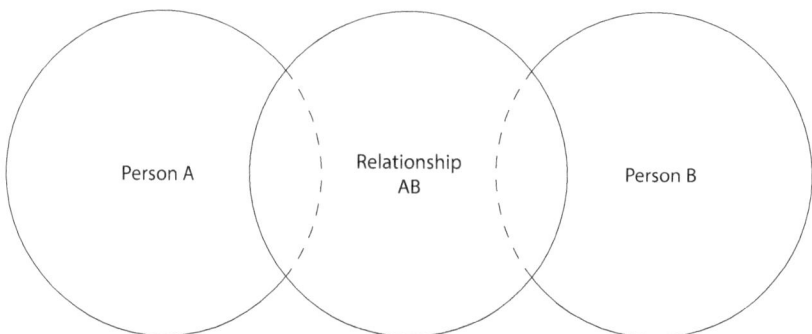

A partnership is not limited to two people. It can essentially be any number more than one. For example, becoming part of a team or committee is also partnering with others to create a new entity in the pursuit and fulfilment of a common purpose and to create an outcome that is greater than anything each individual could achieve on their own. The more people involved in the partnership, the more relationships there are to maintain.

Partnership

Partnership is living from the viewpoint of being in union with other human beings, an entity, team or organisation in the pursuit and fulfilment of a common purpose. It is when you are available to join with others who may share the same values, goals or commitments to create a disproportionate outcome in comparison to what each of you could possibly achieve alone. *Partnership* is the state of confluence where you embrace others and are available to influence each other. It is when you choose to powerfully collaborate and empower each other, irrespective of circumstances.

A healthy relationship with *partnership* indicates that you mostly experience being together, where common purpose, vision, intentions and goals are fulfilled. Others may experience you as being on the same journey with them. You appreciate the company of others and experience being connected, belonging and moving towards the same mutually fulfilling outcomes. You are steadfast in your relationships and will appropriately challenge and support others to bring out their best.

An unhealthy relationship with *partnership* indicates that you mostly experience being isolated and on your own. You may consider yourself independent, although you may also experience frustration and resentment around what is possible to achieve alone. Others may consider you unavailable, overly independent or a loner, and you may experience a sense of not belonging or disconnection. You may tend to initiate transactional relationships based on a trade-off (quid pro quo). You may sacrifice true intimacy and are often oblivious to the value of the contribution of others and the synergy that can be generated of a greater value than you could ever cause alone. Alternatively, you may initiate superficial relationships in the hope of instant gratification rather than investing, building, nurturing and developing long-term relationships.

At this point, you may be wondering how love and connectedness relate to partnership. Simply put, partnership has a more tangible context than love, which is more general. For partnership, there is a clear intention and scope. We connect for the sake of 'xyz'. It's not just a general connectedness with others. With partnership, we connect in the pursuit of a common goal or intention. You may see it as a project or a series of iterations of a project over time. But we partner in order to fulfil a mission, such as building a business or raising a family. Context is critical in any partnership.

The ingredients of a healthy partnership

There is a level of sacrifice and pain involved in anything rewarding in life. Forming a partnership is no exception. A healthy partnership requires each party to be willing to surrender the level of complete independence they had before they decided to join forces. When one party struggles to surrender to that reality, the partnership will be challenged from the get-go. It is not an uncommon scenario for this reality alone to cause so much concern for one party, particularly if they have a relatively unhealthy relationship with their Moods and partnership, that it causes them to withdraw. Imagine if a new player is selected for a soccer team and refuses to make themselves available for some of the team's regular practice sessions because of other priorities. Or if someone joins a committee but is the only member who doesn't put their hand up to assist with duties. Scenarios like this will never be workable. It is also extremely important to be authentic when forming a partnership, to remove the masks and let go of the fake personas so each party knows who and what they are committing themselves to and exactly where they stand.

From a Being perspective, each party in a partnership must be aware of what they are getting themselves into. So it is critical to clearly declare the partnership's intention and the role each party is to play, including their commitment, upfront. It is equally important to periodically revisit the original declaration and commitments, refining or adjusting them over time as things change. Failing to do either step can result in a partnership breakdown. Each party should also be committed to accepting and working through the limitations and challenges that a partnership can create and have a healthy relationship with their Moods, especially care and vulnerability. They must be vulnerable enough not to have their guard up and care about the partnership's contribution and the contribution they will make to the partnership.

To be frank, to form an effective, sustainable partnership, each party should be relatively polished in all Aspects of Being. In other words, they must have integrity as individuals in order for the new entity they create to also have integrity. I am not suggesting each party needs to be perfect. On the contrary, in most cases, each party will bring strengths and weaknesses on board, ideally balancing each other out by not having the same strengths and weaknesses. However, they should at least be willing to learn and grow together over time. When forming any partnership, I would also encourage you to look for people who share similar values to you.

If you ask me what the most critical ingredients are to build a solid foundation for an effective partnership, it would be awareness, vulnerability and authenticity, which you may recall make up the 'Exposure Triangle'. Without the vision that comes with awareness, vulnerability and authenticity, you will never achieve your potential on an individual level, let alone in a partnership, because you will have a distorted conception of reality, including the reality of yourself and others. Furthermore, without the vision you achieve through the Exposure Triangle, you will also struggle with another key prerequisite for a successful partnership – being present to your partner's needs, wants and concerns. My opinion here stems from my extensive studies and also from personal experience, having shaped a successful partnership with my wife Atefeh and with my business partner Ariya Chittasy in developing our company, Engenesis. High-profile examples of successful business partnerships include Larry Page and Sergey Brin, the co-founders of Google, and Mike Cannon-Brookes and Scott Farquhar, co-founders and co-CEOs of Atlassian. These are two notable examples where each individual has mastered partnership as a Way of Being and where each partnership has resulted in an entity far greater than the sum of the two founders.

Being comes to the rescue

If establishing and developing a partnership were easy, we wouldn't see so many divorces and business partnership breakdowns. In fact, working with company directors and board members to address their partnership issues is one of the most common requests my team and I receive. That's because establishing a successful partnership isn't easy. It starts with a relatively polished Being – both at an individual and collective level – and a willingness to continually grow, remembering that anything that isn't growing will eventually wither and perish. It also takes sacrifice on behalf of all parties concerned, which generally involves giving up some personal freedom and choice. It is in the challenges where knowing human beings – the foundation of this framework – comes to the rescue. If you can see yourself and others with sharp clarity and have the tools to break down and articulate your Being and the Being of others, it enables each of you to work on the shadow parts of yourselves before forming a union. This ensures the partnership is built on the strongest possible foundation and a deep level of trust.

In summary, establishing the right foundation for a partnership is essential if your intention is to make it sustainable. This begins with the Being of each individual involved, starting with awareness, vulnerability and authenticity, and a willingness to predominantly give primacy to the relationship/partnership over themselves as individuals. Once a union has been formed, the partnership becomes a separate entity whereby its own integrity is to be nurtured and developed so it may flourish and grow over time. Fail to build a strong foundation, which happens all too frequently, and the result can be both destructive and costly for all parties concerned. Do it right, however, by forming a partnership where purpose and intention are aligned, and the outcome can be fulfilling for all parties, with exponential growth a very real possibility.

CHAPTER 8.15

Forgiveness

B y this stage, you would be aware that we all have shadow sides as human beings. We all make mistakes and sometimes we cause others pain. Sure, some people are more polished than others and are less error-prone and more considerate as a result. There are many variables that determine this, from their upbringing and education to their life experience and, particularly, how well-polished their Being is. However, even the most polished, integrous and effective individual stuffs up from time to time. If you're not making mistakes, you're probably not taking any risks or leaps of faith, which is what all high achievers do. I am not suggesting that one should use mistakes as an excuse for one's misdemeanours or lack of responsibility. I am suggesting that genuine mistakes are a natural part of life. It's how you deal with those mistakes that counts, whether they are caused by you or others. This is where forgiveness as a Way of Being comes in.

We all know at least one person who tends to hold a grudge and resentment. It might be towards an individual, an organisation, a group of people, the government, a system or the whole world. Take a moment to think about someone you know who is like that. How do they come across? Do they seem happy and fulfilled? Are they pleasant to be around? Or are they bitter and negative, often playing the victim and self-sabotaging? You might even recognise yourself here.

Forgiveness is the opposite of resentment. It is a powerful Way of Being that is often misunderstood and greatly undervalued. It can also be easier said than done to achieve, especially if you have been negatively impacted by the wrongdoing or error of another, personally, profession-ally or in business. It requires intention, willingness, patience, time and reason, which are driven by many other Aspects of Being, particularly awareness, vulnerability, responsibility, courage, care, love and compas-sion. Fundamentally, forgiveness centres on giving up the right to be a victim so you can let go and move on with grace. Whether you are playing the victim due to the wrongdoings of others or are constantly victimising and beating yourself up over your own mistakes, holding onto resentment is counterproductive. It will never serve you well in life. This has nothing to do with morals or virtue; it is a practical truth.

Forgiveness

Forgiveness is the quality of being able to let go and move on. It provides access to restoring *integrity* to how it used to be before the act or event you are forgiving. When you forgive, you completely discard any resentment, anger or hurt towards a person (including yourself) in relation to the act in question. *Forgiveness* is not about condoning another's behaviour or actions; it is freeing and releasing oneself from the past while embracing the lesson learned. *Forgiveness* brings about ease and flow.

A healthy relationship with *forgiveness* indicates that you mostly experience freedom from resentment and choose to discard resentment, anger or hurt towards yourself and others quickly and completely. Others may experience you as someone who can move on from negative experiences or issues with ease. You look to actively resolve issues and restore relationships.

An unhealthy relationship with *forgiveness* indicates that you often dwell on and repeatedly bring up past events and have difficulty letting go of blame or shame. Others may consider you vengeful, bitter, or someone who can maintain a grudge for a long time. You may have a tendency to blame circumstances, past events or others for the outcomes you experience in life. You may also consider yourself forgiving of others but hesitate or decline to forgive yourself. Alternatively, you may frequently try to move on too quickly without learning the lessons, resolving any issues and bringing about closure. You may be considered naive and unable to discern the motives of others and often accept excuses to preserve the peace. You may let others take your *forgiveness* for granted and are susceptible to being taken advantage of.

Practising forgiveness is good for you, including your health

It would be naive to think you are in full control of every situation at all times. As mentioned often in this book, we are all vulnerable to unavoidable challenges and hardships in life. And we are also vulnerable in the face of how others behave and act. You aren't able to pull all the strings and, therefore, you are not the only person influencing the outcomes. We need to forgive, not just as a one-off, but over and over again. Forgiveness is not only enormously necessary and beneficial for the recipient but also for the one doing the forgiving.

Studies have found a link between forgiveness and our health and wellbeing, physically and mentally. That's because forgiveness is a release. When you forgive someone or yourself, it frees you from the anger and resentment you would otherwise harbour within and releases you from the fear and anxiety generated by the mistake or wrongdoing. Studies have also shown that harbouring resentment for prolonged periods can compromise our immune system, alter the production of hormones and disrupt our ability to ward off and fight infections and viruses. Have you ever noticed the sense of a weight being lifted off your shoulders after forgiving someone? Once you are no longer carrying that heavy burden, you are free to let go and move on.

I have worked with clients who have been through tremendous hardships in life. While some chose to hold onto the injustices in their lives and kept suffering, others made the powerful decision – after polishing their relationship with forgiveness under my guidance through the Being Framework – not to have their quality of life determined by the will and imposition of others. They learned to let go, in most cases coming away much stronger in the process. Many even expressed gratitude for undergoing the hardship because it gave them new and valuable insights in life and empowered them to tackle future challenges more proactively. I have also coached executives and business owners who were suppressed in their endeavours because they could not forgive another person and/ or themselves, highlighting an unhealthy relationship with forgiveness or its shadow. Once we were able to release the blockage – which mostly centred on forgiving themselves – they were able to move on. As a result, they found a new sense of empowerment and the courage to take on new opportunities and calculated risks.

Forgiveness, vulnerability and responsibility

Some people find it easier to blame others or external factors when things go wrong as a way to protect their pride and ego. This approach lets them maintain the 'perfect' persona they are portraying to the world rather than forgive and move on. Their unhealthy relationship with vulnerability causes them to raise their guard and hold their cards close to their chest for fear of losing the upper hand or control. Let's look at an example. Imagine you have made a mistake at work but you're afraid that if you own it, you are acknowledging your weakness, and that will make you look bad in front of the team and your boss. Your unhealthy relationship with vulnerability causes you to try to hide the mistake or make up an inauthentic story about what went wrong. In most cases, this type of scenario will backfire because the truth almost always comes out. You may have been a victim of circumstances, but it is counterproductive to keep victimising yourself. Consider that a more effective and responsible way to handle a situation like this is to forgive yourself so that you can then respond appropriately to the matter at hand. It shows strength of character to let your guard down and be vulnerable enough to own your mistake, forgive yourself and get on with resolving the error. Then you can move on with grace, knowing you have done the right thing.

If you are a leader, the larger the team or organisation you lead, the more often you will have to forgive. Again, this is a practical matter, not a kind gesture or a matter of virtue. Sometimes it only takes one person on the team to make a mistake for the performance and effectiveness of the entire team to be impacted. As the leader, the buck stops with you. It is your responsibility to let go of any resentment and forgive. If you are unwilling to accept partial responsibility for the mistakes others on your team have made, then you should not be leading a team. Why? Because there is no such thing as a perfect human being who never makes mistakes. Therefore, forgiveness is a must-have quality for every leader. After all, it is people and teams who build products and organisations, so supporting people in their growth and development is a major part of every leader's role, and forgiveness is aligned with that. Without forgiveness, nothing will get done and resentment will creep in. And resentment will cause you to be bitter and self-sabotage. That's going to affect not only your performance but the performance of the entire team and put the revenue and reputation of the organisation on the line.

Should you forgive and forget?

Forgiving is one thing, but forgetting is another altogether. It is actually inauthentic to expect yourself or others to forget a mistake or wrong-doing. After all, you cannot unknow what you know. But this does not mean you should let a matter keep bothering you and getting in the way of your future expression of self and contribution. When you forgive someone, you intentionally let go of being a victim, meaning you can move forward with clarity and without resentment. But that does not mean you should also forget. Why? Because every mistake and mishap offers a valuable learning experience, which contributes to your life experience and makes you stronger. Once again, this is not easy. But the most rewarding things in life don't come easily.

It takes true strength of character to forgive, but not forget, choosing to learn from the experience instead. Not forgetting is different from harbouring resentment. It doesn't prevent you from moving forward like resentment does. Not forgetting means storing the information in the back of your mind for a time in the future when you may need it. As we discussed in Chapter 5: Transformation Methodology, it takes multiple iterations, both in the awareness and application phases, and rounds of refinements to polish ourselves. So when you complete a Conception Worksheet during the awareness stage, track your executions during the application phase and receive feedback, you want to be present to your mistakes and the mistakes others made in the past so that you can learn from them and develop and polish your Being. Forgetting those instances would result in important lessons lost. Each mistake is an access to learning, growth and transformation.

In summary, forgiveness is when we intentionally let go of being a victim and the need to be right. This is easier said than done because our ego is naturally inclined to want to hold someone to account and maintain a grudge when something goes wrong and that impacts us. Resentment is the opposite of forgiveness. The one who suffers most when you hold onto resentment is you. Forgiveness, without forgetting, so you can learn from the experience, isn't easy, but it is extremely empowering.

CHAPTER 8.16

Self-expression

I n the Being Framework, self-expression refers to the expression of your Unique Being, who you were born to be. Much like the proverb 'all roads lead to Rome', all Ways of Being and Moods lead to the expression of self. The more healthy your relationship with your Ways of Being and Moods, the more likely it is that you will discover and project your Unique Being to the world and be self-expressed. Closely related to freedom, self-expression is far more than just being free to express yourself in terms of what you say, wear, do and act. It is the state of being unleashed and unrestrained so that you naturally and consistently project the real YOU to the world through your unique contribution in life.

Self-expression is an innate part of being human, which is why it is classed as a Primary Way of Being. It is there to be discovered, to gradually become aware of and in tune with throughout your life. It is similar to freedom, which is an undeniable prerequisite to being self-expressed. But where freedom is subtle, internal and enables you to see the possibilities, self-expression is when you actualise those possibilities. It's the difference between thinking you can fly and actually flying. Self-expression is clearly visible for all to see in your ideas, decisions, actions, behaviours and in who and how you are being. It's the gateway to how you are perceived and understood by others because it's how you show up in the world, be it through the businesses you create and the products and services you deliver, to your community service, career and educational achievements and so on.

Self-expression

Self-expression is when you intentionally and authentically communicate who you are and how you are, including (but not limited to) your points of view, beliefs, values, feelings, emotions, moods and experiences. You may express yourself freely and creatively in many ways: through your work, speech, body language, facial expressions, music and other creative arts or ways. It is the state of being uninhibited and resonating with life and everything in it and may evolve to become your unique contribution to humanity.

A healthy relationship with *self-expression* indicates that you mostly experience being free to project yourself in various ways with others, regardless of circumstances, leading to satisfaction, joy and fulfilment. You are self-expressed when you unleash your qualities to be seen, heard and appreciated.

An unhealthy relationship with *self-expression* indicates that you may frequently experience being suppressed, restricted and constrained in how you interact with others, commonly leading to a lack of both fulfilment and satisfaction. Others may experience you as inhibited, quiet, reserved or shy in different circumstances or to have hidden or rarely seen talents and qualities. You may hide your passions or interests from others for fear of judgement or ridicule. Alternatively, you may have few filters and be considered blunt or overbearing. You may disproportionately value your contribution and feel the need to outshine others. You may also be uncomfortable with silence or not being the centre of attention.

Self-expression has intentionally been left till last in Chapter 8: Primary Ways of Being because it represents the culmination of everything we have discussed so far. Unless you have a relatively healthy relationship with awareness and all Moods and Primary Ways of Being, it's almost impossible to dare to become fully self-expressed and project your Unique Being to the world. Wherever the shadow is in the way, your ability to be completely self-expressed will be impacted. So, essentially, you need to have integrity (wholeness) in your Being to pursue self-expression. In other words, the ultimate goal of the Being Framework is for each of us to be self-expressed.

Consider that being self-expressed is a reward for polishing and transforming your relationship with awareness, all Moods and Primary Ways of Being. That's because, like a river, your thoughts, actions, decisions and behaviours flow naturally from those deeper, underlying qualities. Then your Secondary Ways of Being bridge the gap between those deeper qualities and the decisions, behaviours and actions you manifest, as discussed in Chapter 1: A Lens into Human Beings. When any of those underlying qualities are impacted by the shadow, a blockage is created, preventing you from channelling or projecting yourself out. It's like stemming the flow of the river with a dam. The greater the blockage and the longer it is there, the harder it will be for you to tap into your Unique Being and be self-expressed.

Let me bring it home by painting a picture of how the projection process could play out. It all begins when you become authentically aware of a matter. You are vulnerable enough to be open to letting the new knowledge in. You authentically check its validity and congruence before slotting the information into your web of perceptions. Free to see the options and possibilities, you responsibly tap into your autonomy as an active agent and courageously step forward, despite the presence of fear and anxiety. You are then empowered to act upon those possibilities rather than finding reasons to tell yourself you can't. This decision leads you to be self-expressed as you cross the bridge to the very moment before your underlying qualities manifest themselves as actions and behaviours. Your healthy relationship with the Aspects of Being mentioned above (and others) feeds into your Secondary Ways of Being, such as your confidence, assertiveness, proactivity and resourcefulness.

You might recall the example of how your Aspects of Being play their role in your life using the scenario of arguing with your partner in Chapter 2: The Being Framework. I encourage you to revisit that now and consider in a more tangible way how the process described here could play out in your life.

What's your 'thing'?

Everything in nature has its 'thing' that is there to be expressed. For example, a rose is here to convey its beauty and express its aroma. We humans are no different in that we also have our 'thing' to express. You will recall from when we talked about the Exposure Triangle that when you have clear vision, you have access to reality and are open and vulnerable enough not to let the stories you have told yourself in the past get in the way of the truth. In other words, when you have a healthy relationship with awareness, vulnerability and authenticity, the Aspects of Being that make up the Exposure Triangle, you have access to who and how you are meant to be – your Unique Being or calling. Once you are present to that, it becomes your 'thing'. Your purpose in life is to express your 'thing' because when you are self-expressed, not only will it bring meaning to your life, but it will also manifest into your unique contribution to humanity. You may recall from Chapter 1: A Lens into Human Beings that everything you do in life is like releasing drops of water into the ocean of existence, creating a ripple effect. So by being self-expressed, you will bring meaning and joy to the lives of others too. The alternative is to become a liability and create suffering for yourself and others.

Self-expression is more than just expressing your personality, traits, ideas and quirks; it is the full and vivid expression of your Unique Being and authentic self, which in turn becomes your distinctive contribution to the world. It is the opposite of being suppressed, restricted and constrained. Imagine how sad and dull the world would be if most of us failed to be self-expressed. All the beauty, literature and innovation created by human beings are the result of individuals being self-expressed, people like the great composers, musicians, artists, authors, innovators, inventors, and the list goes on.

You don't have to be extraverted to be self-expressed

There is a misguided perception that we need to be extraverted to be fully self-expressed because those with introverted behaviour seem naturally inhibited, shy and reserved. This notion seems to suggest we are all hardwired to be a certain way according to how we have been categorised. While it is true that we all express ourselves outwardly in different ways, that has more to do with an unhealthy relationship with certain Aspects of Being than whether we are naturally introverted or extraverted. While we can be a certain way at any point in our lives, that does not mean we should be slotted into a category where we are to stay for the rest of our lives. For example, consider that an individual who has been labelled – or who labels themselves – an 'introvert' is simply someone who hasn't addressed and polished certain Aspects of Being, most commonly Moods, freedom and self-expression. The Being Framework Ontological Model can support them to identify the areas they should work on to be more self-expressed.

Human beings are not fixed objects. We can transform. And transformation ultimately leads to the projection of self (Unique Being). There are many examples of successful transformations, from those who have turned their lives around after living on the streets to amazing health and weight loss transformations and people who struggled to converse with a small group of people who have gone on to build successful professional speaking careers. We all have the potential to express our calling and authentic selves, whether we think we are introverted, extraverted or however we or others may categorise us. If you never actualise your potential through self-expression, then the one responsible for that failure is you. It has nothing to do with your personality type or temperament or any other category you may be slotted into.

Self-expression and contribution

The grandmother of a good friend of mine loved to sing. It was her passion from a very young age and she was also gifted with a beautiful singing voice. Her dream was to perform on the stage one day before large audiences all over the world. However, her parents had other ideas for her and sent her to secretarial school so she could get a 'real job'. Believing it was her duty to follow her parent's advice, she abandoned her dream in exchange for an office job and worked there until she married and had children. By the time she had raised her children and they had left the nest, the flame had been well and truly extinguished. She ended up living her entire life without actualising her calling as a singer and projecting her Unique Being to the world. What a liability to humanity to have missed out on what would have been her unique contribution through self-expression! This is just one example out of countless. No doubt you can think of at least one example like this.

As mentioned, self-expression is linked to all other Aspects of Being in that any gap in your integrity not only impacts your effectiveness but also your ability to be fully self-expressed. The more you polish and transform your Aspects of Being, the more you will be free to express your Unique Being and, therefore, also your unique contribution to the world. There are several ways self-expression is outwardly conveyed. Your presence and actions, tone of voice, facial expressions, body language, energy, what you stand for, the projects you take on, your priorities, the decisions you make, the matters you care about, the way you ARE; all of these factors contribute to your expression of self and how you choose to make your mark.

Whether you are a leader, a parent or both, it is so important to encourage self-expression in your organisation and in your children. It's about empowering individuals to align their Ways of Being with the right career path for them and giving them the freedom to discover their Unique Being and be themselves. In a business context, this is about letting your people be part of the decision-making process and putting systems in place that support high-performing teams and foster a culture of creativity and authentic self-expression. The rewards will be felt throughout the organisation and be reflected in higher staff and customer retention rates and also in the bottom line.

To sum up, self-expression is how you radiate your presence to those around you and how you choose to make your unique contribution to the world by being YOU, your genuine, authentic self. There is only one you in the world and there will never be another one. So I encourage you to make the most of your time here and let the world see and experience the real you. This is precisely what the world's greatest artists, composers, poets, inventors, scientists and leaders, etc., have done.

They were true to their authentic selves and this was conveyed in their actions and shone through their entire Being. Who knows, maybe you are the one who is destined to discover a cure for cancer, write a series of best-selling novels, win an Oscar, clean up our oceans, lead a nation, etc. Ask yourself, 'Am I only seeing the possibilities or am I actually making them happen?'

Conclusion

As we have learned over the last sixteen subchapters, our Primary Ways of Being are the fundamental ways through which we project ourselves in the world. The healthier our relationship with these deep, underlying Primary Ways of Being, the more integrous, effective and self-expressed we can be. In other words, we become a more polished human being, which results in our wellbeing and effectiveness.

To change or transform begins with awareness. The Being Framework Ontological Model gives you access to see and become aware of the health of your relationship with each of the primal qualities we have covered in this chapter. Through this understanding, you will also become more aware of how others are being in terms of their relationship with their Primary Ways of Being.

Why polish your Being and transform? Because that is the access to expressing your Unique Being and contributing to the rich and beautiful tapestry of existence. Every single one of us is a unique part of that tapestry; we all have our special contribution to make. Through my studies, I have come to learn that the world needs more self-expressed people: individuals who are willing to offer their unique contribution to humanity through various vehicles, no matter how grand or humble.

My studies also highlighted that we perform at our best collectively when individuals are given the opportunity to contribute by actively doing what they care about AND are effective at. The greater the integrity at an individual level, the more it will lead to the integrity of humanity. Each of us is responsible for creating those opportunities for ourselves. It all begins with the awareness, vulnerability and authenticity (Exposure Triangle) to create a clear, undistorted picture of reality and to have the vision to see with clarity.

Now that we have built this foundation, it is time to explore the Secondary Ways of Being. These are the more tangible and visible Aspects of Being, the surface-level qualities that bridge our deeper and subtle qualities with our external reality – our behaviours, decisions and actions.

As a practical philosopher, my intention is to do much more than just intellectualise the world. It is to bring meaningful conversations, content and instruments onto the street, into the workplace and into various aspects of our lives.

CHAPTER 9

Secondary Ways of Being
the bridge between primal qualities and our decisions, actions and behaviours

Qualities like assertiveness, confidence, persistence and reliability sound familiar to all of us. They are commonly referred to in both personal and professional settings. They are also qualities many of us spend considerable time reflecting on. You might wish you were more assertive in meetings, confident when asked to present to a group of people or resilient during challenging situations. Perhaps you have a tendency to be reactive in certain situations, forever putting out spot fires rather than being proactive by anticipating what might happen and taking the initiative to influence the outcome. These are all examples of Secondary Ways of Being.

Secondary Ways of Being are familiar to us because they are behavioural factors and are readily observable in most cases. For example, it is much easier to observe if someone is being accountable for their actions or confident on the stage than it is to gauge, let's say, their level of empowerment, freedom or peace of mind, which are deeper, more subtle human qualities. This is why the latter are Primary and not Secondary Ways of Being. We project Secondary Ways of Being through our decisions, behaviours and actions, our body language and even our facial expressions. They are closer to the surface than other Aspects of Being. Secondary Ways of Being are not behaviours themselves but **behavioural**

factors. This means they more directly influence our decisions, behaviours and actions than other Aspects of Being. Metaphorically speaking, they are the bridge that connects the more primal parts of us (awareness, Moods and Primary Ways of Being) with the actual decisions we make and the behaviours we manifest.

It's worth noting that there is a big difference between just acting or appearing confident and assertive and actually **being** confident and assertive. Why isn't it enough to act a certain way? The answer is simple. When you act a certain way, it's like putting on a fake persona and performing on a stage. Your actions won't be congruent with how you actually are. You might come across as though you have it all together, but deep down, you might feel sick with worry and fear, and this will almost certainly influence the outcome. There is a massive difference between a medical practitioner and an actor pretending to be a doctor in a movie. Similarly, you might act confident without actually being confident.

Whenever you act a certain way, you know deep down that it is a pretence. There is a distinct link with vulnerability and authenticity here. Those who choose to work on **being** confident acknowledge their unhealthy relationship with vulnerability and authenticity. They know they need to polish and transform their relationship with both qualities if they want to **become** confident. That is what it will take for more confident behaviour to flow through to their performance and participation in life. This is vastly different from those who care more about appearing to be confident in the eyes of others, be it their spouse, children, parents, friends, social media followers, employer, employees, customers, etc. When qualities like assertiveness and confidence come from within, it isn't just an act. It's authentic, which is an immensely fulfilling and a powerful way to be.

As we have learned so far, multiple relationships exist between our Aspects of Being. Primary Ways of Being and Moods contribute to our integrity, which then flows through to impact our effectiveness, while Secondary Ways of Being emerge from the make-up of our underlying Primary Ways of Being and Moods. There are eight Secondary Ways of Being in the Being Framework: assertiveness, proactivity, confidence, persistence, resourcefulness, resilience, accountability and reliability.

They have been selected due to their impact on performance, influence, wellbeing and fulfilment.

Just as you can transform your relationship with awareness, Primary Ways of Being and Moods, you can also transform how you are being with any Secondary Way of Being. The main difference with Secondary Ways of Being is that for change to be effective, we must dive deeper to find the underlying qualities that are driving the engine. Popular theories today, like Behaviourism, work on 'fixing' one behaviour at a time, which can be an effective short-term solution but is not sustainable long-term. In contrast, the Being Framework's Transformation Methodology requires you to identify, polish and transform the deeper underlying qualities linked to it first. To neglect those deeper qualities would be like taking a pill for a physical ailment rather than identifying and addressing the root cause. For example, it is impossible to be confident if you are not being authentic, courageous and free, among other qualities.

In short, Secondary Ways of Being bridge the gap between the deeper parts of you (awareness, Moods and Primary Ways of Being) and the qualities presented on the surface. As you read the following subchapters to learn more about each Secondary Way of Being, don't be alarmed if you observe the shadow in terms of your relationship with one or more of these Ways of Being. Consider it constructive because you can only grow if you first acknowledge and then confront and transform the shadow parts of yourself. The alternative is to look away and do nothing, which will only lead to regression and suffering. Once you become more present to the shadow sides of these Secondary Ways of Being, you might resonate so deeply with them that it hits a nerve. While you might be tempted to jump in and try to 'fix' them immediately, I would encourage you to address the underlying qualities (awareness, Moods and Primary Ways of Being) first. Our empirical data, together with the collective experience of our coach and practitioner community at Engenesis, indicates that this is a far more effective way to improve the health of your relationship with a Secondary Way of Being.

CHAPTER 9.1

Assertiveness

O f all the characteristics people want to change about themselves, assertiveness would have to top the list of areas that people bring for coaching. Even from a clinical perspective, assertiveness training is trumped only by requests for assistance with anxiety and depression. After all, who doesn't want to be comfortable enough to speak up in meetings, say no to unreasonable demands, make a genuine complaint, express their point of view in a disagreement or stop downplaying their accomplishments. However, it is also one of the most misunderstood qualities. Even dictionaries struggle to correctly define this quality. For example, they use words like 'bold' and 'forceful' to define it. Some even relate assertiveness to 'acting confident' or 'making a confident statement' and 'not frightened to say what you want or believe'. However, the meaning referred to by the word assertiveness within this framework is distinctly different. It is the quality of being direct, firm, straight, undisguised and frank without being aggressive, forceful, manipulative or submissive. When you are being assertive (as opposed to just acting in an assertive manner), you are firm and steadfast and don't passively accept whatever is thrown at you. When you are assertive, you will say no when the situation calls for it and stand your ground, but not just for the sake of being right.

Assertiveness

Assertiveness is when you express yourself effectively and stand up for your point of view while also being respectful of others. It is the willingness to express your thoughts and feelings and communicate your needs and expectations firmly and directly while being considerate of others and aware of any subsequent consequences of being assertive. *Assertiveness* is being resolute, straight, firm and effective.

A healthy relationship with *assertiveness* indicates that you are predominately straight and unambiguous in your communication with others. You rarely resort to threats or attempt to manipulate outcomes and are transparent with your motives. You are bold in communicating your and others' needs and expectations in terms of the outcomes required or expected. You are comfortable letting others know how you feel and express yourself without emotional outbursts.

An unhealthy relationship with *assertiveness* indicates that you may be unreasonably submissive, agreeable or aggressive, or that you predominantly rely on manipulation and domination to get your way, express yourself and communicate with others. You may frequently go along with what others decide to avoid conflict. You may also use inappropriate humour, sarcasm, teasing or underhanded comments to manipulate, bully, control or put others down. Alternatively, you may frequently threaten or use the tone of your voice to dominate or exert your will on others. As a result, they may consider you manipulative or dominating, even though that is not always your intention. Your conversations may quickly spiral or escalate emotionally while issues remain unresolved.

The ramifications of an unhealthy relationship with assertiveness

One of the best ways to explain a Way of Being is to describe what it's like when we have an unhealthy relationship with it and the potential ramifications of that. It might surprise you to learn that most people are not assertive the majority of the time, even those who think they are. I believe this largely stems from a lack of encouragement to be assertive, and our Being Profile empirical data testifies to that. For example, as kids, we were told to be nice, polite, quiet and so on. That's all well and good when you're a child, but being nice in the adult world can lead to being taken advantage of. Children often learn this the hard way, which might lead them to be walked over and feel victimised or disempowered. This, in turn, can lead to the development of a host of self-destructive habits and behavioural patterns. When this happens, we can see a close connection between an unhealthy relationship with assertiveness and an unhealthy relationship with responsibility, a Primary Way of Being. That's because when we are not assertive, we are not choosing power-fully to be in charge of our own lives, the epitome of responsibility. By now, you would know that part of my vision is for all human beings to be more powerful and empowered individuals. As a collective, assertiveness is a significant driver that supports us to be more powerful and is a major part of the mechanism that encourages us to communicate freely, as discussed in Chapter 8.3: Freedom.

An unhealthy relationship with assertiveness is also commonly linked to a lack of awareness, one of our three Meta Factors in the Being Framework. You can't be assertive towards a matter you know nothing about. Imagine walking into an important client meeting without having done any research on the client and their company. Or what if you attempted to negotiate the price of a property without having any idea of the property's value or your financial position. You can't be assertive in these types of situations. I recall a conversation with a startup founder who approached me in the hope of raising seed funding for their new business venture. However, it quickly became apparent that they had no idea how much capital they needed to get the business off the ground. They were also lacking the self-awareness to realise that this was even an issue. Needless to say, the founder walked away empty-handed.

Another potential ramification of an unhealthy relationship with assertiveness is that it can lead people to become aggressive, passive-aggressive or manipulative. A bully is a classic example of someone who has an unhealthy relationship with assertiveness. This might seem at odds with your idea of a bully, especially if you subscribe to the definition of assertiveness as being blunt or forceful. Bullies typically hide their unhealthy relationship with assertiveness behind aggression or passive aggression. However, aggression is distinctly different from being assertive, though it can sometimes be challenging to discern between the two.

Let's say you own a business and you need to put an employee on notice because, despite the many conversations you have had with them and your multiple offers of support, they continue to repeatedly arrive late to work without a reasonable excuse. Your assertiveness in stating your case may land as aggression to the employee. However, as long as you are being straight and direct with the employee and not letting emotions get in the way, you are being assertive, not aggressive. If, despite making things crystal clear to the employee and coming to an agreement with them, they continue to breach their commitment without a reasonable explanation, the reality is that they are 'firing themselves'; it's not about you. There seems to be a significant level of collective confusion around assertiveness these days, particularly in discerning the thin line between aggression and assertiveness. This confusion is the source of many misunderstandings, misjudgements and problems in various aspects of our lives.

Being submissive is another example of having an unhealthy relationship with assertiveness. We all know people who are overly agreeable and nice in a forced way. They are the ones who say yes when they'd rather say no, the people-pleasers, the ones who don't want to create a fuss. They might think they're doing the right thing, however, submission commonly leads to regret and even resentment. For instance, have you ever said yes to an invitation when you really wanted to say no and then regretted it later? Or perhaps you're on a committee and are the one to always step forward to take on the tasks nobody else wants to do, only to resent it later when those tasks take you away from spending precious time with your family. That is not being assertive. Being assertive is saying your real yeses and noes.

If you are a high achiever, do you typically underplay your accomplishments to avoid being ridiculed or appearing as though you are boasting or suggesting that you are better than everyone else? Many cultures value equality so much that it threatens to limit the potential of their citizens. This is commonly referred to in Australia and New Zealand as 'tall poppy syndrome'. It takes a great deal of courage, amongst other qualities, to stand tall and not hide your achievements. You will need to develop a thick skin and be prepared for others to ridicule you or try to 'cut you down'. You need a healthy relationship with assertiveness, courage and authenticity (all three qualities are closely linked in this context) to do this. Traditionally, some groups of people, genders, ethnicities, etc., or individuals have been expected to conform to certain standards or submit to those occupying positions of power. Such expectations still exist in cultures and societies today. If those expected to submit refuse, they are commonly considered rebellious or even aggressive for standing up for their values when in reality, they are being assertive. Being insecure, passive, submissive or 'overly nice' inhibits the growth of any individual. I am encouraging you to rise above such stereotypes and be assertive as much as you can.

Transforming your relationship with assertiveness

As mentioned earlier, Secondary Ways of Being are closely linked to a range of Primary Ways of Being and Moods. In the case of assertiveness, the most notable links are with the deeper qualities of responsibility, authenticity, vulnerability, freedom, courage, love, presence and self-expression. So before you attempt to transform your relationship with assertiveness, it is important to become aware of your relationships with other Aspects of Being first to reveal the root cause of the issue. An effective way to do this is with the support and guidance of a Being Framework accredited ontological coach.

Let's consider an example. Steve and Julianna are Singapore-based entrepreneurs who built an innovative technology company in the retail sector. As the founding partners deepened their knowledge of the Being Framework, they could see several areas within themselves to transform. During one particular session with their ontological coach, Julianna identified how authenticity, responsibility and assertiveness were missing from a recent client meeting that had not gone well. The result? The client conversation became gridlocked and she didn't feel like she got her true points across. At first, she required assistance from her coach to identify how these Ways of Being were showing up for her and the relationships between them. Over time, using the Transformation Methodology, she gradually became familiar with the thought patterns and feelings that would arise whenever her relationship with these Ways of Being faltered. Ultimately, she was interested in producing results. By practising being aware of these Ways of Being as they arose and changing her behaviour accordingly, Julianna became more confident to assertively speak her mind and share her feelings in meetings.

As business partners, Steve and Julianna would sometimes disagree on certain decisions. Therefore they knew that the ability to negotiate effectively was critical. They both came to understand that negotiation without listening and being present to the other party and without being willing to put themselves in the other person's shoes is not being assertive. Both initially struggled with this. Under the guidance of their coach, they individually transformed their relationship with various Aspects of Being, which led to a lack of assertiveness when negotiating. And they haven't looked back since.

Being assertive is at the heart of communication and interactions with others. It supports you to build trust and helps you express yourself effectively and stand up for your point of view while also respecting the rights and beliefs of others. It's about being neither aggressive nor submissive and authentically saying your real yeses and noes. That's the difference between **being** assertive and merely acting assertive.

CHAPTER 9.2

Proactivity

We all know what it's like to procrastinate. But it might surprise you to know that procrastination does not just happen due to laziness. It is commonly the outcome of reacting to whatever life throws at us or when we get bogged down by our thought processes. Being proactive is taking the initiative to act as opposed to waiting for any undesirable consequences to be dealt with. It's when we intentionally make conscious decisions and act upon them responsibly. Proactivity is also about being nimble and resourceful (another Secondary Way of Being), which is why many smaller businesses and teams are often more effective than their larger counterparts at being proactive. Their smaller size facilitates their ability to initiate matters and respond to changes relatively quickly, enabling them to be less reactive and more proactive. Proactivity leads to agility and responsiveness, two key factors if you want a competitive edge in your endeavours.

Being proactive is becoming increasingly important in today's flexible, varied and often remote work environment. Today's employees are expected to use their initiative to identify and address business needs rather than wait for instructions or follow a prescribed set of actions. Furthermore, with innovation on the rise, there is greater emphasis on taking risks and trying out new ways of doing things. People who have a relatively healthy relationship with proactivity have the upper hand in these types of scenarios. They also have an advantage in that they realise they are responsible for their own career and success. The days of having a job for life are over. There are no guarantees in this ever-changing world, making proactivity a valuable Way of Being.

Many refer to proactivity as having a 'can-do' attitude. But that is only half the story. You might know you can do something. The question is, will you? Proactivity is when the can-do attitude results in action. As is the case with all Secondary Ways of Being, multiple relationships exist with other Aspects of Being, with some more apparent than others. For instance, proactivity is strongly linked to awareness and care. When you are aware of the consequences of being proactive versus being inactive or passive, you need to care or value the outcome enough to make it a priority to take action immediately. Proactivity is also linked with fear, anxiety and courage because it takes guts to take the initiative to move forward, particularly in uncharted territory.

Proactivity

Proactivity is the quality of actively influencing, creating and contributing to a situation rather than reacting to it after it has happened. Being proactive moves you to think, plan and act in advance of an impending situation, making decisions and taking appropriate actions beforehand rather than procrastinating or waiting for the outcome. When you are being proactive, you make things happen and take the initiative to bring about a different future for yourself, your team or the organisation as a whole. Proactive individuals are willing to challenge, make suggestions and try new ways of doing things to bring about relevant change.

A healthy relationship with *proactivity* indicates that you tend to take the initiative to move things forward and bring about change. You are solution-oriented and actively seek opportunities to advance in any situation. Others may experience you as someone who is considered, frequently contributes, asks questions, takes action and will step up without hesitation. You may often anticipate what is needed in advance, respond rather than react to matters, and are prepared and willing to do what is required.

An unhealthy relationship with *proactivity* indicates that you may be unreasonably inactive or reactive. You may rely on waiting to be told what to do and procrastinate until you have everything at hand. You may only take prescribed actions and rarely plan effectively. You may often be indecisive and inactive, ignoring what you know needs to be done, leaving yourself exposed to potential breakdowns. Alternatively, you may only address matters when there is a breakdown and then react to the subsequent undesirable outcome. You may frequently be on the back foot, avoid change and defer making decisions. Others may express frustration at your apparent disinterest, lack of engagement, inaction, reactivity or your need to be fully convinced before you move forward.

Inactivity vs reactivity – the shadow sides of proactivity

Responsiveness is a major theme within this book in that, as human beings, we are here to respond to matters or situations, regardless of the source. Responsiveness is the opposite of reactivity and they generate significantly different outcomes. This framework encourages us to respond rather than react to matters, the latter demonstrating a shadow side of proactivity. The other shadow side of proactivity is inactivity and we can swing between the two. When we are inactive, we over-think situations and procrastinate. And when we are reactive, we tend to wait for things to happen before reacting to them rather than anticipating and/or predicting the consequences and outcomes in advance. When someone is reactive, they might be impulsive, charging ahead with projects like a bull at a gate without properly thinking things through. It is not uncommon for people to flip from one end of the spectrum to the other. For example, someone may be inactive at first and then suddenly react in an inappropriate manner when they become aware of their inactivity and start to resent their own behaviour.

Let's look at an example. Jenny was recently hired for her impressive qualifications and experience. Her new role frequently requires her to work as part of a team. The team leader is concerned because, during team meetings, Jenny sits back while others on the team put forward their ideas and suggestions. She seems disengaged, failing to contribute in a meaningful way, even when asked a direct question. This is an example of an unhealthy relationship with proactivity on the inactive side. There can be several underlying reasons for inactivity, including but not limited to an unhealthy relationship with any of the Moods as well as an unhealthy relationship with courage, freedom and self-expression, among others. In Jenny's case, fear and courage might be holding her back. Alternatively, she might be concerned that if she speaks up and then makes a mistake, that she will look silly or get the blame if things don't go to plan, highlighting an unhealthy relationship with vulnerability. She might be unhappy in the new job and therefore lacking the care to contribute. This example highlights why it is so important to dig deeper when there is an issue with a Secondary Way of Being to reveal and address the root cause.

When we are reactive, we commonly allow a problem to grow and fester rather than nip it in the bud early. Once the issue is out of our control, we might behave aggressively and blame others rather than being responsible and accountable by owning the problem. At first, a reactive individual may appear to be proactive because, on the surface, they can make it seem like they have everything under control. They like to impress while others are watching. There is commonly a close link between reactivity and an unhealthy relationship with authenticity, responsibility or vulnerability.

Proactivity starts at the top

If a business leader wants to encourage proactivity in their team members, they need to set the right example by fostering a supportive culture that facilitates taking initiative and being proactive. This is the opposite of a workplace where people are micromanaged. Creating a culture like this is easier said than done because there is a high level of trust involved. Leaders have to trust that their people will be responsible for the outcomes of their actions and they themselves must acknowledge their team members' contributions and be vulnerable enough to accept that their suggestions for improvement and innovation may be better than their own. Effective communication is also critical here because team members need to know when their leaders want them to take the initiative without requesting their permission. At the same time, team members need to understand how important it is to own and clean up their mistakes, be accountable for their actions and forgive themselves. Forgiveness is critical at all levels, from employees to leaders, particularly within a culture of innovation and growth where mistakes will undoubtedly be made from time to time.

There is a danger associated with having too much order in place. The environment is dominated by authoritarian rule and everything is so over-engineered that creativity is crushed. It is virtually impossible for people to be proactive in such a toxic environment, even though proactivity – among other Ways of Being – should be prevalent in all situations and scenarios, not just when everything is safe and comfortable. After all, systems don't design themselves; we design them. Furthermore, we human beings are the ones who choose to participate, follow and conform. Therefore, both the designer and the participant are responsible. We have the autonomy to say no, even if it may come at a cost. The truth is, there will be a price to pay anyway. Polishing and transforming any part of your Being, including your relationship with proactivity, is not necessarily a neat and tidy process. It invariably demands confrontation, going to the uncomfortable zones and dealing with unexplored territories and uncertainties. It requires facing the new and unthought-of, being with unpleasant situations and rising above inauthenticity and deception. At times, we need to be like a lily that grows and rises above the sludge. All plants require dirty, smelly manure to thrive and fulfil their potential. Proactivity is more necessary than ever in today's rapidly changing world. But as you can see, it does not come without risks. However, the rewards are great if this Way of Being is encouraged, nurtured and rewarded in the right way.

CHAPTER 9.3

Confidence

Most people have a sound idea of what confidence means, how it looks in themselves and others, and what it feels like to be confident. Almost everyone wants to be confident. There's nothing like jumping out of bed in the morning full of confidence about the day ahead and feeling like you could tackle anything that comes your way. But when you're lacking confidence, the feeling can be overwhelming and prevent you from being effective, even if you know you have the skills and knowledge to perform the tasks lined up for the day. A lack of confidence can literally freeze you in your tracks and stop you from achieving your goals and living a life of fulfilment. Is it any wonder that confidence is up there with assertiveness as a quality people want to transform within themselves? Confidence is also seen as an attractive and desirable quality in others. When we meet someone who exudes an air of confidence without being arrogant, we are naturally drawn to them. However, when we meet someone lacking in confidence, whether it be in professional or personal circumstances, it's difficult to trust them.

When it comes to the word confidence and the meaning it refers to in this framework, there is a strong focus on trust. From this, we can conclude that self-confidence means having trust in yourself while simultaneously knowing your limitations as a human being in that you won't always have access to all the evidence. More specifically, confidence is the state of being clear-headed and certain, either that an assumption, hypothesis or prediction will turn out to be valid or that a particular chosen course of action or solution turns out to be the best or most effective. And to be certain requires trust in oneself. Someone who has a healthy relationship with confidence knows, through their authentic awareness, that it is impossible to know absolutely everything about any matter, individually or collectively. They take the time to investigate a matter in detail to learn as much as possible about it but acknowledge that there will be parts that they won't be able to fully verify. A confident, authentic and aware individual has sufficient belief in themselves and their process to make educated assumptions about unverified information. In other words, they don't need 100% proof to be confident. They make decisions based on intelligence – the aggregation of their acquired knowledge and educated assumptions. Making decisions based on intelligence in this way is far removed from reacting to matters that don't have solid grounding.

While there are plenty of techniques that teach you how to act or look more confident, they don't change how you really are. Being confident goes far deeper than just a series of surface behaviours. It comes from being aware of your own competencies, proficiencies and the extent to which you are effective at something, like public speaking, for example. Others can trust that when you say you can do something, you will follow through and won't let them down.

Confidence

Confidence is how you relate to certainties, uncertainties, doubts and hesitation. It is the belief or understanding that you can rely on or have faith in someone or something, including your own abilities and qualities. Being confident supports you in gaining credibility and making good first impressions while dealing with pressure and meeting life head on.

A healthy relationship with *confidence* indicates you are predominantly able to forego your doubts and uncertainties and don't allow them to stop your progress. Others may experience you as self-assured or at ease, even in challenging situations. You leverage and effectively utilise available resources to move forward despite your hesitations. You are aware of and trust your strengths and abilities and back yourself fully. You can move forward in difficult circumstances, even though you know your limitations and the risks involved and are not reckless. This may encourage others to trust you when you say you can do something, and they expect you to follow through.

An unhealthy relationship with *confidence* indicates that you may be overconfident, inappropriately confident or unreasonably hesitant. You may ruminate, get stuck or be weighed down by your doubts. You may question your abilities and doubt yourself or others, even in familiar circumstances or situations. You can frequently waver in challenging situations and may experience last-minute doubts or panic you are unable to overcome. Alternatively, you may be reckless, dogmatic, display bravado or undertake excessively risky behaviour with little or no regard for the impact or outcome. Others may feel the need to check if you are okay and may have concerns about your ability to see a task through. You may often worry that you or others will disappoint, let people down or not live up to expectations. You may defer making decisions or taking action unless all uncertainties are resolved.

When we talk about confidence, some people assume we are referring to self-esteem or self-confidence. However, they are not the same. Self-esteem – also known as self-worth, which is outside the scope of this subject – refers to how much you appreciate and value yourself and your contribution. The health of your relationship with all Aspects of Being, including confidence, contributes to your self-esteem and how you perceive yourself. So the more integrous you are, the higher your self-esteem. Self-confidence, on the other hand, is your belief in yourself and your abilities, which, like self-esteem, can change with time and experience. For example, when you undertake training in any new field, you start as a beginner. The more you learn and practise, the more your self-confidence grows. While self-confidence is part of confidence, there is more to confidence as a Way of Being.

When I refer to confidence as a Way of Being, I am referring to how you are **being with** confidence, including self-confidence. Are you certain or hesitant about your abilities? Do you collapse and suppress your expression of self and contribution if you are uncertain of anything? Do you need to know it all to be confident? Or are you confident, despite not knowing anything about a matter? A singer who freaks out every time they are asked to perform despite years of singing training and practice might have an unhealthy relationship with confidence. On the other hand, someone who thinks they can sing, despite being tone-deaf and having had no training whatsoever but who dares to perform every opportunity they can get, is overconfident. The latter also demonstrates an unhealthy relationship with confidence.

Hesitancy and doubt versus overconfidence and bravado

It's important to remember that the Being Framework is concerned with how we relate to our Aspects of Being. This is very different from having or not having a certain quality. For instance, it is not a matter of being confident or not being confident. Like assertiveness and proactivity, an unhealthy relationship with confidence can show up in two completely different ways. A lack of confidence in one person may cause them to doubt themselves, be hesitant and frequently question their abilities, like the trained singer in our example who is afraid to perform. Another person may convey their unhealthy relationship with confidence as bravado, cockiness or recklessness, signalling their overconfidence, like the tone-deaf, untrained individual who thinks they can sing. The latter is just as unhealthy as doubting one's own abilities. Overconfidence is confidence without authenticity, and that can be a dangerous combination.

Consider the following example. Steve has an unhealthy relationship with confidence, but at face value, you wouldn't know it because he often comes across as a 'know-it all'. He can be sceptical and constantly seeks evidence from others in order to be convinced while pretending to be certain about his own abilities. Rather than taking the responsibility to seek evidence himself whenever he is unsure about something, he passes the buck to others on the team. Once a project has been completed, he over-exaggerates his contribution to the successful outcome. Steve's unhealthy relationship with confidence has its roots in an unhealthy relationship with deeper qualities like vulnerability, authenticity and courage. Unless those are addressed first, it is highly unlikely that Steve will be successful in transforming his relationship with confidence. This scenario is all too common in many organisations, especially in management and leadership roles. Think of the type of leader who locks themselves away in their office while ordering others to source information or do the work that will make them look good and then claims responsibility for it. However, the facade always falls away at some point. In short, being overconfident serves no one well.

If your aim is to have more influence, achieve your objectives and be more fulfilled in life, being hesitant and doubtful won't serve you well either. Imagine working for someone who constantly avoids making decisions and is always either deferring the decision-making to another time or delegating it to someone else. Would you trust that this leader was taking the business in the right direction? What if you work in sales and freeze whenever a potential customer starts a negotiation with you? Or imagine having a member on your team who acts without thinking because they overestimate their capabilities. The deeper qualities generally at play in scenarios like this are awareness, responsibility, higher purpose and, most notably, courage. By working on transforming these deeper qualities, we also transform our relationship with confidence over time.

Confidence is not something we are gifted with at birth. It's not a case of having it or not having it. It is how we are **being with** certainty or uncertainty and hesitation, particularly when making decisions and relating to the world and others around us, including ourselves. Like every other Aspect of Being, our relationship with confidence can be transformed through practice. Thinking back to the Transformation Methodology we discussed earlier in the book, confidence is a great one to practise using this powerful yet simple iterative approach. For instance, if you observe that you are hesitant to present to a group and want to improve, use this as the focus of your practice. Start by presenting to small groups, even just one or two people, and observe how you are **being with** confidence – and likely also with courage – each time you practise. Slowly increase the number of people you present to over time. Last but not least, I would encourage you to avoid comparing yourself to others. Once you get to know human beings better through the Being Framework, you will become more proficient at discerning between those who are being confident and those who are putting on an act. Which one would you put your trust in?

CHAPTER 9.4

Persistence

magine being asked to run an ultra-marathon that has no specified finish line or being tasked with a project that has no defined conclusion or end date. What if you are an aspiring actor who is knocked back at auditions time and time again. Would you keep going? Persistence, also known as perseverance, is the quality of pushing on when the going gets tough, as long as the effort is warranted. Persistent people are tenacious. They resist the temptation to give up along the pathway towards achieving their objectives, which can be long, arduous and unfamiliar, even if others try to sabotage their efforts. Many of the world's most revered high achievers have persisted through significant hardships on their journey to success. Well-known examples include Oprah Winfrey, JK Rowling, Walt Disney, Steven Spielberg, Bill Gates, Colonel Sanders, Jerry Seinfeld, Kikuo Ibe, Michael Jordan, and the list goes on.

Persistence is the quality of being steadfast when working on a task, project or towards a goal, despite difficulties or delays. Intelligence, talent, skills and experience alone aren't enough, particularly if you are working towards an important objective. If you aren't persistent and don't have what it takes to weather the unexpected turbulence, knock-backs and frustrations along the way, you are likely to give up. A classic example is someone who has been advised by their doctor to lose weight to avoid severe health consequences. This individual knows that the journey is necessary. But they also know it won't be easy and that there will be many distractions and temptations along the way. Persistence is the key to staying the course and accomplishing the goal.

Persistence

Being persistent is living life from the viewpoint that you are to persevere, stay the course and not give up despite difficulties, challenges and setbacks. *Persistence* is a quality that determines your success in many areas of life, as intelligence and skill alone are insufficient to overcome the obstacles and challenges you face. *Persistence* leads to accomplishment and is the access to greater fulfilment and satisfaction in overcoming life's challenges.

A healthy relationship with *persistence* indicates that you are tenacious and refuse to give up easily, especially in challenging situations. You stay on task, even when facing formidable or daunting circumstances. Others may know you to be determined, resolute, and someone who will follow through and remain focused on achieving outcomes you are committed to.

An unhealthy relationship with *persistence* indicates that you may be unreasonably inconsistent or insistent. You may be easily distracted, wavering, unsteady and discouraged by setbacks and may question your original decisions and lose heart. You may have many unfinished tasks and projects that you are unlikely to complete and justify yourself with excuses. Alternatively, you may be overly insistent – stubborn and dogged to the point of belligerence. You may rise to face the same obstacle time and again while refusing to consider alternatives. Others are less likely to believe that you will stay the course, and you may frequently procrastinate, become despondent, give up or change direction.

Persistence and patience are closely linked. Think about some of the great inventors and pioneers. Do you think the inventors of the various COVID-19 vaccines that are now being used globally would have persisted to achieve what they did in compressed time without patience? There would no doubt have been countless failed attempts in the laboratory and many sleepless nights before they discovered the right combination. A persistent individual lives life from the viewpoint that failure is only a temporary state and an inevitable part of achieving any worthwhile goal. They are so focused, committed and determined that they know they will get there in the end, as long as they don't give up.

Persistence is a quality that is critical for anyone wanting to build their career over time – as opposed to just getting a job – raise a family, build and scale a business, study to be a medical doctor, train to be an elite athlete, etc. In other words, we all need this quality. If you are not being persistent and are constantly jumping from pillar to post in life, you are not going to be effective, and therefore, you are unlikely to ever be truly fulfilled.

Persistence and patience are critical ingredients in the transformation process, which, as you discovered earlier, is an iterative process of Execute > Track > Learn > Refine > Execute. As a beginner, you will need patience when comparing your current Being to the ideal or your current level of effectiveness to an individual who has already attained mastery, to avoid becoming despondent if the journey is taking longer than you had hoped. **Being with** how you are now demands patience, and lasting the distance takes both patience and persistence, so I encourage you to be gentle on yourself.

If you currently have intentions that have not yet been fulfilled, consider that your current position in life is where you are letting your intentions and dreams be crushed by an external reality. You are responsible for where you are at any given point in time, so it is up to you to respond by taking the wheel and steering the course. Maybe you are in a job you dislike but are effective at, purely to pay the bills, and dream of doing something you genuinely care about, or – referring to the Contribution Quadrant – are both effective at and care about. Consider how content and fulfilled you would be if you persevered and refused to be defeated.

It is also worth noting that transforming your Being is not the only process that requires an iterative approach. For example, several iterations are commonly required in computer programming and software development before success is achieved. In fact, it takes rounds of refinement when building anything new, be it a business, product, team, partnership or personal relationship.

The two shadow sides of persistence

As discussed, all Aspects of Being have more than one shadow side, persistence being no exception. An unhealthy relationship with persistence usually presents in one of two ways: inconsistency or insistence. When we are inconsistent, we might waver and dart in and out of our commitment to a project or endeavour as opposed to being focused and all in. When we are insistent, on the other hand, we might be so adamant that our idea is worthwhile pursuing that we stubbornly push on no matter what happens, even if the idea is clearly going nowhere. To use an analogy, the latter would be like continuing to fight a losing battle or banging your head against a brick wall. Insistence or over-persistence commonly results from an unhealthy relationship with the deeper qualities of awareness, vulnerability and authenticity. Sometimes, the most effective thing you can do is stop. Let's look at an example.

Sally led a team of software developers who were tasked with the development of a new app. However, after multiple iterations and rounds of market testing, it became clear that their target market wasn't interested in the app they were developing. Not to be dissuaded, Sally demanded that the team push on, despite the feedback and results that highlighted they were on the wrong track. This may seem like persistence, but it is actually the opposite. Being insistent or stubborn demonstrates a shadow side of persistence. It is when we are unwilling to give up the fight, despite it being the right time and the right conditions to stop and move on.

Sally's Being Profile highlighted that she struggled with vulnerability and responsibility. Ultimately, she was so worried about being seen as a failure if she put a halt to the product development that she stubbornly and irresponsibly insisted the team push on. As a result, the team lost faith in their team leader and the company's leadership team lost faith in Sally.

Ironically, Sally's insistence was setting herself and the team up for failure and disappointment from the start while also wasting the company's resources in time and capital. There will always be serious consequences when we stubbornly press on despite knowing that the endeavour we are working on is ineffective or impractical.

Now let's look at an example of the other shadow side of persistence: being inconsistent or wavering and unsteady rather than committed, focused and all in. As a budding consultant and thought leader, John knew it was critical that he write and publish regular articles to highlight his expertise to his target market. However, he was constantly procrastinating, always finding something that he claimed was more important to do. Each time he made a commitment to sit down and write, he would start and quickly become blocked. Rather than pushing on, he would just give up. Consequently, he became increasingly despondent as he observed others in his field publish article after article while he was yet to publish his first.

After working on his Being with his ontological coach, John realised he was afraid that his writing wasn't good enough and he would be seen as inferior by his peers, highlighting an issue with vulnerability. His coach also helped raise his awareness of the fact that he struggled with care. Rather than caring about sharing his expertise through writing to help his audience with their burning pain, he was focused on a perceived need to publish articles to enhance his profile. By transforming his relationship with the deeper underlying qualities of vulnerability, care and commitment, John transformed his relationship with persistence. He subsequently went from being inconsistent (in and out) to all in with his article writing and gained a strong following of potential new clients as a result.

Whether you're building a business, a team, a product, a partnership, a long-term relationship or raising a family, it's not a sprint but a marathon. It requires consistent effort and patience to persevere. The same is true for many other things in life, such as learning a new language or working on an invention that seems impossible. Persistence is about not giving up easily while at the same time discerning the best time to call it a day on an unworkable iteration and moving on to the next iteration as you strive to achieve your intention. Persistence and daily effort will eventually reward you with accomplishment. However, if you stubbornly and insistently push on with a project or endeavour that is not going anywhere and has no merit, that is not persistence. That is just as counterproductive as procrastinating, wavering and being unsteady.

CHAPTER 9.5

Resourcefulness

'Think outside the box' is a saying we are all familiar with. It's about thinking differently and creatively to find a solution to overcome a challenge and pave your own way. In the Being Framework, this quality is called resourcefulness. Resourcefulness is an extremely valuable Secondary Way of Being because it enables us to move forward towards achieving a goal that would likely be unattainable unless we leverage this quality within as well as the resourcefulness of the people around us. It is important to note that resourcefulness has nothing to do with having resources, including capital and people. We can be resourceful without access to any physical resources.

In my organisation, we are often approached by startups who claim that all they need to break through is capital. However, we have found that in the majority of cases, there are several aspects of their business and, most importantly, themselves (their Beings) that need their attention first. Resourcefulness has an important relationship with awareness, freedom, care, responsibility and commitment, among others. The high achievers of the world don't focus on what they have or don't have. Take Apple, for instance. They have never been known for having the most resources at their disposal. Speaking at the D8 Conference in 2010, Steve Jobs explained how Apple 'chose wisely': 'Apple is a company that doesn't have the most resources of everybody in the world, and the way we've succeeded is by choosing what horses to ride really carefully... And, if you choose wisely, you can save yourself an enormous amount of work versus trying to do everything'. As you can see, it's not about how many resources you have at your disposal but the extent to which you are 'being resourceful' that counts.

Another well-known example of a resourceful human being is Elon Musk, who questions the need to rely on limited fossil fuel resources when there are far more sustainable alternatives freely available. Both

Jobs and Musk epitomise the definition of entrepreneur, as coined by French economist and philosopher Jean-Baptiste Say: 'The entrepreneur shifts economic resources out of an area of lower and into an area of higher productivity and greater yield'. To achieve this Way of Being begins with awareness of what's possible. Then it's about choosing powerfully to take action or be responsible. The outcome when that happens is resourcefulness.

Resourcefulness

Resourcefulness is living life from the viewpoint of abundance and being effective at finding or creating new ways of doing things and solving problems. When you are being resourceful, you will often look beyond pre-existing knowledge, tools, conventional systems and traditional methods to find solutions. You are profoundly related to reality and have the passion and curiosity to discover more. You often see things others miss, love to try out new ideas and willingly drop any preconceived notions or perspectives. You acknowledge that you always have options and can pave a way forward.

A healthy relationship with *resourcefulness* indicates that you rarely stop searching for new options and will primarily look for a way to find solutions, even when there is no obvious way forward. You thrive on challenges, are imaginative and rarely allow existing resources or circumstances to determine when or how you will take action. You utilise and leverage available resources to maximise *effectiveness*, producing disproportionately greater results than others may with the same resources. Others will come to you for ideas when they are stuck and appreciate you as someone creative, with a different perspective and who thinks 'outside the box'.

An unhealthy relationship with *resourcefulness* indicates that you may become quickly disillusioned or discouraged when there is a perceived lack of resources. You may often operate from scarcity and repeatedly perceive a shortage of resources to fulfil your intentions. You may also frequently find it challenging to see and utilise resources beyond those immediately in front of or given to you. Others may consider you to be someone who often fails to complete a task unless all resources are ready and available. Alternatively, you may be frivolous and use resources as though they are limitless with little or no consideration for their value.

Resourcefulness is a Way of Being that allows organisations to capitalise on their people's work, which stems from a combination of their talents, skills and qualifications as well as their individual and collective Beings, not just on their so-called 'hard skills'. What does Being have to do with this? Unless a leader actively encourages and supports their people to polish and transform their Being, they can't expect effective performance from them. For example, a highly talented and intelligent engineer who is not committed, reliable, resourceful and self-expressed will be unlikely to contribute as much as they would if they were given the opportunity to transform their relationship with these Ways of Being. That's why Being matters. Putting this in context with Jean-Baptiste Say's definition of the word entrepreneur, Being can lead an organisation to higher yields, returns and profits. The most effective way to distribute surplus value (profit) in different economic systems has always been a controversial topic. But the truth is, profit matters in a commercial economy. It contributes to a thriving economy, regardless of how the extra wealth generated is distributed. Given that profit matters, transforming and polishing one's Being, including resourcefulness, must matter too because, collectively, our Beings contribute to the wealth of a nation and its GDP, leading to a prosperous economy. Throughout my studies, I have never come across anyone with a relatively polished Being who suffered from poverty.

People who have a healthy relationship with resourcefulness live life from the viewpoint of abundance and thrive on a challenge. This doesn't mean they see the world through rose-coloured glasses. It means they see what's possible. They actively search for possibilities and are forward-thinking and solution-oriented. As you can perhaps tell from this explanation, resourcefulness has a close connection with gratitude. Those who have a healthy relationship with resourcefulness are present to and grateful for what they have and how they can get the most out of that rather than focusing on what they don't have. The opposite of this is someone who lives life from the viewpoint of scarcity, who only sees problems, not solutions. Think of someone you know who fits the description of a person with a scarcity ethos. It could be someone at work, a friend, a family member or a politician. How do they make you feel when you're around them or hear them speak? Do you feel frustrated that all they see is problems and negativity? Are they constantly complaining that everything is working against them and always finding fault in or blaming others? Do they seem to be forever waiting for more resources or a miracle to happen rather than proactively seeking the best way forward? Perhaps you recognise yourself in these descriptions?

Let's say a business owner has five employees, commonly referred to as 'human resources'. While I only refer to people's work as a resource, for ease of understanding, let's refer to them as resources for this example. The business has been offered the opportunity to take on a major project that, at face value, seems impossible with the number of resources available. A resourceful business owner would understand that by arranging their team members/resources in the most effective way through leadership, creativity, innovation, systems and processes, five employees could essentially produce the work of ten or more. The difference between **having** resources and **being** resourceful gives rise to a whole that is greater than the sum of its parts. A leader who has a healthy relationship with resourcefulness would actively consider all possibilities to determine how much more could potentially be achieved with their available resources without taking advantage of their people. For example, they might assess how they could free up additional time to facilitate the work that needs to be done, demonstrating a connection with care.

Global pandemics and other large-scale disasters have given rise to numerous examples of resourcefulness in action. We have seen event management companies find creative ways to host business award ceremonies and other major events online. Apps have been developed to enable trade professionals to provide an accurate measure and quote service without attending a premises, and we've witnessed manufacturing companies pivot their operations in compressed time, just to name a few examples. Those who choose not to be resourceful in times of crisis are doomed to failure. Rather than actively seeking opportunities, they might choose victimhood and self-sabotage. Perhaps an unhealthy relationship with authenticity, vulnerability, awareness or freedom leads them to be unwilling to adapt and rearrange their resources to change course. As is the case with all Secondary Ways of Being, when we have an unhealthy relationship with resourcefulness, there are always underlying issues with the deeper, primal qualities to be addressed and this will differ from one person to the next. Being resourceful as opposed to not being resourceful can literally mean the difference between success and failure.

Many businesses barely generate enough to pay their employees, let alone make a decent profit, due in part to the leaders having an unhealthy relationship with resourcefulness. In contrast, the way many Fortune 500 organisational leaders capitalise on their people's work is extraordinary. Their resourcefulness is largely the result of their authentic awareness of the benefits of nurturing their people's Beings and being of service to their customers. It leads them to attract the best talent and a loyal customer following. This creates a powerful ripple effect: they innovate more, invest more in R&D and therefore have the capacity and capability to serve more people, leading to higher revenue. Consequently, they can offer higher remuneration packages and so on. When results are compounded in this way, growth is often exponential. The phenomenal success of organisations like this and the way they achieve it highlight the importance of resourcefulness and its role in wellbeing, integrity, effectiveness and fulfilment.

Decoding human beings from an ontological perspective gives us greater access to understanding how to leverage people's value through the work they produce and their potential to do even more when given the chance. People who have a relatively healthy relationship with resourcefulness don't allow circumstances to determine when or how they take action. This doesn't mean they don't consider the circumstances; that would make them reactive, which you will recall is a shadow side of proactivity. On the contrary, those with a relatively healthy relationship with resourcefulness give themselves permission to think creatively and consider all possibilities, opportunities and contingencies. They see things in themselves, others and circumstances that other people either intentionally ignore or are oblivious to. Imagine a world in which resourcefulness was more prevalent on a collective scale. That world would be far more productive and sustainable, with far fewer unresolved issues than the world in which we live today.

CHAPTER 9.6

Resilience

By the time most of us reach adulthood, we know what it's like to go through a major challenge, adversity or traumatic event. They are inevitable as we progress on the journey of life. Whether it be the death of a loved one, the loss of a job, the breakdown of a relationship, serious illness, theft, the uncertainties of a global pandemic or whatever it may be, these events stretch us far beyond the everyday problems we all encounter. At times like these, resilience is one of the key Aspects of Being that comes to our rescue because it supports us in restoring our integrity when it is shattered, whether by ourselves or by circumstances. However, the shadow sides of resilience can keep us feeling trapped, vulnerable, disarmed and victimised.

We need resilience most of all in times of crisis because it supports us to bounce back, sometimes stronger than we were before. Resilience is also key to the process of transformation because, without it, we may be tempted to stray off course, especially when the path becomes rocky, as it invariably does at some point. People who have a healthy relationship with resilience don't let the setbacks in life keep them down. Instead, they leverage them to discover the learning that enables them to stand tall and keep going.

When we experience hardship, catastrophe or trauma, we can be so deeply impacted that, metaphorically speaking, it's almost as though our DNA is changed forever. To prevent ourselves from breaking under pressure and ensure we bounce back to the way we were before the event occurred requires 'elasticity'. That's where resilience comes in. It is a Way of Being that enables us to break through rather than break down. Imagine losing your job or the company you have worked so hard to build. Consider the impact of discovering your partner has been cheating on you, impacting your perception of your past and present and shattering your hopes and dreams for the future.

Think of any situation that could lead you to the verge of breaking down. If you have a relatively healthy relationship with resilience, you would be more likely to turn the course by going from freefall to soaring higher to rise above the situation. However, if you have an unhealthy relationship with resilience, you might feel defeated and disarmed in the face of life's adversities. Alternatively, it could lead you to be weak or to victimise yourself, remaining in destructive situations. An example of the latter is someone who remains in an abusive relationship.

When it comes to people's understanding of resilience, we once again strike disparities. It is commonly seen as the process of adapting and adjusting well in the face of adversity, which I would call 'flexibility'. While flexibility is important and connected to resilience, it does not paint the full picture. A meaning that is more congruent with the quality I am referring to in the Being Framework as resilience is 'elasticity': the ability of a substance to return to its original shape after being bent, stretched or pressed. Metaphorically speaking, this definition describes our ability to restore our integrity (return to being whole or unbroken) and wellbeing when pressured or stretched by external or internal forces. In other words, it's our ability to bounce back when we are on the verge of a breakdown, restoring integrity, wellbeing, workability and effectiveness.

Resilience

Resilience is a quality that enables you to bounce back to your original form or even stronger when circumstances in life knock you down. You consistently leverage setbacks to adjust and learn while finding a way to rise up and continue forward rather than letting difficulties or failure overcome you and drain your resolve.

A healthy relationship with *resilience* indicates that you can consistently face difficult circumstances with elasticity, without breaking as you might if you were rigid. You trust your ability to endure hardship. Others may consider you to have the patience, strength of character and capacity to manage pain, discomfort, difficulties and challenging emotions and impulses. People may feel encouraged by you and your presence when things are tough.

An unhealthy relationship with *resilience* indicates that you may often be defeated, distressed, disarmed and broken by life-changing circumstances or events. You tend to avoid uncertainty, change or challenging life experiences. Others may describe you as weak or a victim. Alternatively, you may become entrenched, rigid or fixed to one spot, making you susceptible to fragility. You may take unnecessary punishment while numbing yourself to your pain, potentially causing you to remain in unhealthy situations or relationships.

How badly you want something contributes to your resilience

The more committed you are to tapping into and expressing your Unique Being, the more motivated you are likely to be, which might make you appreciate the need to be resilient all the more when you strike challenges. Particularly if you are devoting your life's work to a significant cause, there will be times when the path gets rocky. There might even be times when you are stretched almost to breaking point. If you don't have the elasticity (resilience) to bounce back, you will break, and your dreams and intentions could come crashing down with you. The opportunity could be lost forever if you are so severely impacted by the failure of your first iteration that you can't bear to face the challenge again in round two. I know many entrepreneurs who attempted to build a business with great passion and conviction. But a harsh failure at some point collapsed them to the point where they gave up. Now they wouldn't even dare to dream of building a business again. This example highlights a relationship between resilience and responsibility, commitment, fear and persistence, among others. Take being responsible, for example. There will always be matters in life to which you must respond, and at times you might fall off the rails. This is where resilience comes to the rescue.

Imagine you have written your first book, only to have it knocked back by every publishing house you approach, crushing your self-worth and causing bitter disappointment. If you had a healthy relationship with resilience, you would not let the knockbacks get you down for too long. Instead, you would seek feedback on where and how you could improve the manuscript in order for it to be considered. Assuming the manuscript has some merit – otherwise pushing on would indicate the shadow of persistence on the insistence side – you would return to the drawing board and push on until it meets the brief. That's resilience as well as persistence driven by the deeper underlying qualities of responsibility, vulnerability and commitment, to list just a few. The author of the *Harry Potter* series of books, JK Rowling, showed great resilience after her pitch for the first book was knocked back by no less than twelve publishing houses before Bloomsbury Publishing eventually accepted it. There are countless examples like this.

You may wonder, what's the difference between resilience and persistence? The principle difference is that, with resilience, there is always an element of emotional or physical pain associated with it. If you have ever been rejected multiple times in job interviews, created a product as a startup only to find that the market rejected it or lost a loved one, you would know how this type of pain feels. To recap, if you are working towards a goal and you know you need to keep pushing through several iterations in order to actualise your intention, you need persistence to persevere. But if, during this process, you get hurt, perhaps from rejection during a product trial, then this might stretch you to the point where you will either break or bounce back with resilience so you can keep going.

Emotional safety has become a buzzword in our era. I would put forward emotional resilience as a more effective alternative. Although it is vital to move towards creating safer environments, it is inauthentic to think that we can rid the world of bullies, aggressive behaviour and uncomfortable or offensive situations. Furthermore, being offended is quite subjective. Not everyone is triggered by the same things and some of us don't realise how our words or actions can offend certain people at times. It is far more effective to develop emotional resilience. When you are emotionally resilient, you won't break down whenever you are offended or bullied. Instead, you would bounce back and stand tall so you can continue on your way with conviction. The main difference between emotional safety and emotional resilience is that with the latter, the power stays in your hands. You are the one who gets to decide whether you will allow a person or situation to get to you and the extent to which you are impacted will be under your control, nobody else's. This is a critical quality to possess if your intention is to be a leader of influence, or even the leader of your own life. I am not suggesting that unacceptable and inappropriate behaviour is to be tolerated or that it should not be condemned. On the contrary, it definitely should be condemned. But to rise beyond that and be responsible – tapping into your autonomy in the face of those inevitable situations – is extremely empowering.

Resilience is not about being tough

It is unsurprising that many people confuse the quality of resilience with being tough. That's because dictionaries like the *Oxford English Dictionary* use the word 'toughness' to define it. Delve into the meaning of the word 'tough', however, and you will realise that it is more closely aligned with being rigid. Being resilient is far removed from being rigid because resilience demands elasticity, which is the opposite of rigidity. Ironically, being rigid makes you more fragile because the right level of force might cause you to break.

Have you ever been involved in a project and, at the eleventh hour before the launch deadline, something unforeseen happened that put a sudden halt to the project? For instance, perhaps a key member of the team fell ill and there was nobody with the skills to replace them, or perhaps a major glitch in the product was discovered just before it was due to be released. Situations like this are often unavoidable. Resilience is being willing to receive challenges gently – not with toughness – and having the elasticity to redirect your energy with clarity and calmness.

At the end of the day, adverse events can be extremely painful and difficult while they are happening, but they don't have to determine the rest of your life. While they may be out of your control, there are many aspects of your life you can greatly influence. That's one of the key roles of resilience. Becoming more resilient not only supports you to get through and bounce back from difficult circumstances, it also empowers you to grow and transform when polished in conjunction with other Aspects of Being.

CHAPTER 9.7

Accountability

Some may question why accountability is included in the Being Framework when responsibility is already there as a Primary Way of Being. I understand the reason for their question because accountability and responsibility are commonly referred to interchangeably, as though they refer to the same meaning, which leads to confusion. However, as Ways of Being, both are distinctly different.

The ontological distinction of responsibility is honouring your relatively high level of autonomy and choosing powerfully to be the cause in the matters of your life. Accountability, on the other hand, is how you are **being with** your responsibilities, including during and after any situation that might have caused the promised responsibilities not to be fulfilled. It's how you choose to be when responding and taking ownership of the commitment you have made and for which you are directly or indirectly responsible. Being accountable means others know they can count on you to deliver on your promises. And, if those promises are not met, they know you can be counted on to own it and fix things without resentment. When you have a healthy relationship with accountability, you are known as someone who is dependable and whose word can be trusted.

Accountability

Accountability is living from the viewpoint that you assume full ownership for promises and agreements made by you or on your behalf, including those inferred or otherwise. *Accountability* is fulfilling, completing and being held accountable for whatever you or your team have agreed to, regardless of the circumstances. When you are being accountable, your word can be counted on fully, without question and in every relationship or situation.

A healthy relationship with *accountability* indicates that you will complete what you or your team have agreed to do when you give your word. You choose to deliver as promised or clean up when or where you don't, without resentment. You expect to keep your promises while treating the promises of others as though they are your own. Others know you to be someone whose word has value, rigour and is powerful. You are also available and willing for others to hold you to account.

An unhealthy relationship with *accountability* indicates that you avoid making explicit promises or committing to projects and deadlines. You frequently push back and make excuses when others ask for your commitment or hold you to account. You may collude with or blame others when deadlines or promises are not met. You may abdicate to others in the hope that the agreement is fulfilled. Others may avoid asking you to commit to tasks and projects or take responsibility for managing others. You may be uncomfortable and resist challenging or confronting others when they miss deadlines or fail to fulfil their promises. Alternatively, you may use inappropriate force or your position to threaten others to complete tasks and may be considered overbearing or domineering.

The relationship between accountability and other Aspects of Being

While accountability is distinctly different from responsibility, there is a close relationship between them. Where responsibility refers to our innate freedom of choice to respond to things in life, accountability is one of the most obvious behavioural factors that springs from being responsible. It is choosing powerfully to meet your commitments and own them when, for whatever reason, you are unable to meet them. It is the quality that stops you dropping the ball or deflecting responsibility when you stray off track. Accountability is also giving others permission to hold you to account and assertively and actively holding others to account when appropriate.

Accountability is also closely linked to freedom, empowerment, vulnerability and authenticity. Someone who willingly owns it and cleans up without resentment when they don't deliver as promised does not have their guard up, and therefore, is likely to have a healthy relationship with vulnerability. Being accountable is also an extremely empowering and authentic way to be. And when someone has a healthy relationship with freedom, they choose powerfully to respond to situations based on their own values without worrying about what others may think of them, which is a natural way to be for someone who has a healthy relationship with accountability. That's because accountability is how we are being with our decision to respond to something for which we are either directly or indirectly responsible. Let's look into some of these relationships in a little more detail.

Being free is when you are present to the fact that you always have options while being responsible is to choose to respond and select from those options powerfully. Then it is through empowerment that you will act upon it. A person with a relatively healthy relationship with accountability lives life from the viewpoint that they always have options (freedom). So they intentionally and autonomously (responsibility) give their word (commitment) to choose an option rather than turn a blind eye to the possibilities available to them. Their authentic awareness leads them to know that they are capable of fulfilling the promises they have made (empowerment). Then, if they don't fulfil their promise for whatever reason, they own up to it (accountability).

We shouldn't ignore the impact of other Aspects of Being here, such as courage, anxiety and vulnerability. For example, you need to be courageous and confident enough to dare to make a promise, despite an educated level of uncertainty. You also need to have a relatively healthy relationship with anxiety and vulnerability to ensure that the what-ifs or concerns over how others may perceive you do not stop you from making the decisions and taking the actions you know to be 'right'. Having others hold you to account along the way as you fulfil your commitment will support you to reduce mistakes and prevent you from going off track. If the outcome is less than your original intention, being accountable will enable you to make progress in subsequent iterations.

Just because you meet a deadline does not automatically mean you have a healthy relationship with accountability. For instance, you may have met the deadline purely because you were worried about losing your job rather than out of a sense of duty. Similarly, if you strike issues that cause you to miss a deadline, owning up to it and getting it done as quickly as possible also does not automatically mean you have a healthy relationship with accountability. On the contrary, you are not being accountable if you only own up to a situation because you know there is no alternative and resolve the situation while holding anger and resentment deep down.

Leaders and accountability

Whether you lead an organisation or a small team, the buck stops with you. This means that if one of your team members causes a commitment you have made to not be met, **you** are the one who is accountable. This notion can be challenging to comprehend. Consider the following example. Let's say you are a team leader for a significant project that involves multiple moving parts, meaning there is a lot that could go wrong. It would only take one break in the chain for the entire project to fall over. With the project deadline looming, one of your team members comes to you explaining that they have been unable to deliver their part in the project on time. You know that this will cause multiple delays down the line, meaning the deadline will not be met and causing significant ramifications for the business. What would you do? Would you make excuses and lay the blame on the team member? Or would you choose to openly and assertively own the issue and ensure it is resolved in the best way possible? If you choose the latter and consider that this is how you tend to be in any situation like this, then it is likely that you have a healthy relationship with accountability. It takes courage and vulnerability to own a situation, especially when you are not directly responsible.

I am not suggesting that you would let your team member off the hook. Once the project is back on track, you would have an open conversation with them to learn what happened, being present to their reasons for letting the team down. You might even discover that your initial instructions weren't clear enough or that you should have checked in more frequently with your team members rather than assume that they had everything under control. The next step would be to forgive both your team member and yourself and move on.

Higher purpose is key in this scenario. Someone with a healthy relationship with higher purpose would go beyond the current time and beyond themselves, knowing that it is more important in the long run to nurture the relationships within their team and generate trust. Building a team and relationships takes time. There will be times when forgiveness is required. Bringing compassion, assertiveness and higher purpose to the equation will lead you to hold the person to account while simultaneously supporting them to fulfil their commitment. When this happens, you will build a longer-term asset – the relationships and trust in your team.

If you lead a team or aspire to be a team leader, consider gradually instilling accountability as a Way of Being into your team. That way, it will become part of the culture for all team members to hold each other to account on group projects. When there is a culture of accountability, team members will not accept anything below the standard. They will not tolerate a team member who is consistently letting the rest of the team down through a lack of accountability. The result is a team you don't need to micromanage.

As you can see, accountability is a critical Way of Being in both personal and professional situations. It is central to producing results and living in harmony, especially in the face of challenges. Without accountability, little can be accomplished and trust is diminished. When we are accountable, we appreciate, acknowledge and accept the consequences and outcomes of our decisions, behaviours and actions, which assures others that they can count on us in any situation. People who have a healthy relationship with accountability also understand that the buck stops with them, even if they are not directly responsible for something going wrong. They are not afraid to own it, clean up, forgive and move on.

CHAPTER 9.8

Reliability

From before the time we are born, we are reliant on others. When we are developing in the womb, we rely on our mother to nourish us and also take care of herself throughout our development. And so begins a lifelong journey of relying on others and, later, on being reliable so others can rely on us too. As social beings, we need and rely on others, from individuals to groups, governments, institutions and systems, in some shape or form and to varying degrees throughout the different stages of our lives. We rely on our life partner or spouse to honour their commitments, our employer to pay our wages, the medical system to support us when we are unwell, the justice system to keep us safe, individuals and businesses to pay their taxes, and the list goes on. Similarly, employers rely on their employees to come to work and meet their deliverables so they can continue to serve their customers and remain profitable enough to not only stay afloat but to grow and provide opportunities for others. A world without reliability would be unworkable. We would not even survive, let alone have any chance to thrive. In fact, one of the primary objectives of transforming our Being is to be more reliable. This makes reliability one of the main outcomes of transformation, which is why I left this Way of Being till last.

Reliability

Reliability is consistently performing as intended while completing what is expected of you or agreed to fully and on time. When you are being reliable, you produce consistent results in line with promises and expectations. You can be depended on to be available, ready, fully present and show up when needed.

A healthy relationship with *reliability* indicates that you are acknowledged as someone who can be counted on to fulfil your promises. Others know that when you agree to something, it will happen as and when you said it would. You expect – and others expect you – to complete all tasks and projects you undertake as promised and on time.

An unhealthy relationship with *reliability* indicates that you often have difficulty completing tasks or seeing projects through to completion. You may be someone others choose not to count on. You may underestimate timeframes and push back deadlines. You may be frequently late for meetings and complain that you have too much to do or are running behind. You may be considered someone who lets others down, over-promises and rarely delivers as agreed. You may be unpredictable, overly spontaneous or frequently change course without considering the consequences. Alternatively, you may excessively go beyond what is required of you or necessary for the project.

When an employer hires an employee, they ideally hire them for their reliability in applying their knowledge, skills and qualifications, not simply for possessing those qualities. You can have all the skills, qualifications and talents under the sun, but if you are unreliable, those assets will go to waste. In short, if you are not being reliable, you are a liability.

Let's say you needed a solicitor to represent you in a legal matter. What if they failed to attend court on time or neglected to do all the necessary due diligence to prepare for your case? It would make no difference that they had certificates on the wall proclaiming their university achievements and admission to the Supreme and High Courts. Or imagine you were told you needed urgent surgery. You would select a surgeon based on their reliability, such as their track record of performing similar surgeries in the past, not one who has never performed that surgery before but has impressive qualifications or an excellent bedside manner. And what if you needed help during a time of personal crisis. Would you call a friend who has let you down in the past or one who has always been there for you? I'm sure I don't need to spell out the consequences of an unreliable World Wide Web or border control authority! These are just some of the many examples that sum up the value and necessity of reliability.

While we are all aware of our need to be reliable and our dependence on others and systems to be reliable, we can also be easily distracted and readily tire of mundane tasks. This can lead to an unhealthy relationship with this Secondary Way of Being. As you can see from the distinction, people who struggle with reliability's shadow often over-promise, struggle to complete tasks and therefore let others and themselves down. It is worth noting that meeting deadlines and commitments from time to time does not make you reliable. To have a healthy relationship with reliability requires you to deliver your promises consistently. Most of us know people we would want on our side or on our team at work. They're the ones we know we can always count on, no matter how challenging the circumstances.

Awareness, all Moods and all Primary Ways of Being play a significant role in our ability to be reliable. For example, it is impossible to be consistently reliable if you haven't established a healthy relationship with most, if not all, Primary Ways of Being. Furthermore, it is futile to attempt to hide a lack of reliability because it is one of the most visible and significant outcomes of polishing your Ways of Being and Moods. The health of your relationship with reliability can be readily seen in your outputs, presence, demeanour and actions or inactions.

Most of us know what it's like to be unreliable, even if it's only happened once. I'm sure you would agree that it's not a good feeling. There are also those who believe they can't rely on themselves to commit to a goal, from changing their unhealthy habits to completing a course or writing a book. The good news is that transforming our relationship with reliability begins with small steps focusing on daily habits. While we might not be able to control how we feel all the time, we can control our decisions and actions. Running a marathon begins with daily runs around the block, gradually lengthening the distance. Writing a book begins with a chapter structure and then committing to one chapter at a time. Changing your diet begins with removing the temptations from your fridge and pantry. Getting to work on time starts with setting the alarm ten minutes earlier and so on. At the end of the day, when we have an unhealthy relationship with reliability, we are prevented from being fulfilled in life. But anything is possible when you know you can rely on yourself to do whatever it takes to achieve what you set your heart and mind on.

CHAPTER 10

The Being Profile
a vivid snapshot of your state of Being

I n this book, we have explored a framework that enables you to see and know human beings – yourself and others – with sharper clarity and more profound understanding. You have also learned that we are not fixed objects destined to be how we are now forever. We all possess the power within us to transform. So what's the next step? The good news is you have already taken the first step by investing your time to read this book. By now, there is a fair chance that you are resonating with the challenges I've laid out. It might be the times you've been impacted by another person's Way of Being and ended up being blindsided, crushed or misled. Or it could be the instances where you realise you've trapped yourself in your own prison. As a result, you're constantly making decisions that don't end up working for you and finding that you're 'putting up with' increasing dissatisfaction in your life. Or you might be in a position where others keep commending you on your external achievements. Yet beneath the surface, you know there is a repeated pattern of attempting to set goals related to what you really want out of life but failing to meet them.

For many, when you generate the willingness to start the process, common barriers already start to appear. Your Aspects of Being are playing a part in how you are reading and receiving this message right now and, as a result, can lead you to dismiss or ignore the solution you've received in this book as nothing more than an interesting idea rather than something that can actually support you to have a transformational shift in your life. For example, a shadow side of empowerment might be active for you, bringing you thoughts like, 'I can see how this might be relevant for others, but it would never work for me'. Or perhaps a shadow side of forgiveness might be dominant, raising the idea that, 'I've tried so many initiatives to change myself before and they didn't work. So I don't want to put myself through that situation again'. Alternatively, a shadow side of vulnerability and authenticity could be playing a role, prompting thoughts of, 'No, I'm perfectly fine and am happy to put up with my issues'.

If you allow yourself to move through these initial barriers, there is a good chance that you will become present to those areas of your life where you've reached the point of 'enough is enough'. Perhaps you see repeated patterns of dysfunction in your relationships that you want to address. You could be present to the tangible and surmounting costs of your self-doubt. Or maybe you're becoming aware that your stressful work-related issues are beginning to have a detrimental effect on both your personal relationships and your health. While you don't need to be going through a difficult situation to benefit from the Being Framework and the learnings from this book, my team and I have found that people become more sincere and determined to shift their results when facing challenges in life. That's when they become more willing to face the shadow, which is necessary for their transformation but can be uncomfortable and confronting.

If you are sincerely seeking change and striving for new levels of results in any area of your life and are willing to cast aside your preconceptions and past experiences, then I invite you to start by gaining an understanding of your current state of Being. This is most effectively achieved by harnessing the power of the Being Framework's measurement tool, the Being Profile®. This instrument will dramatically simplify and reduce the time required to go through the process of transformation and, in so doing, support you with the awareness necessary to break through to new levels of personal growth and results, provided you are willing to do the work. Let me give you a brief overview of the Being Profile and how it works.

As you can imagine, even after reading this book and learning about every Aspect of Being in the Being Framework, it can still be challenging to relate it to your own Being and life. The Being Profile is an ontometric measurement tool: a tool that measures the qualities within an ontological model. It supports you in raising your awareness of how you are being by providing you with a current-state measurement for each of your thirty-one Aspects of Being. It highlights which Aspects of Being you currently have a relatively healthy relationship with and which ones are less developed and might be holding back your level of effectiveness.

People choose to take on the Being Profile for various reasons. For some, the focus is predominantly on themselves in the context of their personal or professional lives. They can see repeated patterns of decision-making and behaviours that bring about results that do not work for them, and they're looking to understand themselves in these areas at a deeper level. The Being Profile has also been used as a tool to support the raising of awareness for professionals who want to advance their careers, those leading businesses and organisations who wish to lead more effectively, and individuals wanting to know more about themselves to gain personal clarity and direction, among many others.

Some people take on the Being Profile to understand others as much as to understand themselves. They want to better read into others' motives, behaviours and decisions to prevent being 'burnt' by the shadow side of others' Aspects of Being while also wanting to harness and nurture their light side. By better understanding how they and others operate on the level of Being, they start the journey towards impacting the business partnerships they build, the performance of the teams they work within, and the romantic and intimate relationships they foster.

How does the Being Profile work?

The Being Profile is taken online and can be completed on your mobile, tablet or desktop. You are challenged with a series of over 240 probing, unique and strategically assembled questions that measure your relationship with each of the thirty-one Aspects of Being in the Being Framework and explored in this book. As a result, many people have reported that their awareness is raised simply by completing the assessment, even before they move to any further stage. It is an informative and insightful tool that plays a critical role in a person's transformational process.

Substantial consideration was given to the Being Profile's formulation and refinement, backed by significant research and testing. My book, *BEING*, provides a more detailed exposition of the framework, including the profile, such as the philosophical and academic background that underpins it. In addition to posing a series of questions that are not commonly asked, the assessment adopts a complex, multi-layered approach, meaning that each question is formulated to provide multiple data points that contribute to various measures that make up your individual and unique profile. Not only does this make the assessment incredibly difficult to manipulate or 'fool', but it also shines a light on the numerous, complex, interwoven relationships that exist between the four layers of your Being: Meta Factors, Moods, Primary Ways of Being and Secondary Ways of Being.

A key aspect of the Being Profile's formulation and refinement was the initial cohort of over twenty professional coaches, and later many more, who collaboratively contributed to developing its effectiveness. Through extensive rounds of in-field testing, the tool's calibration and the report's format and structure were refined to more effectively support the coaching process. The result is that the Being Profile is a unique profiling tool, particularly in terms of its level of practicality. It is also a powerful instrument for leaders who care about the people within their organisations and for its ability to support real transformation for both organisations and individuals. By now, it would be apparent to you how important these factors are and the extent to which they are directly linked to producing key outcomes for an organisation, from increasing revenue and lifting its probability of success to fulfilling its mission in the world. When an individual or team chooses to work with a certified and accredited Thrive Coach, who is not only trained to conduct the Being Profile debrief but also coach a person over time on their Aspects of Being, the insights from the Being Profile translate into actionable and specific areas on which to focus coaching in a seamless and integrated manner.

On completion of the Being Profile assessment, a detailed report with a score from zero to ten for each Aspect of Being is created and either emailed directly to you or to your coach if you have opted for a professional debrief (the two options to complete a Being Profile are explained shortly).

It is important to be aware that a score of zero or ten in any Aspect of Being, while not impossible, is highly improbable. In fact, it is extremely rare to achieve either the highest (nine, ten) or the lowest (zero, one) scores for any of the Aspects of Being it measures. This aligns with reality in that very few people sit at the edge of the spectrum. As part of our mission to cause transformation in the world, my team and I continue to complete research and development in collaboration with our community of active business investors, executives, leaders, entrepreneurs, coaches and academics. This ensures the Being Profile is continually refined, extended and enhanced to more effectively support people to understand their Aspects of Being and the role they play in their lives.

How the Being Profile supports your transformation

The Being Profile is markedly unique in its approach. Many profiling tools focus on identifying 'strengths', 'weaknesses' or 'personality types' that are fixed and/or innate. We are then encouraged to find ways to cope with and manage our limitations to gain incremental performance improvements. The Being Profile does not work this way. Its objective is not to categorise people. Instead, it focuses on how you are being, using the ontological model as described in this book. This enables you to see yourself with sharp clarity – as though you are looking in a mirror – or use it as a lens to decode and understand others so you can make more effective decisions.

You will recall that every Aspect of Being is mutable and can be transformed by any individual, without exception. Therefore, relatively low scores on your Being Profile are not intended to be put up with or managed. Instead, they become key opportunities to adopt and practise the Transformation Methodology for profound and sustainable transformation. A similarly powerful opportunity exists to refine your conception of and master those Aspects of Being for which you display relatively higher scores. By polishing each of your Aspects of Being, you contribute towards your integrity or wholeness and the fulfilment of whatever you care about.

One of the most notable aspects of the Being Profile is its ability to get to the heart of important matters for an individual. This is no easy feat.

The complex nature of human beings and our ability to deflect, deny or obscure the truth can make it tremendously difficult to get to the root cause of an individual's barriers without the support of the Being Profile, even for the most experienced coaches. The Being Profile can provide an accredited practitioner with valuable insights by objectively measuring and mapping a person's thirty-one Aspects of Being. These insights enable the practitioner to form connections between what a person is dealing with in their life and what shows up on their Being Profile. While every person responds differently to their Being Profile assessment and debrief, it is not uncommon for people to be deeply touched, often to the point of tears, when they become present to the cost of how their Being has been playing out in their lives.

Ways to complete the Being Profile

There are two options for completing the Being Profile. The first is an online self-discovery format. This option enables you to complete the Being Profile assessment in your own time and at your own pace before walking through your results in a self-guided way. You are given access via your mobile, laptop or desktop to a series of informative video modules designed to build your understanding of the Being Framework and provide relevant examples and case studies before viewing and reflecting on your scores. By taking the time to consider your scores on one screen and walking through the distinctions and guidance videos on another, you'll be able to deepen your understanding of how your Aspects of Being are playing a critical role in your life and the results you are producing. If at any time you would like further clarification, guidance or support, you also have access to the accredited practitioners within the Engenesis community.

The second option is to work one-on-one with a Being Profile Accredited Practitioner who will walk you through your Being Profile results and support you in relating your scores to the context of your life. Being Profile Accredited Practitioners undertake rigorous certified training through the Engenesis Coaching Academy that enables them to work carefully within each layer of the Being Framework to support their clients to form a crystal clear picture of how their Aspects of Being are playing out in their lives. They can also support a client to identify more subtle connections and patterns between multiple Aspects of Being that can interact with one another to strengthen or block the results they're seeking.

While a Being Profile Accredited Practitioner is trained to complete a debrief session and walk a person through their Being Profile, a Certified or Accredited Thrive Coach is a specialist Being Framework ontological coach practitioner. They have undergone additional training, including an intensive thirteen-week program facilitated by Master Coaches at the Engenesis Coaching Academy. They have also completed substantial requirements in logged coaching hours and passed a rigorous interview process. A Certified or Accredited Thrive Coach has the skills and qualifications to guide you through the transformation process, supporting you with coaching to unlock the barriers that may be holding you back. Many of our accredited practitioners and Certified or Accredited Thrive Coaches report that the key to making a sustainable difference to the people they work with is their continued personal transformation and development of their own Being by facing the shadow or troubled aspects of themselves in conjunction with their coaching community.

Case studies

Let's explore a few examples of people's experiences completing the Being Profile assessment and debrief.

Vicky was a management consultant with over ten years of experience in her industry when she first worked with a Being Profile Accredited Practitioner. In coming to complete her first Being Profile, she already knew herself as being confident, ambitious and wanting to accomplish great things in her career. However, she would receive repeated feedback from managers that she was quiet and introverted and that this was getting in her way of making the progress she wanted. In commenting about her experience completing her Being Profile, Vicky said, 'In answering the Being Profile assessment questions, what came up immediately was that I actually have to deal with myself and be frank and honest with myself'. In adopting this approach, Vicky was able to transcend the perceived limitations of her 'introversion' being a fixed and unchangeable character trait. She identified clear and specific ways to develop her Aspects of Being to transform this.

Not long after completing her Being Profile assessment and debrief, Vicky found herself back at work and in a meeting with one of the company directors. This time, she was fully aware of how her Being played a direct role in her communication and performance. At one stage in the meeting, she noticed a critical issue not being addressed. Instead of feeling like it wasn't her place to speak up, she practised being assertive and raised the issue with the director. Her assertiveness had an immediate and positive ripple effect. Not only did the director take on her input, which subsequently led to project improvements for the client's benefit, but Vicky also felt a stronger connection with her director from that day forward, which contributed to her sense of fulfilment at work. She has since been promoted to a senior management position.

Kristina owns a yoga studio in Sydney, Australia. As a first-time business owner, she felt held back and blocked by procrastination and hesitation. The circumstances surrounding the business were challenging. However, determined to make it work, she committed to completing the Being Profile. In reviewing her results, Kristina uncovered some Aspects of Being that she expected for herself and others that were surprising and unlocked new domains of enquiry and growth that she hadn't considered before. By working on specific Aspects of Being related to her leadership, she lifted her ability to positively influence members of her community to become paying customers of her business and developed the leadership capacity of certain members of her team. Astounded by the changes Kristina was making, her business partner remarked, 'What's going on? I'm hearing you're on fire!' Her transformation went beyond how she thought and felt. It translated into a 20% increase in profit within weeks. Kristina said, 'In my experience, completing a Being Profile is a very fast way to transform some of those Ways of Being that are holding you back and that are going to massively impact everything in your business and the way that your business moves forward.'

Being Profile for teams and organisations

As well as being an effective tool to support an individual to transform their performance, effectiveness and influence, the Being Profile can also be used to support the growth of a team. This can be achieved by having each team member complete their Being Profile and combining the results of team members into a Team Profile. In this way, a team's Being Profile provides a snapshot of the collective Being of that team.

Those who initiate the Being Profile within their team range from CEOs and company directors to team leaders, managers, HR leaders or those responsible for people, performance and culture within their organisation. These individuals may either become accredited practitioners of the Being Profile themselves or hire an accredited practitioner to come into the organisation and facilitate the conversation through individual debrief sessions, team workshops and facilitated discussions. Let me share with you a few examples of how the Being Profile has been used in an organisational context.

The CEO of a not-for-profit organisation that supports men in need initiated the adoption of the Being Framework, not only in his organisation but also within the context of a partnership with another not-for-profit that supports women in need. Over the last two years, several leaders within these two organisations have undertaken coaching and training in the Being Framework. They not only chose to conduct initial coaching and training with the Being Profile but they also participated in a number of our advanced training programs that have enabled them to shift the overall culture of their organisations with exceptional results. In the Being Framework, the core focus is not to change individual team members' behaviours one at a time. Instead, multiple individuals and behaviours are impacted by transforming their Aspects of Being. The CEO of the first not-for-profit observed the following as his team undertook the training and practised the Being Framework under his guidance. He said, 'I made a promise that I will create an organisation where people love to come to work every day, and there have been so many times over the last eight years that have been heartbreaking to me not to be able to fulfil that promise. But what I've seen in the Being Framework is that I now have a methodology that speaks to every single person who works for us and creates leadership.'

An international company in the agricultural technology sector chose to invest in adopting the Being Framework within the organisation. They started with members of their leadership team, with each leader completing their Being Profile assessment, undergoing a debrief session and participating in coaching and a team workshop. Subsequently, one of their directors became accredited as a practitioner in the Being Profile and undertook the thirteen-week Thrive Coach Training Program. He said, 'The company provided the means and space for me to be trained and developed as a coach, using these two platforms: the Being Profile and the Thrive Coach Training Program. They now affect the way we recruit. We now incorporate the Being Profile into our recruitment process – how we train and how we develop all of our teams. We integrate the methodology into our leadership conversations and decisions all the time.'

In the next section – Where to from Here? – I will also share where you can access more case studies and similar relevant material if you are interested to learn more.

Our growing community of accredited practitioners and coaches has worked with many organisations that have integrated the Being Profile into their boardrooms, with their leadership teams and across their entire operations. They work with them to create awareness around the key qualities that determine a healthy relationship with their team while also shedding light on the team's collective shadow or troubled parts. This information supports their understanding of why the team is producing the results they do in different areas and what they can change. Like individual Being Profiles, Team Profiles are also used to facilitate transformation, though on a collective scale. Organisational directors and leaders acknowledge that it is a viable, tangible and methodical way to build and maintain a strong culture and relationships within their team. Rather than leaving the organisation's culture to chance, leaders who adopt the Being Framework can support their team members to pull the organisation's culture forward together.

Summary

To recap, the Being Profile is not a personality test. It is an ontometric measurement tool that assesses a series of predetermined qualities within an ontological model. In this way, it enables you to harness the true power of the Being Framework by giving you a vivid snapshot of your Being at a given point in time. Completing a Being Profile also dramatically simplifies and reduces the time to undergo a process of transformation by supporting you with the awareness to see how you are being in relation to the thirty-one Aspects of Being it measures. Importantly also, the Being Profile is a tool that is being refined and enhanced over time to support people more effectively as the world and societies evolve and we discover more about human beings.

While you don't necessarily need to use the Being Profile to adopt and apply the Being Framework, you will rely on guesswork without it. Here are a few further benefits of incorporating the Being Profile into your life:

- The questionnaire challenges you with a series of over 240 probing, unique and strategically assembled questions that measure your relationship with each of the thirty-one Aspects of Being in the Being Framework and explored in this book.

- Its methodical, objective and non-judgemental approach minimises inherent biases.

- It acts as a third-party reference point that can ground the conversation when working with someone else on their Aspects of Being.

- It supports transformation as it clearly highlights the Aspects of Being you have an unhealthy relationship with, including the deep, underlying qualities at the heart of an issue. The same is true for someone you are supporting, such as a team member.

- It can be completed in an online self-discovery format or with the support of a Being Profile Accredited Practitioner, the latter being the most effective.

- It can be taken once every six months, enabling you to track progress over time.

- The Being Profile can also be used to support the growth and development of a team by combining individual profiles into a Team Profile. A Team Profile simplifies the process of working with a team as it enables you to compare and contrast each individual, assess how they contribute to or detract from the performance and effectiveness of the team and identify the Aspects of Being that need to be collectively addressed.

Conclusion

It takes courage to shine a light on your Being, but the results are immeasurable when you do. The more you polish and transform your Aspects of Being, the easier it will be to support others in polishing and transforming too. Eventually, you will reach a point where you undergo a continual series of transformations, which is how high achievers ongoingly adapt to new and ever-changing environments. And this is how you will manifest your Unique Being – the one-of-a-kind, one and only YOU – to the world for true fulfilment in all your endeavours and for the greater benefit of others and humanity. That is the ultimate objective of this paradigm. Who knows, maybe you are the one who can sing like no other. Or perhaps you will cure that commonly perceived incurable disease or invent a device that could solve a deep pain point for humanity. So while we all come to this world for a very short period of time and are eventually blown away like a speck of dust, as individual beings, we are also a node in the network of humanity. Therefore, what you say, the decisions you make and the actions you take matter and make an impact, no matter how big or small.

I wish you well on your journey. Please feel free to reach out via the Engenesis Platform at engenesis.com and to use that platform for access to multiple resources, including the Being Profile and our community of ontological coaches and accredited practitioners.

Where to from Here?

Resources for further action

I believe that entrepreneurial ventures, businesses and not-for-profit organisations are among the best-suited vehicles in the world to solve key problems and pains for humanity. However, when the shadow sides of our Being take control of our decisions and behaviours as leaders of these organisations, it leads to suffering for ourselves and causes suffering for others. Unpolished Being is the root of dysfunction in the world. At Engenesis, we use the vehicle of business as a springboard to bring about transformation and fulfilment.

Those who are continuously polishing their Aspects of Being and attending to their integrity make decisions and take actions that reduce corruption and alleviate unnecessary suffering. If we carry out entrepreneurship and business effectively and foster a thriving economy led by integrous individuals, we will reduce poverty, suffering and related crime in the world. This is why I've spent years building – and am committed to continuing to build – programs, products, services and a platform that serves people and supports them to attend to their Being.

Who would benefit from adopting the framework laid out in this book and why?

Coach or Consultant – If you are in the business of developing and nurturing human-to-human relationships for the benefit of supporting your clients to effectively fulfil their goals, adopting the framework laid out in this book will significantly enhance what you do.

Leader – If you want to be coached for your own personal growth or would like to incorporate coaching into your approach to leadership within your organisation to lift your people's ability to meet the organisation's goals, there are multiple resources available for you.

Professional – If you aspire to rise to leadership and authentically have your organisation fulfil its mission in the world, the Being Framework will support you to address the areas where your Being is getting in the way.

Visit ashkantashvir.com/human-being for a complete list of resources and other information.

Further reading: *BEING*, by Ashkan Tashvir

If you are curious to learn more and wish to delve deeper into the background research and philosophical underpinnings behind the Being Framework, I invite you to read my book, *BEING*. More akin to a body of work than a standard book, reading *BEING* requires a significant investment of one's time and attention. However, it will give you greater clarity around the rigorous work that laid the foundations of this paradigm and will leave you with a more detailed and comprehensive understanding of it.

BEING is available in both hard copy and e-book formats at ashkantashvir.com/being, or can be ordered directly on Amazon through the links below.

Amazon Paperback
beingbookpaperback.ashkantashvir.com

Amazon Kindle
beingbookkindle.ashkantashvir.com

Connect with me

I am personally committed to supporting the leaders of the world to raise their awareness and shape a more accurate conception of reality. Connect with me at ashkan.engenesis.com to access my latest articles, videos and other content.

To learn about my other projects and interests, visit ashkantashvir.com.

Join our global community

Through the Engenesis Platform, you can get free access to the latest articles, videos, materials, workshops, courses and programs, many of which centre around the Being Framework, from our community of leaders, coaches, consultants and professionals. Create your free account at engenesis.com.

You can also join one of our many communities, which bring together those ready and willing to **be with** and attend to the shadow side of their Being and spur on effectiveness through a process of transformation to fulfil their objectives in life. Find a relevant community for you at engenesis.com/community.

Key articles and resources related to this book's content

I'd like to make specific mention to the following articles that may be of interest and relevant to you now that you've finished reading this book.

- Article: Why Being matters
  engenesis.com/a/why-being-matters
- Article: How your Way of Being determines the results in your life – An introduction to the Being Framework
  engenesis.com/a/how-your-way-of-being-determines-the-results-in-your-life
- Article: How the integrity of our Being is critical to an organisation's performance – The application of the Being Framework in the workplace (includes 5 workplace case studies)
  engenesis.com/a/how-the-integrity-of-our-being-is-critical-to-an-organisations-performance-the-application-of-the-being-framework-in-the-workplace

More resources, including whitepapers, case studies and articles, are continually being added to support the community. You can keep up to date by visiting and registering an account on engenesis.com/c/being.

Being Profile® Self-discovery Course (online)

Now that you've read this book, if you're interested in taking the next step towards awareness, integrity and effectiveness, a popular place to start is to complete your Being Profile as part of the Being Profile Self-discovery Course. Not only will you be able to go through the full assessment and receive your unique results, but you can also be guided through key Aspects of Being in a self-paced, convenient, online video course format.

You can access the course online at engenesis.com/courses/being-profile-self-discovery.

Being Profile Assessment and Debrief

If you're ready and willing to authentically confront what is not working for you by starting with your Aspects of Being, the one-on-one Being Profile Assessment and Debrief is for you. After completing the in-depth online assessment – which takes around forty-five minutes – a Being Profile Accredited Practitioner will walk you through your Being Profile and map your Aspects of Being to the results you are experiencing in your life. You can begin this process at beingprofile.com/assessment.

One-on-one ontological coaching

Working privately with an ontological coach who has been professionally trained by Engenesis is a radically effective way to build clarity on how you are being so that you can fulfil your objectives. Your coach will support you to cast a light on each of your Aspects of Being to ensure they shine bright and reveal their shadow, the key to effecting change. By working through the issues that typically sit behind your facades and go unaddressed, you will be supported to shift issues that could otherwise remain unresolved and undergo a process of transformation. Our community of Thrive Coaches and Master Coaches span the entire globe, work across all industries and bring their unique experience and skills to serve you. To connect with a coach that is best suited to you, contact our team at beingprofile.com/get-in-touch.

Engenesis Influence™ Leadership Program

Are you a manager or leader within an organisation that would like to implement positive change, address conflict constructively and grow your team and team culture successfully? The Engenesis Influence™ Leadership Program operates over twelve weeks and provides a transformational process where you will develop your leadership capabilities to the next level by adopting the Being Framework and leveraging the Being Profile in challenging business scenarios.

You can learn more at engenesis.com/program/engenesis-influence-leadership-program.

Become a Being Profile Accredited Practitioner

Are you a coach or a leader who wants to incorporate the Being Profile in your endeavours to support others to gain profound insights and access breakthrough performance? Then apply to become a Being Profile Accredited Practitioner here: beingprofile.com/accreditation.

Thrive Coach Training Program

Would you like to take your coaching to the next level and coach others to produce even greater results? Coaches, those interested in coaching, directors, managers and leaders from around the world are participating in a unique thirteen-week program founded on the Being Framework that gives them the training and tools they need to thrive in a coaching capacity while being surrounded by a community of peers equally committed to deep personal growth and fulfilment. To learn more about how the program works, register your interest at engenesis.com/program/thrive-coach-training.

Being Mastery® Program (invitation only)

If you want to change the entire trajectory of your life by tapping into your Unique Being and transforming yourself inside and out, right down to the very fabric of your Being, the Being Mastery™ Program will be an unforgettable experience for you.

As a participant in this unique program, you will completely transform your relationship with and conception of reality itself. Run over twelve months, the program will take you through a process of discovery, application and practice, including the Being Framework Transformation Methodology. You'll learn and grow alongside other changemakers, leaders and those committed to addressing the problems in the world, starting with themselves and their community. In this program, participants have the opportunity to understand, adopt and practise the body of work laid out in my book, *BEING*.

This program has a series of prerequisites and participation is by invitation only. You can learn more at beingprofile.com/being-mastery.

The Being Profile video case studies and stories

Access practical examples and stories of how you can apply the Being Framework in your life and/or business. Enjoy the ever-evolving library of videos that showcase the extraordinary work being achieved by our community by visiting youtube.com/engenesis.

The Being Profile for teams and organisations

Take your entire team or organisation through the Being Profile and develop a common language and approach for accessing new levels of growth, performance, effectiveness and leadership. When combined with our private group workshops, your team will experience a shared discovery process as they explore how they can impact performance collectively. Speak to our team to learn more at beingprofile.com/get-in-touch.

Author Biography

Ashkan Tashvir built and launched the first of several businesses at the age of fifteen and subsequently led a series of businesses to become thriving and successful enterprises across various industries. With a master's degree in information systems management, he has worked on various technology projects. Over the years, his interest in business and entrepreneurship continued to evolve and he led or advised several startups and SMEs to become sustainable, scalable ventures before becoming an investor and venture builder himself.

In addition to his business and technological engineering qualifications and experience, Ashkan is a thinker, researcher, voracious reader and philosopher with a profound interest in and knowledge of metaphysics, ontology, epistemology, phenomenology and ethics. For more than a decade, he was driven by a quest to discover why there is so much dysfunction and suffering in the world and to find the answer to a burning question: 'Why are we human beings the way we are and what drives our decisions, behaviours and actions?' His quest led him to a crossroads between the realms of technology, business, leadership and philosophy. His interests extend beyond theory and abstracts of philosophy to their application in the economy, particularly in business and organisational leadership contexts.

Over the next ten years, he embarked on a journey of discovery, tapping into ontology, epistemology, phenomenology, philosophy, anthropology, literature, analysis and spiritual disciplines. Possessing a rare gift of being able to connect the dots between multiple domains, Ashkan applied a uniquely structured and holistic approach to the study of human consciousness, leadership, transformation and Being. This systemised, ontological approach, coupled with his broad and in-depth practical knowledge and experience in the field, led him to discover the answers he sought.

Observing a distinct lack of logical, ontological and systematic thinking in the areas of human consciousness, transformation and leadership, particularly in terms of how they empower people to generate opportunity and wealth for themselves and others, Ashkan set his mind to using his discovered knowledge to devise a series of practical frameworks, tools and methodologies, one of which is the Being Framework. This framework, which incorporates the Being Profile assessment tool and the Transformation Methodology, is now supporting people from all over the world to create significant economic and social benefits in their organisations and personally derive fulfilment from their contribution in life. He has since also designed and built the Genesis Framework™, a revolutionary business venture building paradigm.

Shifting his core focus to the human side of business, transformation and leadership, Ashkan and his team committed to serve millions. To date, they have supported thousands of startups, entrepreneurs and SMEs to amplify their effective exercise of leadership and build scalable, sustainable businesses from nothing more than their Being and the seed of an idea. He holds the belief that entrepreneurship is the greatest vehicle that exists to solve the most complex problems for humanity. His vision is for a new wave of the economy to develop and grow, where people are not only driving a healthy economy but are also minimising wastage and finding genuine meaning in their work.

Ashkan's extraordinary ability to see through human beings' false pretences arising from inauthenticity and a lack of vulnerability allows him to extract the hidden and unspoken truth and support people to confront what typically remains unaddressed. His personal commitment is to advocate for the truth seeker within by supporting human beings to raise their awareness and shape a more accurate conception of reality. His mission is to bring about transformation in the world, one story at a time, through individuals focused on who and how they are being in the world and leveraging their potential to tap into the power that lies within. Ultimately, this leads them to cast the light of their Unique

Being out into the world and build a life of service, contribution, success, prosperity and fulfilment.

As founder and CEO of Engenesis, Ashkan heads a business movement of global venture builders, professional investors, business management consultants, advisors and coaches who adopt and apply his frameworks while also encouraging and facilitating their use by others for personal and organisational transformation. When not writing, studying, coaching or building his businesses, Ashkan spends his time close to nature with his wife, daughter and the family's beloved dogs. He enjoys cooking, singing and playing the oud and harmonica.

Acknowledgements

Firstly, this book would not have been possible without the humble contribution of many of the world's greatest truth seekers, such as Martin Heidegger, Mulla Sadra and numerous others. This content was built on the foundation they shaped, and I would like to acknowledge them.

I would also like to acknowledge and appreciate the contribution of many great leaders and entrepreneurs who are actualised examples of authentically aware, integrous and effective human beings. Without studying them, it would have been impossible to come up with a framework of this kind.

This book would also not have been possible without the many corporate organisations and startups, small and large, and the individuals I have worked with who gave me the chance to understand and support them through their highs and lows, pain and suffering. Every leader I had the opportunity to work with expanded my awareness and understanding of the real problems out there and enabled me to develop and test insight-related discoveries through projects, workshops and coaching and consulting engagements. Furthermore, my work could not have turned into a valuable framework had I not had the opportunity to work side-by-side with professional and experienced coaches on a daily basis. I would like to acknowledge their generosity and the privileges I have been given to shape this body of work.

I would also like to express my gratitude and appreciation for all that the universe has brought to me as part of my diverse and intense personal journey so far. While some of those messages were dark and hard to digest at the time, every experience, trigger and inspiration they sparked helped shape the person who was able to write this book. Today, I feel blessed for all my lack of accomplishments, expensive mistakes, adversities and catastrophes. So, I convey gratitude towards existence and all its manifestations, as even the tiniest particle was a sign that taught me a lesson and contributed to my desire to polish my own Being.

I am compelled by the universe to acknowledge all four of my grandparents who instilled the courage in me to dare to BE out there in the world with kindness and care, and my parents who, in raising me, introduced me to what they knew to be virtuous.

There have been many other people that directly or indirectly contributed to this work, its expansion and the person I am today. While it is impossible to name them all here, I would like to express my gratitude to each and every one of them and acknowledge their significant impact.

I owe an enormous debt of gratitude to those who gave me detailed and constructive comments and feedback throughout this journey, especially our community of Being Profile Accredited Practitioners and Thrive Coaches who courageously use this work every day with their clients and within their teams.

Thank you to my beloved friend, John Smallwood. John's extensive industry knowledge and decades of practical experience in coaching and coaching coaches continues to support the Being discourse to be relevant, practical and applicable in the real world.

My special thanks to John Lowe, who contributed by providing valuable intellectual insights as well as contributing to the initial formation of the Being Profile.

A special thanks to my dear friend and business partner, Ariya Chittasy, whose support makes it possible to operate and grow our multiple businesses while simultaneously allowing me to complete the writing and research to extend this body of work.

To my team at Engenesis, thank you for playing your role and supporting me on this front. I would like to particularly mention and thank Odette Abrenica for her work in designing the front cover of the book.

I would also like to acknowledge Phaedra Pym, the editor of this work, who went beyond her professional responsibilities and has persisted with me through the challenges in continuing to articulate this work. Her care and obsession with the content have made a significant difference to what is now available to you. An additional thanks to other integral members of the production team, Eric and Thymen Hoek, who have done a brilliant job of making the book easier to read in their design and production of the structure and layout, and Caroline New, who graciously sub-edited the work with sincerity and care.

Last but not least, I would like to thank my wife, Atefeh, for her exceptionally unique insights, feedback on the content and inspiration when the path of continuing this body of work was rocky, and for her understanding and patience over my incessant disappearances into my home office. Her constant contribution and partnership eased the suffering and served to restore my peace of mind and integrity when challenged. A lifelong partner makes both the journey and destination worthwhile.

References

A full list of references used to shape the main body of work, *BEING* is listed in the link below:

ashkantashvir.com/being/references

Lightning Source UK Ltd.
Milton Keynes UK
UKHW050146300722
406564UK00013BA/566